THE
People Specialists

THE
PEOPLE
SPECIALISTS

AN EXAMINATION OF REALITIES
AND FANTASIES IN THE
CORPORATION'S VIEW OF PEOPLE,
AND THE PLAIN AND FANCY
SPECIALTIES AND SPECIALISTS
THAT ARISE THEREFROM

STANLEY M. HERMAN

Alfred A. Knopf  NEW YORK

1 9 6 8

THIS IS A BORZOI BOOK

PUBLISHED BY ALFRED A. KNOPF, INC.

Library of Congress Catalog Card Number: 67–18606

The author gratefully acknowledges permission to reprint from the following works:

Psychiatry for the Curious, by Dr. George H. Preston. Copyright 1940 by George H. Preston. Reprinted by permission of Holt, Rinehart and Winston, Inc.

A Business and Its Beliefs, by Thomas J. Watson, Jr. © 1963 by Trustees of Columbia University in the City of New York. Reprinted by permission of McGraw-Hill Book Company.

To SHAN, LISA, MIKE, ANDRA, and MATT, who suffered sometimes silently, but sometimes not so silently. And so I always knew they missed me when I went off to the "dungeon."

For their great help—their ideas, criticisms, encouragement, and labor—I would like to thank especially Angus Cameron, Shan Herman, Tom Wickes, Cy Lehrer, Helen Lay, and Michael Magzis. I also owe much to Joseph Johnston.

C O N T E N T S

THE
People Specialists

Introduction

A CONSIDERABLE NUMBER of words have been written in recent years about life and times in The Organization. Many have been disapproving. From "liberal" critics have come denunciations on a variety of subjects, from executive washrooms through luxurious expense accounts to the threat of a military-industrial conspiracy. Capitalistic economics have been elaborately mated with business ethics (or the lack of them), and the resulting progeny, in the form of what are seen as the executive's deteriorated life values, have been speculated upon at length and in depth.

On the other hand, we have been hearing with increasing frequency from the new breed of articulate public conservative. He has rallied the heretofore befuddled defenders of the faith, reforged their pugnacious pragmatism into finer-edged philosophies, and has pointedly reminded us all of the divine and inseparable bonds between free enterprise and free men.

The wide interest and strong feelings on the subject of men in organizations is understandable. In the United States over thirty-five million people congregate every weekday in the plants and offices of American corporations. During forty to fifty years of his life each of those working Americans will spend from about two fifths to well over half his waking hours within one or more companies.

People live in corporations. There is a significance in this statement that may not be immediately apparent. People do not turn a switch and shut themselves off during the time they work, although some of them try to. They experience. They think. They feel—excitement, anxiety, pleasure, annoyance, boredom, lethargy. They face challenges—physical, intellectual, and emotional. They struggle, adapt, or surrender. What they think, how they feel, and how they act are largely determined by two things—their own natures and the environment within which they operate.

This book is concerned with people in companies. More specifically, it has to do with what in American companies is called personnel relations. Within corporations there are technicians who specialize in the matter of how the organization's people think, feel, and act. Their primary task is to assess the natures of employees and to develop means of influencing employee attitudes in favor of corporate purposes. These specialists are called personnel men, and they will be central characters in the discussion to follow. But while the personnel man is industry's most readily identifiable people specialist, our picture would be incomplete if we limited our attention solely to him and his activities. We also need to consider the underlying intentions of personnel work and its actual performance. In large corporations many of the personnel man's most important intentions are determined by those above him; and much of personnel work is actually performed by operating executives, supervisors, and managers at all levels, who in their daily direction of their subordinates utilize personnel technology. In very significant ways they too are people specialists.

In this book, then, the primary purpose is not so much to describe a particular group of business technologists called personnel men, although such descriptions will be included. Rather, it is to portray the personnel relations *function*. What comes out of that broader intent is really a description of the organization environment for those who live within it, and an explanation of why it is the way it is.

History, for the most part, has been written as the record of the acts and intentions of the great. Emperors and generals have been the historian's star characters. He has seldom dwelt long on second-line ministers or civil-service officials. It is also true that most of the business literature of our time has concentrated on the top of the organization hierarchies. The character and the style of those who currently occupy the pyramid's peak, as well as those in the process of following their rising destinies to it, have been examined, but there has been little attention to the people just below. Probably there is some parallel between the historian's neglect of history's supporting cast and the current scarcity of comment on the functions of those men who find their permanent homes some distance below the pyramid's peak, those who are—and often comfortably so—the second-line administrators, the implementers.

In the mural of the corporation's structure, the personnel man does not loom large. He is a second-liner and an implementer. Bitter as this morsel may be to some personnel men, it is there to be chewed. Staff men (excluding high-level financial officers) are, in general, lowlier than operating men, and personnel men are not standouts even among staff men.[1]

But the real poverty of the personnel field stems from the failure of personnel men to determine the purpose of their function. Except for the shallowest generalizations and most bromidic platitudes, they have neither philosophized nor theorized. Few are realistic about the societies which exist within their corporations, and fewer still have been able or inclined to see and understand the greater society which exists outside of corporations. And because of these fundamental failures they have inevitably failed as well in establishing an adequate under-

---

[1] A quick comparison of salaries paid to executives of various kinds —manufacturing, engineering, personnel, and so on—such as those regularly reported by Arch Patton, McKinsey and Company's compensation expert, provides what for those of the competitive ethic must be proof-positive on the point. Personnel executives are the lowest-paid. Interestingly, according to Patton's international surveys, the pattern seems to apply not only in the United States but in Europe and South America as well.

standing of, or relationship with, what is supposed to be the subject matter of their field, namely, *people at work.*

All of which may seem unkind. As this book goes forward there will be more unkindness. It is not that the personnel landscape is an *absolutely* barren one. Personnel men do some worth-while things, and in these pages notice will be taken of a number of them. But considering its potential, the personnel field is an impoverished land, and the intent of this book is to highlight the poverty as starkly as honesty and a sense of proportion will allow.

The fact is that this book is not being written primarily for personnel men. Though I readily admit that I hope personnel men read and admire it, I am not optimistic. Although the plea of this book is for a more fruitful personnel function, it is addressed primarily to "those other people" who work in corporations, especially the professional, managerial, and technical nobility—those of the button-down white collar—who are being affected each day by the methods and myths of personnel work.

The reason this book is directed toward those subject to the personnel function rather than toward the personnel men themselves is that in my judgment the only pressure to which the majority of personnel men are likely to respond with any urgency is external pressure—the strident sounds of discontent from voices outside their function. Most personnel men are too well insulated by their own mythology. They are not likely to respond to or even feel pressure from within.

John Kenneth Galbraith has observed that the greatest force for changing outmoded ideas is not the introduction of new ideas but the pressure of events which make the outmoded ideas untenable. This is surely true in the realm of most physical sciences and their applications. Here ideas are tested as a matter of course, and if they are unsound they usually fail substantively. A rocket falls. A guinea pig dies. But ideas in the personnel field are much less tangible than either rockets or guinea pigs, and they always exist in the midst of an almost limitless number of variables. Thus, it is as difficult to pin-point the cause of their failure as it is easy to avoid recognizing that they failed. It can be a long while indeed before an idea *must* become untenable, especially to its sponsors. A new personnel program may be, and often is, begun in moments, to the accompaniment of drums and trumpets. The admission of its demise may take years. In the interim its cadaver may be propped up in the middle of the parlor and pointed to with pride.

The personnel man is confused. At the center of his confusion, though he does not realize it, is the issue of his role in the organization. Shall his prime concern be the welfare of employees, or their maximum utilization in the production process? Shall the personnel man be the keeper of the corporate conscience or the chief expert on the manipulation of its "human resources"? Shall he join his fellow managers in their clear and single-minded devotion to the profitability of the enterprise, or shall he stand apart?

The case to be made in this book is that the personnel man ought to stand apart, that his prime concern should be with matters other than profits. Many other matters. To those who may have begun to wonder, no, I am not about to propound a socialist economy. I do believe in profits. I also realize that companies that do not make profits (except in a few special cases) eventually go out of business. When they do they stop employing people. And without employees, personnel work becomes a very superfluous function indeed. The point is, however, that business organizations already have enough people whose job it is to concentrate on making money. They can afford to have a few who concentrate on other purposes. In fact, the case I shall make later is that they can hardly afford not to.

Before we proceed, a word about one aspect of this book's style. In the following pages a good many excerpts from the internal publications of a number of companies will be used to illustrate particular cases. None of these publications, so far as

I am aware, was ever meant to be a secret document. They came to me over the course of a number of years in the normal exchange of information among people working in any field. I have also included a considerable number of quotations from the speeches and writings of other people, especially business executives. Some of these will not place the speaker in a very flattering light. In fact, sometimes the words may seem rather foolish.

We all say foolish things from time to time, and they appear even more so in print. Both wisdom and inanity are fairly transient states for most of us. The more you talk the more risk you take, and many executives do talk a great deal. My purpose, though, is neither to reveal companies' "inside information" nor to make individuals seem silly. Rather, the excerpts and quotations are useful in conveying the spirit as well as the substance of a prevalent pattern of ideas or a "party line."

Finally, I do not mean this book to be unfriendly. Severe, perhaps, but not unfriendly. I am a personnel man. I have friends and acquaintances who are personnel men. Some are good and bright people, some are good and not so bright, and a few are neither bright nor good. That is about the same distribution one would find in most other specialties. From certain friends I have heard the plaintive demurrer that is sometimes made to explain or excuse personnel's condition: that, as professions go, personnel is little more than an infant.

Perhaps, but if for none other than my own selfish reasons, I would rather see it finally begin to toddle along into a more robust childhood than expire in its infancy.

Part One

THE
SOURCES

1

The View from Above

SEVERAL YEARS AGO a cartoon appeared in one of the personnel journals that portrayed a wispy-looking man sitting at a desk with a sign in front identifying him as a personnel manager. Across the desk sat another, healthier-looking man, an applicant for employment. The personnel manager was saying: "Well, frankly, Mr. Brown, what I have in mind is an efficiency expert who will stay strictly away from the personnel department."

I remember that the cartoon struck me as a significant comment on the happy state of the personnel business at that time. One just doesn't fool around that way about things that are really worrisome. You would not expect to find the teamsters' house organ, for instance, treating a forthcoming Justice Department investigation so lightly. Nor, for that matter, would you expect the General Electric annual report to jest much about antitrust indictments.

No, it takes a certain blitheness of spirit, a cavalier quality, to publish such a cartoon in your very own journal. It bespeaks nothing but serenity and optimism. Those are marvelous feelings, and from time to time personnel men have enjoyed them.

A combination of things tend to make a personnel man happy. They are not much different from the kinds of things which make people in most occupations happy. Mainly, it is a matter of feeling needed. Other factors being equal, the man who programs computers is more likely to find occupational satisfaction today than the man whose specialty is painting hex signs.

The people who determine the need or lack of need for personnel men are those above them. In most companies today the main outlines of the personnel mission are drawn by the kings and princes of the corporate hierarchy. Their decisions are based mainly upon their perceptions of the climate of the world around them. At present, that climate is not perceived as healthy, so the personnel man should be happy, for he can feel needed.

A major portion of the personnel work which goes on daily in most companies is basic and routine. It is directly responsive to the organization's obvious needs—people must be recruited, interviewed, and hired; wages and salaries must be paid; employees need to be trained. But other parts of the personnel function are less apparent, more subtle. They are intended to affect people's attitudes, in both the short and the long run. They have an ideological basis, and the content of that ideology is important. To understand personnel work as it is currently being practiced in the United States one needs first to understand part of the ideology which lies beneath it. And since current business ideology really does not originate with operating personnel men, but with those high above them, at the top of the structure, that is where our examination ought to begin. So for a while we will be talking not about personnel men but about their bosses and their bosses' bosses.

The high business community dislikes a good many things about the way the world seems to be, and with increasing frequency its members have been accompanying each other in a rising chorus of lament. The best way to find out what these things are, I think, is to pick some of the richer voices out of the solemn choir and listen awhile to the lyrics.

Mark Cresap, Jr., then president of Westinghouse Electric, put it this way in a message to the Pittsburgh Personnel Association in February 1959: "Big business—the corporate community—is one of the key elements in our society, yet there is evidence to indicate that it is little understood, and certainly not fully appreciated, by the people it serves. Because of this lack of public understanding, corporations have long been vulnerable to political criticism and action. Those with political axes to grind have capitalized on this situation by initiating or supporting restrictive business legislation, or at the very least by publicly censuring business in order to win votes."

More recently, another voice, G. L. Phillippe, president of Westinghouse's rival, the General Electric Company, proves the two firms are in harmony at least on this theme. Speaking as a member of a panel at his church in Scarsdale, New York, Mr. Phillippe intoned: ". . . sometimes individuals outside of business seem to resent, or even find faintly immoral, the businessman's preoccupation with economic matters such as producing goods and selling them at a profit. This is the businessman's vocation, his proper concern, his function in society. In my view, it is no more or less wrong than the government official's preoccupation with politics, or the educator's preoccupation with education, or the minister's preoccupation with religion."

And in especially elegant style, W. L. Lohrentz, a vice president of U.S. Steel, said to another group of personnel men, this time in Chicago: "Modern industry . . . seems to many people to be a great monolithic giant, crushing the individual, robbing him of his power to think, and destroying his personality. The men who work in big industry, they say, are reduced to faceless anonymity, all carrying the same lunch pails, punching the same time cards, running the same machines, or wearing the same gray flannel suits. Modern industry, they charge, is extinguishing the bright flame of human personality." It goes without saying, of course, that Mr. Lohrentz doesn't agree with a bit of this, and later in his speech he provides his own point of view, informing the assembled personnel men that "any large corporation is just as surely the result of individual effort as is the one-man grocery."

Business attributes its bad-image problems to various causes. The National Association of Manufacturers states in a pamphlet on Individualism that "the typical union official . . . [has] had a relatively easy—as well as unhindered—way to plug very effectively the charges that: The business manager is a crook, and the private business system is simply a device to aid the undeserving few to exploit the deserving many. . . ." Rightist sections of the business community continue to blame what they see as a dangerous minority of reds, pinks, and fellow travelers, joined by a few fuzzy-minded but still harmful college professors.

The current and more prevalent trend among the corporate spokesmen, however, is to trace the reasons for the public's disenchantment with business to sources within the business community itself. The deterioration is a result of neglect. Business has been too modest and too reticent. The corporation is virtuous and lovable, but people don't know this. Businessmen have not spoken out loudly or frequently enough to get the message across.

What to do? For management men of action, the answer, quite naturally, is action. C. Virgil Martin, president of Carson, Pirie, Scott and Company, told a 1962 conference of American Management Association personnel: "The business community must develop universal acceptance of the basic truth about our free-enterprise system—the fact that business is not only *interested* in human values; it *creates* them. . . . We had better get busy by every known, acceptable means to convince the public of the basic truth . . ."

Lawrence Appley, long-time president of the American Management Association, who frequently says things in a straightforward way, announced in the May, 1963, issue of the AMA-published journal *Personnel:* "Management has failed miserably to develop the correct image the public should have of business." This is not a very unusual statement. But Mr. Appley then added: ". . . it has also failed in the development of constructive relationships between manager and manager, worker and worker, and manager and worker," which opens up an entirely different box.

A few others have raised the same lid. In 1961 the National

Industrial Conference Board sent questionnaires dealing with employee attitudes to forty major personnel executives. NICB asked whether or not the personnel executives believed that the average employee (1) does not feel his company treats him with respect; (2) believes most improvements in benefits and working conditions have come about through actual or threatened union pressure or because of intercompany competition for manpower, not because of management's interest in its employees; (3) feels management puts profit above everything else; (4) thinks he can get back at management only through pressure, restriction of production, and alliance with his fellow workers; (5) feels little or no pride in the company product or in his part in its production. The majority of the personnel executives questioned found at least "some validity" in all but the final statement.

Whatever the worker may feel toward his company, his company often professes, in its published messages, to care about him.

Says United States Steel: "We believe in the dignity and importance of the individual employee and in his right to derive personal satisfaction from his employment."

Says Standard Oil of New Jersey: "We in the Standard Oil Company (New Jersey) believe in the individual. We believe in *you* . . . and want you to believe in *us* as a company . . . and to all employees, old and new, we reaffirm the friendly interest of the management of the Standard Oil Company (New Jersey) in you and in your well-being and progress."

And Westinghouse: "We believe that the most important asset of Westinghouse is its people—in every plant, office and community, wherever they work and live. We believe in the dignity of every employee in Westinghouse and the importance of his work . . ."

And Cluett, Peabody and Co.: "[The] relationship [of the business toward its employees] creates certain rights, duties and responsibilities. Their improvement is not only a material advantage, but a moral obligation."

In summary, as expressed by R. W. Johnson, chairman of

the board of Johnson and Johnson: "Economic life today is interdependent . . . The idea that business is impersonal is fiction. In business, as elsewhere, we deal with our fellow man and with all the aspirations of his nature. There is no 'economic man,' motivated only by thoughts of gain . . . men have a conscience and a sense of justice. They do not change their nature when they put on their business suits or working clothes."

The personalism-morality-interdependence themes in these statements can be evaluated in a number of ways. For the "accepter" they are signs of the new managerial ethics, industrial statesmanship, and an unfolding of business maturity. For the old guardsman they are the signs of entrepreneurial softness and incipient organizational decadence. For the simple cynic they are only camouflage, a coldly calculated attempt to seduce employees and to fool the public.[1] For the sophisticated cynic they are an expression of the corporation's confusion as it struggles to justify and humanize itself in its own as well as the public's eyes.

But whatever the motives, the means so far have produced too little. Inside as well as outside the corporate walls the images remain heavily tarnished. And like it or not, many love neither the businessman nor his system. They do not understand the function of profits, nor the debilitating effects of creeping socialism. They do not understand that they cannot, as the NAM puts it, "live the good life—by theoretically passing the buck for [their] most important bread-winning and life-living decisions to people in government or union headquarters . . ."

And if they don't love it well enough, they won't work hard enough for it. "For instance," continues NAM, "there is ample proof that at least a 20% increase in productivity can be secured —with no one going home tired and everyone benefitting— through simply correcting these false expectations and explaining the facts as to where the individual and common interest do

---

[1] The cynic might, for instance, read into some of the creeds— especially those of U.S. Steel and Standard Oil of New Jersey, with their emphasis on "the individual"—no more than another thinly disguised attack on labor unions and their "collectivism."

lie and as to why cooperation toward the ends of a business service that individual and common interest."

In another version, J. S. Parker, vice president of General Electric, says: "[There is] greater individual output which remains substantially untapped, pending solution by management of complex problems of human motivation and communication; there are informed estimates that individual output could be increased by as much as 20%[2] if management would both deserve and get employee confidence and cooperation."

Parker is optimistic and believes that, with the help of a dynamic personnel effort somewhere down the line, management will achieve these aims. But not everyone is hopeful. Lawrence Appley, AMA's president, is an older, more nostalgic man than Mr. Parker, and when he compares generations of workers he despairs of the current run. "A person who is born into a world of legislated and sizable security benefits," says Appley, "must have a different point of view from one who is not. An individual who starts work in a world of great organized union strength has work philosophies that are different from one who does not. That individual who expects, receives, and is accustomed to high pay, unrelated to quantity or quality of work done, must think differently from one who does not . . . while deliberating upon these things, I have little hope that anybody is going to do anything about them, but I do believe management people would be far less frustrated if they at least took the time to understand them."

Thus the song of the entrepreneurs is a sad one, not melodious, but poignant, and it has numerous stanzas: The Federal Government is suffocating us with regulations and bludgeoning us with taxes. The public does not understand us

[2] The 20 per cent figure and the way it is used by Mr. Parker and the NAM is rather interesting and reflects their different styles. What for Mr. Parker is "informed estimates" of increases of "as much as 20%," for the NAM is "ample proof" of "at least 20%"! As far as I can tell, the 20 per cent figure actually stems from a very rough guess by a few behavioral science academicians, based on some productivity experiments with a few small groups of production workers.

nor does it trust us. The intellectuals in particular dislike us, and almost no one recognizes the value of our contributions to society. The unions have too much power. They have too much influence in Washington as well, and furthermore, a lot of our employees have more loyalty to them than they do to us. The public isn't sufficiently committed to free enterprise and our employees are hardly committed at all. Neither the public nor our employees know enough about business economics and they do not seem particularly eager to learn. And besides all this, our employees aren't working hard enough.

All in all, as those who ride the highest rising elevators at company headquarters see it, people are not thinking right. People of all kinds—those in Washington, those in the colleges and universities, those on the street, and even those inside the corporate compound itself. As Mr. Cresap, Mr. Phillippe, and Mr. Lohrentz have said, business is neither understood nor appreciated.

How important is it? Crucially and immediately important, if you take the presidents and vice presidents completely seriously. But, for the enterprising spirit, recognizing adversity is by no means tantamount to accepting defeat. On the contrary, adversity is a call to action. And so, in the best traditions of modern management, responsibility has been assigned, and some specialists have been put more or less in charge of things. They are the personnel men. It seems a logical choice. The personnel men have, after all, been around for some time, and moreover, as Mr. Cresap of Westinghouse put it in his address to them: "Remember that four out of every five individuals who earn incomes today are *employed persons* . . . employees are at one and the same time a company's most valuable asset, and potentially its most articulate spokesmen. As personnel people, you have direct and continuing communication with this vitally important group and therefore have the opportunity to build employee support and understanding for the policies, practices, and objectives of your company . . . By winning employee understanding we win potent allies who can tell the business story with the authority that comes from personal conviction."

We have listened to the business chiefs' community sing. Its predominant notes seem to be blue ones of sadness and high ones of alarm. For the personnel man, what seems to emerge is a clear directive: to win allies to the company's embattled cause. How the personnel man has been responding is, of course, in some measure the product of the personnel man's nature. We need now to discover what sort of nature he has, and how it got that way.

2

Personnel Men

In his introduction to a neat little book called *Psychiatry for the Curious,* Dr. George H. Preston says:

> If I look up and you look down
> Upon the biggest man in town,
> You'll see his head and ears and nose,
> I'll see his feet and knees and toes.
> And though it is one man we see,
> You'll swear he's A, I'll swear he's B.

This holds about equally true for the personnel man. People do have a variety of opinions about personnel men. The friendly, up-looking opinions sound something like this: The personnel profession is the broadest one in all management. Within its compass lies the responsibility for industry's human resources, the vital element in all productive effort. Sometimes the sentiment is implicit. For instance, in 1960 Louis B. Neumiller, chairman of the board of the Caterpillar Tractor Company, told a National Industrial Conference Board interviewer that personnel work was "very close to the heart of the business . . . No business can achieve its true destiny unless its management is properly employee centered." Other times it is explicit, as in the words of James M. Symes, president of the Pennsylvania Railroad, an old-style, up-through-the-ranks executive: "One of the surest ways to keep in the front ranks of industrial management today is to have the support and counsel of expert personnel men. I'm not sure that it was true back when company presidents of my generation were starting their careers, but I am sure it is true now and will be true from now on."

People say other nice things about personnel men and their deeds: that they help bring the right man to the right job; that they help the organization and the individual to utilize the individual's talents to the fullest, thus making both parties happy; that their efforts foster labor peace and harmony and provide rationality and equity in the systems that determine how people will be rewarded in the organization; and that they provide the means for the communication of the virtues of each company in particular, and free enterprise in general, to those who labor.

But not everyone is enthusiastic about personnel work. Some people are downright negative about it. Damnation of personnel work comes from a number of sources. One is the public liberals—the anti-establishment men. Their lament has to do with the smothering of individuality, the decline of business morality, the growth of executive autocracy, and so on—all of these being the unhappy by-products of organization life. For the liberal critics, especially on the subject of individuality-smothering, personnel men are the symbol of the big pillow. Conformity, say the anti-establishment men, is the watchword of the personnel function. From the selection of successful job candidates through the determination of their pay and progress within the organizational hierarchy, personnel men pet, protect, and reward the universal gray man, whether he wears flannel suit or coveralls.

What is more, say such critics, work within the corporation has become a dehumanizing process, and life within the corporation has become an alienated experience—an existence in a limbo, where people no longer relate either to each other or to their own labor. Goals and purposes have been replaced by a consuming concentration on means. Means have indeed become ends. Small, selfish ends—the production of goods and services without any real consideration of their value to the society that is to be their consumer. Nor does the question of value even matter much, because the society will be manipulated into their acceptance anyway.

Within the organization the people who produce are also manipulated. And chief-in-charge of the organization's internal machinations is the personnel man. His most diabolical implement—"the science of human relations"; his mission—to seduce those who labor into cheery acceptance of an industrial milieu that would otherwise be an anathema to them. Thus, say his accusers, the personnel man is immoral, or at best, amoral; a pale-eyed specialist in the using of people.

Professor Malcolm McNair of the Harvard Business School, in the March–April, 1957, issue of the *Harvard Business Review,* expresses his disapproval of the manipulators this way: "I am essentially disturbed at the combination of *skill* with *human relations*. . . . [It] has a cold-blooded connotation of proficiency, technical expertness, calculated effect . . . I am totally unable to associate the *conscious effort to practice human relations skill* (in the sense of making people happy in spite of themselves or getting them to do something they don't think they want to do) with the *dignity of* an individual person created in God's image."

Solomon Barkin, former director of research for the Textile Workers Union (CIO), sees the personnel man as no ally in the working man's cause. The primary purpose of the personnel man, according to Barkin, is to win employees away from their unions so that management may once again return to individual rather than collective bargaining with the workers. In a style somewhat cooler than Professor McNair's, he writes in another issue of the *Harvard Business Review:* "Traditionally, a personnel program is simply one of management's tools for the control and direction of the enterprise. Like the others, it seeks greater efficiency and higher profits . . . The personnel program pursues these ends by seeking to induce the worker to accept or adapt himself fully to management's code of values and management's goals . . ."

Barkin then enumerates the means personnel men use in trying to achieve their goal. These include employee selection, assignment, promotion, and discharge; employee counseling and interviews; communications with employees; and efforts to promote the formation of "new groups" among employees. In all cases the goal is the same: to separate the worker from his union and to convince him that his interests lie in a common cause with management.

The most interesting thing about this particular indictment of the personnel man is that a considerable number of personnel men spend a lot of their time trying to convince themselves and their bosses that it is true.

Personnel men, like other specialists of the organization scene, are devoted to "research." They have a fondness for surveys and questionnaires which tap the flow and flavor of employee attitudes, and they often use similar techniques for gauging conditions of life among themselves. The result is a relatively complete picture of personnel practitioners—who they are and what they are like.

Personnel men are no longer rare. According to the census, their number almost doubled between 1950 and 1960. There are about a hundred thousand of them now. It may or may not be of some comfort that, according to a study made by the Industrial Relations Institute in 1964, the typical personnel executive "might also be cast as a rather typical American homeowner." What that means is that he is middle-aged (43.8 years old), married, has two or three children, and is buying a house rather than renting an apartment. He is also a *he* rather than a she by about 99 to 1, and apparently fares well in his marital relationships, since only 2.3 per cent of him are widowed or divorced and only 3.9 per cent are single. Further, the personnel man is well educated, or at least he is certified to be. More than four fifths of the surveyed group had a bachelor's degree; and of these, 20 per cent also held master's degrees, and 9 per cent, doctorates. About a third of the personnel men won their bachelor's degrees in business administration, economics or accounting, with the next most popular specialties being liberal arts (15 per cent) and science, technology, and mathematics (15 per cent). Interestingly, only 14 per cent majored in industrial relations or personnel administration. Sociology and psychology accounted for 12 per cent.

When they were asked to recall which of their college courses had been most worth-while the personnel men reported that business-related courses were of most use to them in their present jobs, and psychology courses next. In third place were courses in industrial relations and personnel. The relatively low rating given to the personnel courses probably ought to reflect favorably on the judgment of the personnel people. Undergraduate personnel courses which were examined by the Ford Foundation, and later by Professor Winston Oberg of Michigan State's Graduate School of Business Administration, were strenuously criticized and dismissed with such accompanying phrases as "little more than a description of routine administrative procedures."

People become personnel men in many ways. Some say too many. For a long time the personnel function served as a snug harbor for many an over-the-hill castoff who had been gently steered out of some other part of the organization. The personnel department was a comfortable place to wait out retirement. There is less of that sort of thing now, but there is still some. More than 60 per cent of the personnel executives surveyed by the Industrial Relations Institute came into personnel work from other specialties—sales, manufacturing, finance, industrial engineering, and so on. But it was not specified how many of these were still considered to be under full professional sail at the time and how many had been moored.

In the organization scheme of things a man is known not so much by the company he keeps as by whether or not he reports to a corporate officer. The higher the reporting level, the higher the status. About one third of IRI's sample group of personnel people reported directly to the chief executive of their corporation. Approximately another third reported to a vice president. This is not a very impressive showing by comparison to other functions. However, IRI looked upon these

statistics as an encouraging trend, since they reflect a fairly significant gain for personnel over the last decade or so in the how-
important-is-your-boss competition.

But some statistics are even more interesting than these.
Dollars, for example. Personnel men do pretty well when compared to employed people in general, but not so well in comparison to other specialists within the organization. With exceedingly few exceptions, in the golden books of executive
compensation, personnel men's names follow all the rest. Only
about 14 per cent of the IRI survey respondents earned $20,000
or more in 1963. An additional 18 per cent made only $15,000
to $20,000. About 8 per cent were paid over $25,000 (which is
about the floor for salaries connoting true executivedom).[1]
One would really expect the personnel men to do better, especially since the salary administration function in most places
has been moved from the comptroller and finance departments
into the personnel department itself.

Personnel men react differently to their lower pay level. Some
(for example, 37 per cent of the IRI respondents) complain
about it. Others seem philosophical about it. Activist-type personnel men regularly make unhappy contrasts between their
own pay and the pay of engineers.[2] In the current age of homage
to technology, engineers, even at nonsupervisory levels, earn
two to three thousand dollars more per year than do personnel
men at comparable levels. At the time of the still-unfurrowed
brow—the entry level just after the bachelor's degree—the personnel recruit is apt to start his career at $6,000 to $7,000 a
year, while his more technically trained classmate, the engineer,
starts at $7,000 to $9,000.

At present, a kind of generalized inferiority complex
pervades the personnel field. You often find it reflected in

[1] The situation isn't really quite as bad as it looks if you want to limit
the view to big companies. Among companies employing ten thousand or
more people, over half the personnel men made $25,000 or more.

[2] Engineers, quite naturally, almost never compare their pay to personnel men's pay. They compare with doctors and lawyers (who do, of
course, earn substantially more).

the personnel journals, and you can hear it alluded to almost anytime two or more personnel men assemble. The IRI reports it this way: "The man directing his company's industrial relations/personnel program has mixed attitudes as to management's viewpoint on the function. On the one hand, he feels that the IR/P [industrial relations or personnel] department lacks status in comparison with other major elements of the company, and on the other, he believes, on the whole, that the value of the industrial relations/personnel function is recognized by management."

To confirm what the Industrial Relations Institute investigators probably expected to find, they asked each of the personnel executives to rank the various departments in his company according to its status in the eyes of top management. The personnel men ranked sales and production highest and *their own function lowest*. They further particularized their plight with a list of specific indignities they had suffered. Almost 25 per cent of them complained that they did not get advance information of company plans and actions affecting their own function. (This is a sort of apex of irony when one considers the emphasis the personnel department has been placing on the subject of "communications" during the last several years.) The personnel men also complained of "inconsistencies in top management attitudes," and more than a third were unhappy about the excessive detail work and clerical routine in their own jobs.

The Industrial Relations Institute study is only one of a number that report on personnel's unhappy state. A study made in 1962 by the American Foundation for Management Research, Inc., which concentrated not only on personnel executives but also on their top bosses' opinions about them and their functions, turned up similar results. They arrived at such depressing conclusions as this: "One of the major findings of this study is that as the importance of the employee relations function has increased, the influence of personnel executives has decreased . . . Noting their waning influence, the more articulate and perceptive personnel executives are concerned with the gaps in understanding between themselves and company colleagues, particularly in top management."

And under the heading of what the foundation researchers themselves call "The Trashcan Hypothesis," they conclude that their study confirms that "Chief executives . . . view the personnel department as a dumping ground for a broad array of functions having little to do with the major goals of personnel administration."

Life, it seems, has not been kind to the personnel man. Nor has this harried and neglected steward of the corporate household found it generous, either. The IRI report sums up bleakly: "Many [personnel executives] feel they are working with staffs either too small or of insufficient caliber to handle the job as they would wish it done . . ."

How would they wish it done? In the personnel men's own words, as the IRI reports, the objective is to make "a larger contribution to corporate profitability." Or, as Solomon Barkin said it for them more specifically, in a way that would enable the personnel man's chiefs and peers to see his function as clearly a tool of management control which produces greater efficiency and higher profits.

Personnel's commentary on itself is not always one of sadness or sulkiness. Occasionally a strain or two of optimism can be heard. But even then there is an overtone of the familiar self-scoldings. The National Industrial Conference Board, in its own study of the personnel executive, concluded in a wondrous burst of dynamic, hard-hitting penitence: "He is an executive who is profit-minded, who is knowledgeable about his company and the industry of which it is a part, and who backs away from the old 'do-gooder' image that, rightly or wrongly, has been attached to personnel administration . . . At the same time, in the majority of cases, he feels the personnel executive still has a distance to travel before he takes his place in the inner circle of top management . . . It is part of his job today, as he sees it, to shorten that distance by convincing the unconvinced of the substantial contribution that personnel administration can make in achieving corporate goals."

And with equally firm resolve, a special feature in the May, 1961, issue of *Management Review* is promisingly titled "Farewell to the Happiness Boys." Up to now, explains the writer, "personnel experts busily pumped the milk of human kindness into industry's veins, and many executives believed that the one-big-happy-family concept of management was the golden road to achieving corporate goals." But that was yesterday, and now the "happiness boys" have had it. Their just fate: to "limp off into the sunset, their bright but tattered banners dragging behind them."

And so personnel men keep on making the point: They are no longer do-gooders. The happiness boys are dead. In their place stands a new breed of virile he-men—tough, hard-headed, and as profit-minded as any old-line sales or production men.

But while they proclaim this image publicly, the personnel men themselves are not quite sure of it. Among themselves they keep talking about the do-gooders as though they were still very much alive and dangerous. The subject comes up at almost every personnel conference. The do-gooders are the enemy, and their pernicious effect on the personnel function's image is discussed with passion. Apparently, while each personnel executive is personally convinced that he and his organization are clean, he remains suspicious of his brother specialists. In the IRI survey only 59 per cent of the personnel men believed that the do-gooder was indeed gone from the field even today.

Is the do-gooder dead or alive? Which ought we to believe— the public announcement or the private talk? Oddly enough, this time the public announcement. The do-gooder is no more. One never meets him at the conference, nor does one discover his doctrine in the personnel journals. What remains is only a ghost, a ghost which continues to be conjured out of fragments of the past, because although do-gooderism has gone away, personnel's image problems have not. The unbusinessmanly blur on the personnel image remains. The personnel man still does not come through as virile, tough, and profit-minded. What most personnel men have not realized, though, is that this failure in projection is not a result of do-gooder subversion at all. It is less sinister but, alas, more inevitable. Though the personnel man wants desperately to be seen as one of the corporation's hard men, this is an unrealistic ambition. In the organization store he has not been given charge of a hardware counter. His principal merchandise is software—employee morale and attitudes—and it is tough to be tough on such soft subjects. The effect on the personnel man's psyche is ambivalence—ambiguous, confusing, nerve-wracking. It is the root source of his neurosis, his ambivalent jitters.

And out of the personnel man's ambivalent jitters come incongruity and absurdity. As illustration, there is a 1960 white paper from the employee relations department of Standard Oil of Ohio. After a cool prediction of the probable slowdown in the economy of the early sixties, which "suggests that it will be necessary to adjust employee relations policies and practices to hard economic realities," the Sohio personnel writers continue: "In the past Sohio has been characterized as a 'people company' with highly developed sensitivity to customers, employees and the public, and with a deep concern for human relations . . . [but] The trends and developments in industry cited above and the anticipated rapid growth of Sohio will inevitably create a different corporate image which may be characterized as more efficient, more technical and scientific, and less in direct contact with people."

In the spirit of Standard's view of the new decade, the company personnel men promise that the employee relations staff will concentrate on hard-hitting productivity increasers such as "Criteria of performance, Measures of performance, Self management and discipline through better controls, and Organizational design to improve working relations." No manufacturing superintendent could have said it better. But that is on page five.

Two pages later is a list of the Sohio personnel men's items of advice to their company, including: "Stress the importance of developing and maintaining a 'climate of confidence and caring for individuals.' . . . We regard [employee] self-realization as a worthy end in itself, and perhaps even the basic purpose of life . . ."

Then there is Shell Oil Company. Say Shell's personnel men straightforwardly, on page four of the *Shell Management Course Study Outline:* "Shell is a commercial enterprise organized and operated for the purpose of returning a profit to those who have invested their funds in the venture . . . To discharge this responsibility, it is necessary for Shell to employ and maintain an adequate work force, train them in the performance of their tasks and organize their efforts to achieve required results, all to the end that maximum production may be secured at the minimum cost."

No do-gooderism here, apparently. But again, alas, after bravely asserting personnel's responsibility "to help management operate the Shell enterprise profitably," the Shell personnel men conclude self-consciously: "It will be noted that most of [the previously mentioned] policies and practices appear to relate more directly to employee welfare than to achieving maximum production at minimum cost. However, it is the firm conviction of Shell management that satisfied employees have a high degree of morale and the 'will to work,' and that individual productivity is increased by these same elements."

It may be a firm conviction but, unfortunately, there is no clear evidence to support any direct relationship between high morale and high productivity.[3]

In 1964 the National Industrial Conference Board called together six vice presidents and a college professor to talk about personnel work. It was an unusually august conference. The idea was to reflect on how the personnel field has changed over

---

[3] For instance, as some researchers have pointed out, morale tends to be very high in work groups which have successfully induced all their members to adhere to the group's own output standards rather than management's standards, and the former are nearly always lower standards.

the years. Said one vice president in his opening remarks: "The biggest difference is that personnel administration today is recognized as a basic function of management. Let me explain that. I haven't heard anyone in the last 10 years say, 'Yes we hire welfare workers for the personnel job.' " And declared another vice president forcefully some moments later: "Let's come right out and say the personnel man has to make his contribution toward the *profit* of the enterprise as much as anybody else."

But time passed, just as pages do, and in the closing moments of the discussion, the first vice president, still talking of the personnel function, said: "In spite of how much decentralization you have, there is one thing you should not decentralize— that is the kind of show you want to run, the principles that you want to follow. Call them *ethical principles* if you like. This is something that should not be left to every little whim and caprice of a decentralized unit."

The appealing image of the production-minded personnel man has reached the campus too. Some years ago, when you asked a bright young college man why he wanted to go into personnel work, you could count on him to reply: "Well, sir, I guess it's because I like people." One does not hear that much any more. The new graduate today is more likely to respond: "I want to go into personnel because I think it affords a tremendous opportunity for achieving business results through human resources." Which is a bit chilling.

Since the mid-fifties, management journals, like more general periodicals, have been covering a variety of cold-war themes, particularly the them-and-us comparisons. In this spirit the June, 1959, issue of *Management Record* featured "Management and Personnel Administration in Russia." The article recounted an interview with Mr. Leonid Rumyantsev, then second secretary of the Soviet embassy in Washington. Announced the lead of the article: "Personnel administration in the USSR today, as described by a Russian Embassy official, has a very different meaning in that country than it does in the United

States." The *Record* soberly continued, "The fact that data which would be considered irrelevant to any discussion of personnel administration here make up the greater part of a Russian official's remarks on the subject is a clear indication of basic differences in outlook of the two countries."

What were the differences, and which were the irrelevant data? I looked for them. What I found was that the Soviet second secretary talked about management development, trade unions, fringe benefits, automation and employee training. No difference so far. But in Russia, said the *Management Record* editor, emphasis is placed on productivity rather than people. (Another "difference" was that Mr. Rumyantsev was not, according to the editor, immediately familiar with the term "coffee break.")

There is at least one straight and sure trail to occupational prestige. Professionalization. A guarantee goes with being "professional." It is not an extravagant one—not like knighthood or British peerage—but professionalism does ensure legitimacy, at a minimum level, anyway. And nobody takes professionalism more seriously than do some personnel men. But when the IRI survey looked into the question of personnel professionalism it found some first-class surprises. Despite the personnel man's dedicated quest for improved status, about half the respondents felt their work was not a profession, *nor did they want it to be.* (Five years earlier, in a similar survey, three quarters of the personnel men had felt their occupation was a profession.)

The apparent caprice of this increased number of recalcitrant personnel men becomes more understandable, though, as yet another manifestation of the ambivalent jitters. For the recalcitrants the price of professionalization was too high. Professionalism is a threat to the ideal of hard-headed businessism, toward which they mightily strive. There is a feeling of softness in it. It gets entwined with such things as codes of ethics, standards, motives of public service, and so on. The point is not that the anti-profession personnel men are so much against these things. The trouble is, rather, that these things do not ring very clangingly the big bell of corporate profitability.

Under the circumstances it might, in fact, seem strange that even as many as half the personnel men still wanted to believe that their field *was* a profession. A possible explanation could be in the definition of "profession" some had in mind. One executive supported his views that personnel work was a profession with this argument: "Although savings that can be made through a sound IR program such as accident prevention and promotion of high employee morale . . . are usually harder to determine than [those made by] various engineering professions, rapid expansion of the function involved now makes IR on a par with engineering."[4]

In a small but popular study of personnel men in seven companies, Maynard N. Toussaint of the University of Michigan's School of Business Administration identifies several widely accepted personnel failings—too many big words, too much professionalism, and too little profit-mindedness. Toussaint concludes that the major troubles between personnel men and operating men arise from three sources: Line managers see themselves responsible for operating results, while they see the personnel department concerned only with its own special function, and frequently so preoccupied with it that they miss the whole point of the business as a whole. There are sharp differences in the education and training of the two groups. Line managers are "practical common-sense" types, while personnel men are regarded as "impractical, ivory tower dwellers," often indulging in professional jargon that no one else can understand. And thirdly, while the line managers identify with and

---

[4] A number of personnel men had a more sensitive and specific view of what a profession was—including its philosophical and ethical aspects —and still felt personnel work was a profession. Others had the broader view but drew different conclusions, such as: "This profession kick we get on every so often seems to be a status quality more than anything else. Let's recognize we get status through results, not sheepskin."

[5] Toussaint's advice to the personnel specialist is to change his ways. Be more responsive to the desires of the line managers, for "while they may have little technical knowledge about industrial relations, successful managers usually have a good idea what it is they want." Also: "Avoid playing the expert. . . . The wise staff man will see to it, therefore, that others take most of the credit for successful changes in personnel practices."

give their loyalty to their immediate work group, personnel men are more likely to turn toward their professional colleagues and to the company as a whole.[5]

There is so much self-reproach literature in the personnel field that at times one can hardly imagine a personnel man anywhere who faces his morning shaving mirror with other than a grimace.

"Why Doesn't Everyone Love the Personnel Man?" asks a personnel manager's essay in the January-February, 1963, issue of *Personnel*. But it is a rhetorical question, and he answers (again): Because they use too big words, and because they too frequently do not have the "practical know-how" of production experience. "To gain real acceptance of himself and his proposals," concludes the author, "the personnel man must put them in terms of the operating man's own interests—and this means describing and defining goals in hard-headed quantitative terms."

There is no doubt that to be hard-headed *and quantitative* is even better than just to be hard-headed. For years, off and on, some personnel men have been trying to be quantitative. They call this Measurement. There are all kinds of measurement systems, some more nonsensical than others. A simple example is the personnel department's own productivity measures, which keep tabs on the number of certain kinds of things the personnel department turns out. These things are usually pieces of paper—like the number of job descriptions written, the number of transfer notices processed, the number of positions evaluated, and so on.

But the best measurements are the ones where the numbers come out with dollar signs attached, the ones that show how much money you helped the company make (or save). The trouble is, though, that for the most part it is very difficult even to pretend to measure the dollar values of what personnel work is concerned with. As a result, many times the personnel department has to fall back on "might-have-been" and "might-have-done" estimates—what the union might have done (and its cost) if the negotiations team had not done such a masterful job of negotiating the contract, for instance; or on the other hand, what might have been the improvement in production if the personnel department had been allowed to put its new communications program into effect.

There are some fairly sophisticated ways of handling the might-have-beens. Temco Aircraft Corporation's personnel department measures its contribution to company profits through its administration of employee-training programs. The Temco approach tests an employee before and after he has gone through a training program, then multiplies the worker's minimum hourly wage by the number of hours he supposedly will use his newly acquired skill, multiplies this result by the actual percentage of improvement, then multiplies *that* result by the number of employees in the classification. Then they subtract the cost of the training. The final figure, according to the Temco personnel men, equals a dollars-and-cents index of the personnel department's worth in training people. So far as I know, nobody looks to see whether or not, or to what degree, the employees actually use the new skill, nor whether it might not have been cheaper to hire someone new who already possessed the skill.

Most splendid of all, though, are the super de luxe master measurements, such as the Employee Relations Indexes used by firms like General Electric and Crucible Steel. The indexes consist of readings on a number of separate indicators of employee-relations conditions—absenteeism rates, separations from the company, visits to the dispensary for work-related causes, the number of suggestions submitted through the suggestion system, grievances, disciplinary actions, and others. A complicated mathematical formula is then applied to the individual items, and ultimately a single index number comes out which supposedly shows the quality and worth of the personnel effort in the particular plant where the measure is being applied. General Electric's man in charge of the Employee Relations Index explains that it is a statistical method of "adding apples and oranges by totaling their sugar content." GE uses eight factors in its system. Crucible Steel uses twenty-eight. The GE system, however, is not widely applied in the company. It never caught on very well, largely because of the complexity of the formula.

By and large, as any personnel man can tell you, personnel men do not become company presidents. There are, however, some exceptions. In 1960 the National Industrial Conference Board unearthed ten ex-personnel men who had made it to their company's presidency or board chairmanship. But these ex-personnel men chief executives did not seem to look back upon their personnel time with special fondness.

After noting that in many ways his personnel experience was "the most valuable experience" he could have had, Charles R. Hook, Jr., president of the Kudner Advertising Agency, nevertheless concluded: "If the stockholders fired me tomorrow, I would not go back into personnel administration at any level. It's too frustrating, and the rewards very seldom match the expenditures of oneself that is required. If any individual has his heart set on personnel administration, I would strongly suggest he become a C.P.A. first."

C. V. Martin, president of Carson, Pirie, Scott and Company, said: "I would suggest to any young person that he not refuse an assignment in personnel administration, but that he not be discouraged either if such an assignment is not available."

The most positive thing that was said about the field as a route to the corporate top was: "I cannot say that the personnel executive is in a better position than a sales, manufacturing, financial, or any other executive to acquire [chief executive] skills. I am confident, however, that his position provides as good an opportunity as any other for full development of his talents and that he can most definitely fill a top managerial position as effectively as other capable executives with backgrounds in other functions of business." (John C. Whitaker, honorary chairman of the board, R. J. Reynolds Tobacco Company.)

They are not ringing endorsements of personnel work. At best they barely tinkle. The chief executives had not, however, ever been asked merely to give testimonials on personnel work; they were also called upon to instruct. For the most part their lectures were in perfect harmony with the proprofit, anti-do-gooder symphony we have so far been hearing.

Said Mr. Hook: "A personnel man must first and foremost be and act like a businessman. Too often personnel managers seem to fail to get at the guts of management problems— whatever they happen to be. On the other hand, management too often considers personnel managers nuisances whose efforts are not sufficiently well directed toward profit goals—immediate as well as long term."

But then, among the Conference Board panel members there was Ellsworth S. Grant. Not that Grant, president of Connecticut Manifold Forms Company, was exactly a booster of the personnel field, any more than his fellow chief executives had been. He had said, for instance: "Once in personnel, it is very hard to get the time or opportunity to learn, except vicari-ously, how other functions are handled. Personnel men are not usually regarded by their superiors as capable or worthy of being transferred to another area . . ."

After that, however, Ellsworth Grant said something quite different. In sad, clear tones Mr. Grant made his point: "I found personnel work challenging, fascinating, ever varied, and taxing of all my abilities and energies. Personnel work, in my opinion, can be as creative as engineering; it is and always will be more of an art than a science. Its degree of personal satisfac-tion is directly geared to the individual's interest in serving others. . . . The more the personnel man becomes cost-minded or profit-centered rather than human-centered, the less will be his feeling of accomplishment . . . Not that he must be a starry-eyed social worker, but his business is primarily people—not machines or dollars—and if he puts something other than people first in his thinking or behavior, he will do better as a production manager or accountant . . . Yet many companies expect him to be some kind of magician who increases profit through the manipulation of employees. That is why personnel men get discouraged—at least those who are worth their salt."

For his own sake it was undoubtedly a lucky thing that Mr. Grant had already made the presidency because this was heresy of the worst sort.

3

×══════╪

The Trouble with Grandmother

IN ATTEMPTING to understand a man it is often useful to find out what he is trying to live down. The personnel man is trying to live down his origins. He hardly ever talks about them even to his fellow personnel men.[1] The truth is that the personnel man's forebears are mixed. And if his grandmother's heritage of charity embarrasses him in the company of his hard-minded organization playmates, his grandfather's toughness ought to make him proud. The personnel man's grandfather was Scientific Management. His grandmother was Social Welfare. Scientific Management is still alive (though somewhat

[1] This became quite clear to me in doing the study required for the next few chapters. Others have noticed this fact too. For example, in the introduction to a bibliographic survey by Professor Frank B. Miller and Mary Ann Coghill, called *The Historical Sources of Personnel Work,* the authors write: "It is astonishing how little attention has been paid to the historical development of personnel administration, considering that it has been an item in college curricula for over forty years and that its practitioners have pretensions to professional status."

The material for this section on the history of personnel administration had to be gathered in small parts and from many places, some of which could hardly be considered the literature of personnel at all. I do want to mention as especially useful, besides Miller and Coghill's study, the following: Henry Eilbert in *Business History Review,* Vol. XXXIII, No 3; Thomas Spates, *The Scope of Modern Personnel Administration;* Daniel Bell, *Work and Its Discontents;* Loren Baritz, *The Servants of Power.*

feebler) today. Social Welfare, as a part of personnel administration, died after only about a decade and a half of life. And that was fifty years ago. Yet her specter continues to haunt.

Both of personnel administration's grandparents were born around the turn of the century. In 1895 Frederick W. Taylor began to tell American engineers about Scientific Management, a new analytical method for the systematic observation of men at work. Taylor was an engineer who had specialized in tooling and industrial belting. He was competent and successful, and even in his childhood he had loved efficiency with a devotion most children reserve for teddy bears. Taylor's turn from machine steel and conveyers to human nerves and muscle had profound effects. His new system enabled the specialist trained in the Taylor method to reduce each manual job into its smallest units of movement, and then to reconstruct the pieces into a revised pattern of motions which were more efficient. At about the same time and in about the same spirit, Frank Gilbreth, a contemporary of Taylor's, identified eighteen basic patterns of physical movements. He called them "therbligs" (Gilbreth spelled backward), and after minute examination of their use in every possible combination he could think of, Gilbreth developed his principles of "motion economy," a catalogue of "one-best-ways" of doing things.[2]

But it is Taylor who stands as the taller giant in the history of efficiency. Four years after the introduction of scientific management Frederick Taylor achieved immortality. His instrument was Schmidt. Schmidt was a steelworker. Specifically, Schmidt's job was shoveling pig iron. Before his encounter with Taylor he shoveled about a dozen tons a day. Taylor trained him to shovel forty-seven tons. Schmidt thereby won the championship among pig-iron shovelers and Scientific Management won true and lasting reverence among production managers.

The direct link that was ultimately to bind Taylor to person-

---

[2] Gilbreth ultimately attained even wider fame for his procreative and child-rearing practices, which were the subject of the Hollywood movie *Cheaper by the Dozen*. Gilbreth was played by the late Clifton Webb.

nel administration rather than industrial engineering was the scope of his concerns.[3] Taylor's interests went beyond the mechanics of a worker's body movements to concern about the whole man and his proper fit into the factory scene. Taylor was among the first to recommend to industrialists the appointment of a special foreman to serve as "shop disciplinarian" and the establishment of an employment bureau for scientific personnel selection. On the subject of scientific selection, for example, Taylor wrote: "One of the very first requirements for a man who is fit to handle pig iron as a regular occupation is that he shall be so stupid and so phlegmatic that he more nearly resembles an ox than any other type." On the other side of the same coin it ought to be noted that Taylor also wrote of the employer's duty "to see that each workman is given as far as possible the highest class of work for which his brains and physique fit him."

Another aspect of Taylor's philosophy emphasized that the dictates of efficiency required that decision-making and control functions be withdrawn from the hands of the workers and centralized in the hands of management. Planning of the work to be done, in terms of scheduling, pace, and methods, should be done by management. Wherever practicable, standardization and simplification principles should be applied. Taylor made it clear in his *Principles of Scientific Management*. "What I demand of the worker is not to produce any longer by his own *initiative,* but to execute punctiliously *the orders given,* down to their minutest details." (Author's italics.) Nor was Taylor oblivious to the social implications of his demand. There is real ingenuity in the way he anticipated his critics head on. Said Taylor:

"When through all of this teaching and this minute instruction the work is apparently made so smooth and easy for the workman, the first impression is that this all tends to make

[3] In most companies nowadays the personnel man owns only a piece of the Taylor heritage of scientific efficiency in production. The time-study man, who is usually a member of the industrial engineering department, has charge of the methods and measurements aspects.

him a mere automaton, a wooden man. As the workmen frequently say when they first come under this system, 'Why, I am not allowed to think or move without someone interfering or doing it for me!' The same criticism and objection, however, can be raised against all other modern division of labor . . . And it should be remembered that the training of the surgeon has been almost identical in type with the teaching and training which is given to the workman under scientific management."[4]

Scientific management had an almost immediate appeal for American managers, but it also had admirers in unexpected places. In a 1919 speech Nikolai Lenin said: "The possibility of socialism will be determined by our success in combining Soviet rule and Soviet organization or management with the latest progressive measures of capitalism. We must introduce in Russia the study and teaching of the Taylor system and its systematic trial and adoption."

On the other hand, Karl Marx did not feel that way. He despised what he considered the deadening effects of specialization, whatever its alleged advantages in terms of efficiency. Said Marx: "It becomes a question of life and death for society . . . to replace the detail worker of today, crippled by life-long repetition of one and the same trivial operation, and thus reduced to the mere fragment of a man, by the fully developed individual, fit for a variety of labours, ready to face any change of production, and to whom the different social functions he performs are but so many modes of giving free scope to his own natural and acquired powers."

It was an interesting argument, and while the voices have changed, it has not been settled yet.

Meanwhile, above the clamor on the factory floor, personnel's other grandparent was beginning to stir in the office. She was called a social secretary, or sometimes a welfare secretary,

---

[4] It is hardly necessary for me to say so, but there are some significant differences between the specialization of the surgeon and the assembly-line worker. Even if there were not, the surgeon does not perform the *same* operation on identical patients eight or more hours of every day.

and according to the 1908 issue of the *New Encyclopedia of Social Reform,* her main duty was "to study the welfare of the employees in every way, to suggest improvements in their conditions, and to organize them [in] . . . various forms of improvement." These suggestions often came out in the course of lectures on such subjects as home beautification, music appreciation, and other cultural topics. The organization efforts included providing bathrooms and requiring employees to bathe at least twice a week.

Employers gave welfarism a fairly substantial start. By 1919 a United States Bureau of Labor Statistics study reported that over four hundred companies had some form of employee-welfare program. Undoubtedly, the most spectacular was Henry Ford's sociological department.

In 1914 Ford revolutionized American industry, incurred the burning emnity of his fellow industrialists, and got himself called, among other things, a socialist. He accomplished all this by raising the minimum pay rate of his work force from $2.30 to $5.00 a day. His reasoning, Ford insisted, was neither altruistic nor charitable but based on sound business sense. He would get his pick of the best workers, win their best efforts and loyalty, and increase manyfold the market for Ford cars by making common men potential customers. But Ford had another concern. He wanted to make sure that his employees' new affluence would be devoted to "proper living" and that they would not, as Garet Garrett, then editor of *The New York Times,* reported, succumb to the demoralization which most other employers predicted for them.

No wishful thinker, Ford, with characteristic practicality, decided to do what he could to make sure that the extra earnings would be well spent by his employees in clean living, sobriety, and a proper sex life. So he set up a company sociological department staffed at first by thirty—eventually by a hundred—field investigators, later retitled "advisers." Each of these investigator-advisers, supplied with his own Ford car, chauffeur, and interpreter, had the authority to enter any employee's house and investigate all manner of things personal and sanitary. Any employee who, in the judgment of the company investigator, did not meet the required standards of exemplary living lost his $5.00-a-day rate. He could, however, regain grace and the $5.00 after a suitable probationary period of demonstrated clean living.

Another employer that took its responsibility seriously was Carson, Pirie, Scott and Company. Company rules for workers required regular Sunday-school attendance and contributions to the church, and included such advisories as the following: "The employee who is in the habit of smoking Spanish cigars, being shaved at the barber's, going to dances and other places of amusement [would] surely give his employer reason to be suspicious of his integrity."

According to the judgments of the day, such company guardianship of employees' morals was marvelously effective. For as Edwin L. Shuey put it in his 1900 book *Factory People and Their Employers:* "Through the means of their strict discipline, [such employers] have been able to keep from drink men who, otherwise, would have been confirmed drunkards."

In her day-to-day way, the social secretary helped too. She kept busy, and constructively so. She saw to it that the tables in the company lunch room were left tidy, and she kept employees reasonably quiet at meals. She took charge of the welfare room, where cases of illness and unsatisfactory deportment went sent. And, as other contemporary descriptions of her work reported, she was responsible for speaking to girls about keeping themselves neat and clean, advising on marital problems, and generally acting as "guide, philosopher, and friend." Not the least important bit of guiding and philosophizing must have come from one secretary who was reported to have "studied hygiene and sanitation," and thus was able to be a "constant adviser, warning [female employees] against imprudence."

Two things hurt most when the modern personnel man recalls these early days of his field. First, almost none of the first personnel men were men at all, they were women. Second, the qualifications of these women were in social welfare and philanthropic work, not very appetizing specialties. Even in their own time, many people on the industrial scene were contemptuous of welfare secretaries. By 1920 writers of the period were referring to the "besmirched connotation" of the title. One industrial physician labeled it "hell-fare" rather than welfare. Another commented: "It is evident that there can be no such profession as that of a . . . welfare secretary . . ." And very soon there wasn't.

By the early 1920's much of the welfare secretary movement was gone or going fast. Fortunately, however, there were replacements—new and more respectable things for personnel men to do. Some were already under way.[5]

For one thing, in the early 1920's more than twenty states passed (and the United States Supreme Court upheld) Workmen's Compensation laws. Before this time, while employees had the legal right to sue their employers for industrial injuries suffered as a result of employer negligence, their access to the courts was more theoretical than real. Few had knowledge of the law's intricacies, the required cash for legal fees, or the wherewithal to risk the ire of a sued employer. The new laws changed the picture substantially. They protected the workman's interest and made it quite possible that an occupational injury could mean money paid out of the company treasury.

Thus evolved another link in the lineage of the personnel man, the safety specialist, whose job it was to prevent occupational accidents where possible, and to investigate their circumstances when they did occur. Unlike the disappearing social secretary, the safety specialist adapted and flourished. By 1913 there were enough of them to form a national association. (The

[5] This and the next few chapters will be on personnel administration's history. This makes problems, because for the sake of coherence one has to talk as though each of the "periods" in the field's development were clear and discrete, with all of personnel's practitioners operating in the same way at the same time. In fact, of course, that is not so. As in other fields, some are as much as a decade or two behind and others a decade ahead of the prevailing mode.

associative urge, as we shall see many times hereafter, is a strong instinct among personnel and other management men.)

Still another fortunate development for personnel administration at about this same time was the discovery of "labor turnover" and the fact that it too could cost companies money. When a skilled worker left a company, whether he was fired or quit, it often took time and effort to find and train a replacement for him. Multiplied by large enough numbers of incidents, such time and effort might involve a good deal of money. The solution? What Frederick Taylor had suggested years earlier: more selective hiring practices at the start. Someone more skilled and sophisticated than the foreman or straw boss was needed to separate the wheat from the chaff, someone who could distinguish the durable young job applicants from the perishable ones. Avoid the physical misfits and you could probably lower the accident rate. Avoid the temperamental misfits and you would lower the agitation level as well. It was a worthy-sounding idea, and from it was born the employment department.

This same idea also accounted for industry's discovery of the now-omnipresent industrial psychologists. Not many companies possessed the kind of daring or liberality of view which would permit them to turn to so strange a resource, but a few did. Very early in the period, one New England manufacturer even co-operated with the staff of the Boston Psychopathic Hospital in exploring the possibility of using mental patients on some of his factory jobs. More typically, though, the psychologists concentrated on selection factors for "normal" people—like salesmen. As early as 1915, for instance, a division of applied psychology was established at Carnegie Institute of Technology, and about two dozen companies, including H. J. Heinz, Ford, Armstrong Cork, Packard, and Westinghouse, each contributed $500 (and later an additional $1,000) to a research program aimed at identifying the ingredients for success in selling.

With the employment department came other seedlings of

still-thriving personnel activities. One was employee and supervisor training. Injuries could be reduced (and workmen's compensation costs as well) not only by minimizing the safety hazards of the environment, but also by training foremen and workers to observe safety practices on the job. Job methods themselves might be better and more quickly passed on to new employees by a training specialist. And with perhaps a faint echo from the recent welfare secretary days, it was felt that once the better workmen had been selected, they were more likely to remain if they were treated more considerately than they had been in the past.

Thus, while the social secretary slid her unhappy way to oblivion, the employment manager's fortunes were on the rise. It was an optimistic time for personnel. It was time to institutionalize. By 1912 the first association of employment managers had been formed in Boston. By 1917 there were ten local associations, with nearly a thousand member companies represented among them. And on a grander level, as the safety specialists had legitimized themselves with the National Safety Council, so the employment managers followed suit with a National Association of Employment Managers.[6] The educational community too took notice of the young function. In 1915 Dartmouth's Tuck School offered college-level training for employment managers, and within few years more than a dozen other schools had incorporated similar programs into their curricula.

But no gift was greater than the one bestowed upon personnel by the Federal Government. It was the Government's War Industries Board which insisted that employment departments be installed in munitions, war-supply, and shipbuilding plants. Thus the style was set, and with the wartime scarcity of labor it was a popular one for companies to follow. An estimate in the July, 1919, *Journal of Political Economy* reported

[6] With the training men also came a National Association of Training Managers. All three—safety, employment, and training specialists—were ultimately to combine in what is now the American Management Association.

that two hundred new employment departments were started during the war. An article in *Mechanical Engineering* of the same year commented on "the truly marvelous expansion" of employment departments that had taken place during the war, and explained: "The impelling motive has not been entirely that of fostering good industrial relations . . . The major reason in the minds of most industrial relations executives . . . has been to secure employees during the period of labor scarcity and find out why men leave."

Nor was personnel's growth during the war years solely a matter of proliferation. The personal authority of the personnel specialist also increased vis-à-vis the operating supervisor. A 1919 bulletin of the Bureau of Labor Statistics stated exultantly: There has come into being "a separate employment department which makes a point of engaging and placing help with ceremony and politeness, which follows up the new employee, and avoids misfits by a system of tryouts in various departments, which has a ready ear for suggestions and grievances and which alone is empowered to discharge."

It was a powerful change. At its newly scaled apex the employment department was taking away the foreman's divine rights. He was no longer absolute monarch of his crew. He no longer hired the people who worked under him, nor could he discipline unilaterally or fire summarily. Worse yet, not only had his authority been limited, but a new avenue, wide and inviting, swept right around him and into the personnel office, where his men could initiate grievances against *him,* and where his decisions could be overruled.

It was called enlightened management. The personnel man had been assigned a new role. To some extent, at least, he was the guardian of company justice and the administrator of company mercy. It was a noble role, and many employment managers assumed it eagerly. A Bureau of Labor Statistics survey of managers in about a hundred firms during 1919 showed that a majority of them believed that only the employment manager ought to have the power to fire employees (though some qualified their answers). An even higher percentage indicated that the employment department ought to have sole responsibility for employee transfers.

But while the personnel men beamed, the foremen scowled. So did the old-line shop superintendents and general foremen. The foreman, not the employment manager, had the responsibility for meeting production quotas, getting the work out, and keeping discipline in the shop. If the quotas were not met, and if the men got balky or insubordinate or slovenly in their habits, it would be the foreman and not the employment manager who would feel the wrathful tongue of the works' manager. And how could the foreman expect his men to pay him the slightest mind under these new rules? To the foreman this new enlightenment was all a mistake.

Time and circumstances were on the foreman's side, and the personnel man was naïve in not anticipating the inevitable. The inevitable was that the war ended, and so did the cost-plus-10-per-cent Government contracts. Soon to follow was the 1920–1 depression, and with it came bad days for the personnel business. The labor shortage had ended. In its place was a labor surplus. Without cost-plus contracts each "overhead item" on the payroll was a drain on profits. Employment departments were overhead items. It wasn't essential to be nice to employees any more, but it was important to reduce costs. Life began to change rapidly even for personnel men still fortunate enough to be on the company payroll. Much of their power was taken away, and many found themselves shifted into the paler roles of "staff men" and "advisers."[7]

The personnel men felt they had been slapped hard. After so quick and pleasant a rise during the war years they suddenly found themselves dispensable. Many personnel men were out of work. (Of course, others were out of work too, but that was beside the point.) The fault, they concluded, must have been

[7] Interestingly, though, the line foreman did not recover the full measure of his old authority, for a number of reasons—not the least of which was the impending advent of The Union.

theirs. They *must* have done something wrong. What was it? The quest for a moral commenced.

It was not a long search. The answer came in a plethora of self-scoldings. As many personnel men saw it, the trouble was rooted in the softness of approach with which they had come to be identified. As the champions of business heart they had interfered with business muscle (not much, but some). And in that brightest, clearest, coldest light which the depression had spread over the land of enterprise, conscience had been seen for what it really was in the world of making and selling— namely, irrelevant. From time to time since 1920—especially after depression- or recession-based object lessons—personnel men have re-searched their brains and souls to discover ways to make their work as aconscienced as possible, and thus make themselves less expendable.

But in the twenties the time of remorse was short, for soon the American economy began to rally. Everyone began to rally as the 1920's roared, jazzed, and boomed ahead. By the middle of this loudest of all decades almost nobody remembered its muted beginning. Business expanded in one of its happiest periods, and as it did businessmen too tended to be expansive. It was a time for rich men to be nice. And *responsible.*

The era of *systematic* welfarism commenced. In contrast to the individual kindnesses dispensed by the social secretaries of old, a growing number and variety of company-wide programs for the planned improvement of working conditions were begun. Medical services for employees, savings plans, credit unions, insurance plans, and pension plans started to blossom. At Westinghouse Electric, the practice established by the company founder of distributing turkeys at Thanksgiving time was terminated. In its place began a system of benefits for retiring employees and their widows and orphans.

Some people called the new trend corporate paternalism. Its source in some cases was, undoubtedly, very real altruism. In others a more complicated mixture rationalized under the theory (still living) that a happy worker is a productive worker, and its corollary—that if management, as a good parent, would take care of its sons and daughters well, they in turn would respond with obedience, devotion, and contentment. Contentment was important, for as business leadership lectured itself, it was one of the best bulwarks against the threat of the emerging unions.

As the National Association of Manufacturers viewed the situation in the mid-1920's, the bulwarks were thick and solid. Said S. B. Peck, chairman of the Open Shop Committee of the NAM: "The assertion may be boldly made that the decreasing membership in most of the unions and the great difficulty they are experiencing in holding their members together, is due to the fact that the employers—notably the once so-called 'soul-less corporations'—are doing more for the welfare of the workers than the unions themselves."

And what is more, concluded the Committee on Education and Labor of the Seventy-sixth Congress in 1926, the NAM had done its work in combatting unionism so well that it was now able to settle back "to the quiet enjoyment of the fruits of [its] efforts during the years of prosperity."

Meanwhile, the systematic approach was being applied to other facets of personnel work besides welfare. Newly reinspired personnel men, especially in the most progressive corporations, were getting systematic about all sorts of things. There were personnel record-keeping systems and labor-report systems, job-classification systems and suggestion systems. Personnel activity was blossoming into a technology. Explorations were already under way to increase worker productivity through scientific wage-payment plans and scientifically designed training programs.

Perhaps most promising of all, though, were the psychologists. This was not an entirely new tribe to the corporation men. A few of the business community's more daring explorers had discovered university psychology departments years before, but the contacts had been rare. World War I changed the picture significantly. Relatively large numbers of psychologists had worked with the armed services during the war, especially in developing and administering psychological tests for inductees. With the restoration of peace, the psychologists could turn their attention in new directions, so they offered their scientific selection methods to industry. Much of the business community was still suspicious. It doubted that the psychologists could or would make the long climb down from the towers of academe to the hard-packed plains of profit-and-loss country. But some company managements were willing to give them a trial and a number of psychologists accepted the challenge. Their adaptation to the hard-packed plains was little short of magnificent. There was, for example, Edgar J. Swift, who captured the conversion spirit classically in his aptly titled book *Business Power Through Psychology*.

Said Swift: "Galileo failed because he was an investigator and not a salesman. Consequently he could not get his goods marketed . . . Galileo thought that only facts and arguments were needed to sell goods of guaranteed quality, but he was so greatly mistaken that at the end he was compelled to deny publicly everything which he had said about the value of his wares. His competitors, Aristotle, Moses, and the church fathers, had monopolized the market and their stockholders would not let him do business."

It was practical advice in practical language to his fellow psychologists. Swift knew the score, as even a common garden-variety businessman could plainly see.

Some things that came out of the selection-testing movement of the early twenties were valid and useful. A. J. Snow, a Northwestern University psychologist who became director of psychological research for a taxicab company, once more rediscovered Frederick Taylor's old truth: It was not only possible to "underhire," by selecting people with inadequate basic intelligence to do a particular job; it was also possible to "overhire"—to pick someone with too much intelligence for a job. This overqualified employee was likely to become bored with his tasks, neglect them, and even use his excess underutilized mental capacity to foment trouble among the rest of the crew. He was also likely to quit his job at the first opportunity for better, more challenging work.[8]

But much that accompanied the reputable work, especially as "scientific" personnel selection rapidly became fashionable, was aberrant foolishness. A significant portion of it had been spawned from such irresistible but already discredited sources as the theories of Cesare Lombroso. In 1876 Lombroso had theorized that criminals were a distinct type, characterized by certain stigmata or anomalies of physique. They possessed, said Lombroso, such features as a long lower jaw, a flattened nose, scanty beard, and low sensitivity to pain. Anyone with more than five such stigmata was clearly a criminal type. Anyone with from three to five was open to suspicion. Lombroso's claims were fairly widely accepted until the early 1900's, when Dr. Charles Goring systematically studied several thousand criminals and noncriminals and found no significant physical differences between them.

The Lombroso idea, however, was too appealing to give up. Dr. Katherine Blackford applied a comparable system of analysis to the industrial situation. She claimed that personality traits could be tied to physical traits. Blondes, for instance, were more aggressive than brunettes, and therefore they would be better salesmen. Many of the early psychologists were enthralled by these shortcut methods of selection. Eliott Frost presented to the American Psychological Association his theory that "the laborer's attitude toward industrial relations is determined by his nationality more than any other single factor." Jews were "radical" and "keen-witted," Italians were "highly emotional" and "sullen and moody," Germans and Swedes were "placid,"

---

[8] Snow's lesson was apparently not widely learned. It is tough to resist what looks like a bargain, and during the depression of the thirties overhiring (using college graduates for menial work) was fairly common. The results were often as Snow had predicted.

and Poles and Croats were best for the "dirty work in the plant."

Besides the too-loose speculation of the professional psychologists, though, there were even wilder activities by a host of charlatans who descended upon an overeager management with schemes for sure-fire people-picking. There were head-measurers and handwriting analysts, experts who could judge a man's ability by the way he walked, and other experts who could do it by determining whether his facial configuration was convex or concave.

Some personnel people found the whole business shocking. Mary Gilson, a personnel woman of the period, writes in retrospect that it was "incredible that certain well-known men, holding important positions in business and industry, shrewd in their competitive activities, could be so naïve in adopting charlatanry in their attempts to judge human beings."

It didn't last. By the middle of the twenties most of the companies had given up testing. By 1925 less than 5 per cent of even the best-known companies still used tests. The testing movement was destined in the future for a magnificent resurgence, but for the next five years its progress would be stopped almost stone cold.

4

From Mayo to Starkey

TWO OTHER THINGS affected the personnel field in the late 1920's. One was the stock market crash of 1929. It resulted in a second blow to personnel's ego in less than ten years and brought the old inferiority complex back with a rush. The other thing that happened was less noticeable, but from the standpoint of personnel administration, its effect was probably even more profound. On April 24, 1928, Dr. Elton Mayo of Harvard's School of Business made his first visit to a small plant of the Western Electric Company just outside Chicago. The plant was called the Hawthorne Works. Though nobody knew it at the time, a conception had occurred and Human Relations was about to be born.

The subject of human relations, past, present, and future, will be given a good deal of attention later in this book. It is complicated, wide in scope, and has a variety of meanings for social scientists and personnel men. There are those who call Elton Mayo's offspring the single most important development in all social science. There are those who believe it has already begun the process of revolutionizing American industry in a way which ultimately will reconcile the causes of management and labor, and end industrial conflict forever.

There are others, though, who call Mayo's offspring "cow sociology," and see in it the technological refinement of mass manipulation, something which had previously been only an art.

And among this latter group there are those who believe that human relations is the forerunner of what may soon become a fearsomely powerful means of controlling people.[1]

There were about thirty thousand employees at the Hawthorne Works when the Mayo experiments began. Hawthorne management, in common with most managements, believed that its workers could be more productive than they were. Hawthorne management also shared the commonly held assumption that physical working conditions could have a significant effect upon worker morale and effort. Thus, with the cooperation of a committee of academicians from the Massachusetts Institute of Technology, the company began a series of experiments to determine the effects of differences in work-area illumination.

Fritz Roethlisberger, an associate of Mayo at the time and subsequently an elder statesman of human relations in his own right, has described the earliest stages (pre-Mayo) of the Hawthorne work. He tells how "the great *éclaircissement,* the new illumination," came about. In a carefully planned and executed experiment, workers were divided into two groups. For the first group work-area lighting intensities were increased gradually from 24 to 46 and then to 70 foot-candles. For the second group, which was to be used as a control on the experiment, lighting was held as constant as possible.

It was a fairly standard experiment, but the results were curious. Each time illumination levels were raised, productivity rose too—which was all well and good. But oddly enough, when the illumination levels were reduced, productivity *continued to go up.* And when they were lowered even further, productivity still rose. What was still more confusing, even in the control group, which had been selected as a part of the experiment but for whom *no changes at all* had been made in lighting levels, production also rose.[2]

[1] Loren Baritz's book *The Servants of Power* provides one of the best over-all tours of Mayo's work and its effects by a guide who strongly holds the latter point of view.

[2] In a later experiment employees were led to believe that their lighting had been increased, though in reality it was not changed at all. The employees expressed their appreciation to management for the improved illumination.

Concluded Hawthorne management: Something other than lighting must account for the difference. The question was, *What?* With no adequate answer forthcoming from its existing research staff, Western Electric decided to assemble a new collection of scientists to consider the puzzle. One of these was Dr. Elton Mayo. So began a research program that was to last more than two decades and would cost Western Electric well over a million dollars and thousands of man-hours. Eventually, the program would change significantly the form of the personnel function as well.

Under the guidance of Mayo and his team, further experiments were framed. These investigations focused upon variations in methods of doing the work, rest periods, wage-payment systems, and a number of other presumed productivity factors. Again, the experiments were carefully devised and closely monitored, but no matter how conditions were varied production continued to go up.

Still more experiments were devised. One of these was the now-classic study of the relay-assembly girls. Roethlisberger explains: "The idea was very simple: A group of five girls was placed in a separate room where their condition of work (assembly of a telephone relay) could be carefully controlled, where their output could be measured, and where they could be closely observed. It was decided to introduce at specified intervals different changes in working conditions and to see what effect these innovations had on output. Also, records were kept, such as the temperature and humidity of the room, the number of hours each girl slept at night, the kind and amount of food she ate for breakfast, lunch, and dinner."

Detailed records showing the quality and quantity of the girls' productivity were scrupulously compiled. The girls were also given regular physical examinations. Under these conditions the girls were studied for five years and "literally tons of material" were collected and analyzed.

Possible correlations were sought between the amount of rest a girl had the night before and her production output the next day. No significant correlation was found. The scientists did not give up. An attempt was made to correlate each girl's productivity to her rest *two* nights previously. Again, to no avail. Other variables were tested. They produced no meaningful outcome. The results of the relay-assembly experiments proved nothing more than the original lighting experiments had, even though, as Roethlisberger reported, "a skillful statistician spent several years trying to relate variations in output with variations in the physical circumstances of these five operators." There was not "a single correlation of enough statistical significance to be recognized by any competent statistician as having any meaning."

If Dr. Mayo's statistician was skillful, he must have been even more patient, as must all of Mayo's crew and Western Electric management. The quest to capture the elusive essence of productivity continued. Not only were the experiments' results carefully examined, the conditions under which they had been conducted were re-examined as well. Slowly, a new thought stirred among the experimenters. *It was not the physical but the social environment which mattered.* The workers who had been chosen to participate in the experiments had become a *group.* Not only that, they had suddenly also become *important people,* people to whom both the Mayo experimenters and management were paying rapt *attention.* This was the great "*éclaircissement.*"

Mayo's men persisted. What else was there to learn—what were the specifics? For one thing, the workers in the groups had been *talked to and listened to* by the investigators. In developing the individual experiments they had, as Roethlisberger described it, been "questioned sympathetically about their reactions to the conditions imposed, and many of these conferences took place in the office of the superintendent." They had also been allowed the uncommon privilege of chatting with each other while on the job, and their minimum production quotas had been eliminated. But most important of all, "their physical health and well-being became matters of great concern [and] their opinions, hopes and fears were eagerly sought."

It was a spectacular discovery, and it was only the beginning. Stimulated by their new-found success, Mayo and his staff expanded their investigations. In another series of experiments they rediscovered the phenomenon of productivity restriction among Western Electric workmen. Despite the company's cleverly designed wage system, which paid an ever-increasing bonus for higher production, the workers still limited their output.

But Mayo was not satisfied merely to identify the phenomenon (others had surmised it before), he wanted to know why and how. And he found out. Productivity rates were not controlled by management standards but by *work-group* standards. The group controlled its members' behavior and prevented deviation; thus it protected itself from management control.

The group's values, or "sentiments," as Roethlisberger called them, were these: "(1) You should not turn out too much work; if you do, you are a 'rate buster.' (2) You should not turn out too little work; if you do, you are a 'chiseler.' (3) You should not say anything to a supervisor which would react to the detriment of one of your associates; if you do, you are a 'squealer.' (4) You should not be too officious; that is, if you are an inspector you should not act like one."

The individual worker needed to belong, and almost invariably the threat of ostracism was enough to keep him in line even if he did not accept the premise that regulating output was in his own as well as the group's long-range best interests.[3]

Ironically, Mayo, who had started his career with the orientation of a psychologist, but whose work had led him into matters sociological, contributed a hurtful blow to the other industrial psychologists of his era. He had shown that it was

[3] "Pacing," as the restrictive practice is commonly called, is even now almost universal among production workers, despite modern "incentive" or piecework wage systems. By quite realistic estimates the effect of pacing is to reduce production by half or even two thirds of maximum potential. Nor is the practice really "irrational" or merely a matter of antimanagement attitudes. As the production worker sees it, pacing helps stabilize earnings, extends employment, and can be used as a "weapon" to protest management actions when a strike would be too drastic or otherwise inappropriate.

not basic intelligence, dexterity, and latent ability which were most important in determining productivity among workers, as the psychological testers had presumed. Most important was the relationship of the individual to the work group of which he was a part, and that group's relationship to management.

But the most significant thing which the Mayo team had discovered in the service of management was that employees liked to talk and be talked to. The reason productivity had risen in the illumination experiment series was that the experimenters had talked to the participating employees. They had told the women what the experiments were about and had asked for their comments and suggestions. As Loren Baritz puts it, "it was a faulty social science, but faulty social science turned out to be profitable management practice." Nor was the point lost on Western Electric. The company, after some further tryouts, established in 1936 a "personnel counseling" program with five "counselors." In two years there were ten, and by 1941 there were twenty-nine. At the program's peak in 1954 there were over sixty counselors in the system. More than half a million counseling sessions were conducted between 1936 and 1955. Mayo had discovered that people in the shop felt good after they were given an opportunity to "blow off steam," and that became the technique of the counselor. Baritz describes it unkindly: "Regardless of all the technical gobbledygook that has been written about the functions of the counselor, it all simmered down to the plain injunction that he was to listen to any problem of any employee, good worker or not; that he was not to give advice or argue; that he should make no promises about remedial action. The counselor . . . was just to listen to the employee talk."

In addition, according to the company description of his responsibilities, the counselor was to watch constantly for signs of unrest and to try to assuage tension by discussion before the unrest became active. He was to try to dilute or redirect dissatisfaction by helping the employees to think along constructive lines.

Mayo's work had its impact on the personnel function. Foreman- and supervisor-training programs in "leadership"—applying human relations in a nice way to get employees to do what you want them to do—proliferated through the personnel departments of major companies. By 1935 a survey of thirty of them showed that two thirds of the company representatives believed that leadership and human-relations skills were the most important ones for a foreman to have. Often, however, though the human-relations training programs were ostensibly based on Mayo's work, in actual fact they were nothing more than reheated versions of good old, practical supervisors' maxims that had been around for years. If Mayo himself noticed them at all it must have left him cold and uncomfortable.

Elton Mayo and human relations were not all that happened to personnel during the 1930's. There was also Franklin D. Roosevelt's New Deal. Howard S. Kaltenborn, vice president of Westinghouse Electric, recalls the period this way: "As economic conditions worsened, employees and the public lost confidence in business leadership. There was a tremendous expansion in the power, influence and range of activities of government. Government encouraged a swift and unprecedented growth of the labor movement." Kaltenborn goes on to tell how both management and unions turned to Washington to solve their problems rather than working them out between themselves. For many companies the unaccustomed requirement of dealing with suddenly more powerful—or at any rate, Government-protected—unions was strange and anxiety producing. Kaltenborn recalls that companies became preoccupied with it to such an extent that most other aspects of their relations with their employees were neglected. There was an ever-present peril of possible union charges of unfair labor practices and an obvious receptivity of New Deal labor referees toward hearing such charges. These conditions made some employers so nervous that in many companies first-line supervisors were forbidden by higher management from even talking to employees about any subject which might, however vaguely, be construed as an industrial-relations subject.

It was a bad time. As the Westinghouse vice president remembers it, employers had "lost initiative [and] management fell into an attitude of hopelessness, even of cynicism, in industrial relations matters."[4] Unionism was advancing with rapidly increasing momentum. Many business chiefs accepted it as a tragic fact of life, but some thought the rush could be slowed, held, and with a little help from a shift in the country's political winds, eventually even be stopped. It was a chance, but it would involve hard work and careful strategy. First, obviously, relations with the unions could no longer be entrusted to ordinary supervisors. They needed skilled attention. So they were removed from the foreman's hands and given over in total to the union-relations expert—then, and now, the most powerful of all personnel men.

Second, it was necessary to find out what was bothering the workers. This needed to be done quickly and, if possible, inexpensively. There was a way—through the attitude survey. Surveys had been used in market and consumer research before, and there was no reason to believe they would not work with employees as well. To the personnel men they were welcome as could be. With management's growing attention to union-relations specialization and attitude-survey administration, many more personnel men would remain at their desks and off the pavements.

Attitude surveys were developed in a number of styles. Essentially, they aimed at tapping the pulse of employee morale

[4] There is one puzzling note in Mr. Kaltenborn's summary of the unhappy 1930–47 situation (1947 being the year of the Taft-Hartley Act). He concludes that had "these trends continued unchecked," there would have been serious "consequences to the economic system under which we operate." The fortunate advent of Taft-Hartley saved us. But when management "again turned its attention to good industrial relations practices [it] found that many of its old problems had been solved—or rather, had simply disappeared." One can only wonder who it was that solved those old problems or made them disappear, since Mr. Kaltenborn had just told us that employers had lost initiative and that the strongest power, influence, and activity were coming from Government. Could he possibly mean what it sounds as though he is saying?

in the plant and discovering trouble spots. The surveys could be administered by interview or questionnaire, or both, and they inquired about the worker's satisfaction or lack of satisfaction with such items as his pay and working conditions, his relationships with his supervisor and his fellow workers, his opportunities for promotion, and his feelings about the company as a whole.

In some surveys the questions became pretty pointed. The following are from a "guided interview" survey of General Finance Corporation:

Is there anyone in your group who you feel is better qualified to be your leader than the one you have now?
Are there any troublemakers in your department?
How would you rate your boss in his ability (a) to handle personnel (b) to handle his job?

Procter and Gamble, Armstrong Cork, Kimberly-Clark, and Sears, Roebuck were all early users of attitude surveys. General Motors had its own unique approach. GM hired the Pinkerton Detective Agency, and Pinkerton men made visits to GM employees' homes to find out how they felt about things. Some people didn't like the idea, and eventually it came to the attention of the United States Congress. In 1937, the La Follette Committee held hearings on the matter. When Harry W. Anderson, GM's labor relations director, was asked about the Pinkerton-style survey by the senator, Anderson explained logically that many times employees were more willing to talk freely in their homes about whether or not their foreman was treating them fairly. Somehow, though, La Follette was not completely satisfied with this answer and he pressed Anderson a bit further. Finally, Anderson admitted that there might be another explanation. "We are interested," said GM's man, "to know if there was any particular labor organization going on in town, and if so, why . . ."

Thomas G. Spates was a remarkable personnel man. His career took him to the vice presidency for personnel administration of the General Foods Corporation, and subsequently to a professorship in personnel administration at Yale's School of Engineering. He is one of the relatively few genuine folk heroes of personnel's history. There was a grandness about Spates which, in a way, personified the ebullience of the personnel function during the 1940's.

Spates was a man of action, in the enterprise tradition, but he was a philosopher too, and in some ways a radical. He spoke of industry's responsibility to the public welfare. He recognized and referred openly to the fact that inherent selfishness was as much a part of the makeup of management as of any other segment of society. He said that "the people on our payrolls are citizens of a democracy . . . [and] unless we make sure that the actual daily work experiences, for at least a majority of our citizens, are a confirmation rather than a contradiction of the Declaration of Independence and of the Bill of Rights, it is quite likely that our form of government will be changed." Spates talked too about such things as "increased participation in decisions that shape human life and affect economic equality and justice," and of "helping individuals to realize all that is within [their] capacity to achieve."

But it was not the radicalism of Spates's ideas which made him the idol of his own and subsequent generations of personnel men. Almost no one now seems to remember much about his ideas except that they were "human-relations oriented." What enthralled them was the extravagant sweep of his view of personnel work. Proclaimed Spates in his book *The Scope of Modern Personnel Administration:*

"Through the influence of [economic pressure] we trace the origins of a great new profession [personnel administration], destined to take its place alongside the four learned professions of law, medicine, pedagogy, and theology in advancing the spiritual and material well-being of humanity . . . There are no troubles any place in the world, arising from relations of people at work, that cannot be alleviated by good personnel administration." And, promised Spates, "Now employers everywhere who really want maximum utilization of their human resources with the highest degree of individual satisfaction, and who are willing to work hard to attain that objective, can be told what to do and how to do it with extraordinary assurance that predicted results will be achieved. The consequences of ignoring or violating this code of personnel administration can be forecast with a degree of accuracy not usually expected in the social sciences."

The "great new profession" was ready for action. But were the corporate chiefs ready for the great new profession? They were. The pendulum had arced again. Once more it was a decade of war.

Manpower shortages had never been so acute. Fifteen million service men and women of prime working age were suddenly no longer available to industry, while at the same time the requirements of the war effort multiplied production demands as much as ten-fold. Previously unemployed, marginal, even unemployable workers suddenly became vital parts of the labor force. There was an epidemic of all the old industrial diseases— absenteeism, tardiness, turnover, goofing-off, griping, and the rest. Something had to be done.

If it were handled right there might even be a new chance to recoup on the old front. Spates himself had sounded the note in his advice to management: *"Refuse to accept the doctrine that the spread of unionism in the United States is inevitable* —There is overwhelming evidence to support the conclusion that Americans prefer good personnel administration to unionism . . ." (Author's italics.)

The theme of good personnel administration in the 1940's was *"The Company Cares."* It cares about employees and their satisfaction. "Morale" was the word of the decade. For soldiers first, but soon for civilians as well. The prototype tools for treating morale had been cast during the preceding decade. In this one they would be ground, polished, sharpened, and mass produced.

The era of victory gardens for the war effort was accompanied by human-relations gardens for the industrial peace effort. The assortment of their flowers varied from the profuse, simple, and direct "morale-booster"—company-sponsored bowling leagues, swimming pools, picnics, and so on—to the most rare and esoteric investigations and speculations about semantics and emotions, consultative and persuasive management, role-playing and sociodrama.

The use of attitude surveys expanded. By 1947 about 250 firms were administering them. Employee counseling multiplied, especially among the aircraft and shipbuilding firms. Leadership training for supervisors became an indispensable program which no up-to-the-minute company could do without. Personnel record-keeping—inventories of worker skills, seniority lists, wage-progression charts, and transfer and upgrade eligibility rosters—was developed and elaborated to awesome proportions. Employee-performance ratings were introduced, and more supervisory training was required to teach the foremen and other managers how to use them.

Employee-benefit programs such as pension plans, hospital insurance, and severance pay were expanded in their coverage —not, management insisted, primarily for their financial value to employees, but rather because they proved that management *cared*. Chester Barnard, president of New Jersey Bell Telephone, warned personnel men against any attempt to "buy off hostile states of mind" among employees. And James C. Worthy of Sears, Roebuck, after explaining that "nonwage payments" in 1948 had cost his company more than 84 million dollars, said: "Important as the economic aspects of the benefits may be, their chief significance as regards employees' morale is the fact that they are tangible evidence to the organization of management's concern for the welfare of its employees."

But if, as Barnard and Worthy announced, money was not most important to employees, nevertheless not many workers had yet abandoned the habit of picking up their weekly pay envelopes. Thus management was still ready to spend effort on capturing the devotion of the economic man as well as the spiritual one.

The forties became a time of renewed concentration on developing more effective wage-payment systems. Incentive pay plans, arrangements whereby a worker's earnings were tied by some formula directly to his output, were not new. Even before the age of "scientific management" there had been rough-cut systems of the sort. Frederick Taylor had himself developed a differential piece-rate plan in which workers who met their quotas were paid a higher amount per piece than those whose production fell under quota. As far back as 1789, Adam Smith had expressed concern about piecework methods of payment, for he feared that workers were "very apt to overwork themselves" under such arrangements.

As Elton Mayo had learned at Western Electric's Hawthorne Works, however, Smith need not have fretted. The findings of William F. Whyte and his intrepid crew of Cornell University graduate students in the following decade were equally reassuring.

In his book *Money and Motivation,* Whyte tells of the experiences of these student-researchers, particularly one of them, Donald F. Roy, who spent eleven months as a drill-press operator in a steel-fabricating plant. In one of several high points in the book, Roy describes a conversation between Starkey, a veteran plant employee, and a new man he is breaking in. Starkey's fatherly advice to the tyro lacks academic finesse, but somehow it suffers little from that fact in portraying the relationship of worker versus system.

Said Starkey: " 'If you expect to get any kind of price, you got to outwit that son-of-a-bitch [the time-study man—a management specialist who sets the standards of "bogeys" from which incentive rates derive]! You got to use your noodle while you're working, and think your work out ahead as you go along! You got to add in movements you know you ain't going to make when you're running the job!' " When the younger man replies that he had done his best to run the job as slowly as possible under the eye of the time-study man, Starkey answers that it wasn't slow enough. " 'Remember those bastards are paid to screw you, and that's all they got to think about. They'll stay up half the night figuring out how to beat you out of a dime. They figure you're going to try to fool them, so they make allowances for that. They set the prices low enough to allow for what you do . . . It's up to you to figure out how to fool them more than they allow for.' "

In a way, then, the economic man had been found, though he was not as simple a phenomenon as management had expected. He had not merely adopted the equation that the harder you work, the more you turn out, the more you get paid; he had taken it a step further and come up with a corollary: the better you fake, the less work you need to do for the same amount of pay.

But there was more than economics involved. As Donald Roy, and others more permanently assigned to the assembly process, had pointed out, working at a faster pace was not in itself repugnant to factory workers. In fact it resulted in less fatigue and boredom at the end of the day. The real appeal was to "beat the system" and thereby beat the system designers— management. It was a contest, and the production workers were by no means overmatched.[5]

Psychology flourished during the Second World War even more than it had during World War I, and with it flourished the prestige of the psychologists. Not only did they refine their tests for the selection of recruits, officers, and all varieties of military specialists, they also became key contributors on the glamorous new front of psychological warfare and trainers of the super-mysterious agents of the Office of Strategic Services.

By war's end the presence of a psychologist in the company personnel department seldom threatened the respectability of even the more conservative business executives. In a 1946 survey of one group of large firms 30 per cent had at least one professional psychologist on their staff, and over 50 per cent

---

[5] A survey of several hundred companies by Scott, Clothier and Spriegel in 1940, and another in 1947, showed that the use of almost all varieties of incentive plans had declined during that period and that "straight-time" pay had increased by almost 20 per cent.

thought it would be a good idea to have one. Even more companies employed psychological consultants on a retainer basis. General Motors, Marshall Field, Sears, the aircraft companies, and many more found use for the behavioral scientists. The Ford Motor Company began a half-million-dollar research program in the psychology of human relations.

Industrial sociology shared the new place in the sun. Fritz Roethlisberger, Elton Mayo's close associate during the Hawthorne days, became an important voice of the times. Roethlisberger had continued to be deeply involved in the study of workers in the factory social system and the application of the Hawthorne wisdom. Like Thomas Spates, he saw the potential of the personnel function in large proportions, but he had reservations about how well prepared personnel's practitioners were to assume their places on Olympus.

Roethlisberger gently told the personnel men that he thought their conventional approach to their mission through such specialities as employment work, training, safety, wage administration, and so on was not what it should be. "My plea," said Roethlisberger in his book *Management and Morale,* "will be for a personnel program that addresses itself to the concrete human situations in a particular plant."[6]

As Roethlisberger saw it, and as he managed to convey to a few of the more conceptually oriented personnel executives themselves, there were three major problem areas:

First, the problem of communication—how could those at the top of the organization be kept informed of what was happening below them. And, on the other hand, how could those at the base of the pyramid be made aware of the organization's major purposes. Awareness here meant more than recognition. It meant sympathy with the purposes and active support. It later came to mean support not only of the company's production and sales

---

[6] Roethlisberger proceeds to clarify his own orientation to "concrete human situations" (and the italics are his): ". . . the first human problem of any business organization is *how to secure the cooperation of people in attaining its collective purpose.*"

goals, but also of the whole free-enterprise–American-way-of-
life package.

Second, there was worker morale. But it was a much more
sophisticated formulation than the average personnel man had
ever heard before. The problem was one of integrating individuals into the organization in such a manner that, as Roethlisberger put it, "a comfortable, working equilibrium [could] be
maintained between the various social groups in an individual
enterprise such that no one group in the organization will
separate itself out in opposition to the remainder . . ."

Third, there was the problem of worker motivation—how to
get people to work better and harder and be happier than they
were. How to arrange the work situation, as Roethlisberger
said, "so that the satisfactions from the job do not fall too far
short of the demands that are being made of it . . . [while on
the other hand,] helping individual workers to modify the excessive and impossible demands which they may be making of
the job."

In fact, the impact of the Roethlisberger formulations on the
personnel field during the 1940's was more symbolic than
substantive. For the field captains of the company personnel
programs the social science research was not very relevant. Except for a very few conceptually oriented personnel men—and
these, by and large, still safely tucked away in the far-removed
offices of company headquarters—the writings of the social
scientists were largely unread. It would be midcentury and later
before these "egg-head" personnel men would begin to come
out to meet the field personnel men. With them they would
carry some new and fancy implements, such as interpersonal
communication theory, group interaction theory, needs hierarchies, and positive and negative motivators. For the field
veterans, it would begin as an amusing encounter, but eventually
become a frightening experience.

5

White-Collar Time

AND SO, after our brief historical review we have arrived at personnel's modern era and the principal subjects of this book. By now personnel's foundations have been poured and are fairly well hardened, but some intriguing things are still happening to its superstructure.

For one, the personnel business has been getting more complicated. A piece of *prima facie* evidence for this comes out of a study made by the National Industrial Conference Board in 1963 when it examined 147 company personnel procedure manuals from firms in the United States and Canada and put together a composite index of subjects covered by the manuals. The list contained over two thousand entries. Another impressive discovery was that 40 per cent of the companies included in the board's sample reported that they gave training courses in the use of their manuals. The training program of one company, Polaroid Corporation, consisted of ten sessions of an hour and a half each!

But there have come to be more serious and troublesome difficulties in the personnel man's work than the complexities of the company manual. The personnel man has had to start to worry about whole sets of people he never had to worry about before: the office workers and the professionals. Until the mid-1950's, one thing had been crystal-clear and concrete-firm for the old-line personnel professional. At the starkest level of reality there was always one undeniably solid reason for the company to have a personnel department:[1] *Because it had a union.*

Labor costs affected profits. Labor costs, obviously, were determined in the shop. So, the *real* job of the *real men* of personnel was to keep wage and benefits packages within bounds, get productivity up without triggering a walkout, and lastly, but only hopefully, get the shop people to like management a little more.

It would be unrealistic to suggest that concentration on the task of dealing with unions had been de-emphasized. It is still a very important concern of the personnel function, but a number of other matters have become important as well. In a 1964 survey of personnel executives by the Industrial Relations Institute, for example, the general area of "employee relations" was rated as their "most pressing problem today" by more executives than was "union relations." In a similar survey only five years earlier more than twice as many executives had rated union relations rather than employee relations as their top problem.

The view has changed because times have changed. The shifts in our economy and technology over the last ten years have resulted in about a million and a half fewer production jobs and about the same number of additional jobs for nonproduction people. Extrapolating this trend, the Bureau of the Census estimates that by 1975, the number of manual workers in the United States will decline to 35.6 per cent of the work force. And for the same year, professional, technical, and clerical employees should comprise 46.7 per cent.[2]

And that is how it has come to pass that enterprise's brightest

---

[1] Often called an "industrial relations" or "labor relations" department.

[2] When the booming growth of service industries, where almost all the jobs are nonproduction, is also considered, the changing nature of work and workers in the United States is even more striking. In 1930 there were about 10 per cent more workers employed in manufacturing than in service industries. In 1960 the percentages had reversed to equal but opposite levels. By 1970 service enterprises are expected to employ close to 20 per cent more workers than will manufacturers.

godling, Efficiency, has leaped up from the factory floor and now stalks the office corridors. For those of the white collars perilous times have commenced. Nor is it the proletarian ranks of clerks and technicians alone that Efficiency's fine-edged axe threatens. The management nobility is not immune.

The pendulum is in full swing back from the 1940's and early 1950's. During that era the sheer *volume* of analysis and decision-making required by corporate growth became too much for the small coteries of top managers who controlled corporate destinies. Their reluctant but necessary response was decentralization—the delegation of analysis and decision-making functions to more people at lower levels in their organizations. Thus decentralization meant the proliferation of middle-level managers.

But computers have enabled fewer individuals to handle a hugely increased volume of data, to analyze it, and to make decisions based on the analyses much more quickly. One thing about top executives is that they usually believe that nobody below them makes decisions as well as they do. By and large, they are right. That is how they got to be top executives. The consequences for decentralization, and for the managers to whom it gave birth, are apparent.

The spread of "computerization" has been wide and rapid, and there has been some decline in the number of middle managers relative to industrial output. Previously, independent operations such as purchasing, warehousing, inventory control, and production scheduling have been eagerly gathered in by the data-processing units of many firms. By incorporating the accounting function as only one element of an over-all control system, the computer has in some cases eliminated entire financial record-keeping organizations, and simultaneously the need for the managers who ran them.

If the drive for increased efficiency beyond the shop has begun to press the management elite, it has been pressing the nonmanagement salaried people longer and harder. The work of clerks and technicians, what might be called the production

work of the office and laboratory, is the kind most easily trans-
latable into computer programs, automated processes, and other
forms of mechanization. Preparation of plant payrolls that once
required dozens of girls can now be done in the *spare time* of a
computer used primarily for other purposes. Claims and records
processing in the insurance business are highly amenable to
electronic data processing, or EDP, as it is called. The telephone
industries, which use a high proportion of clerks and technicians,
have increased the volume of their operations by about 25 per
cent since 1957 but now employ about thirty thousand fewer
people.

The full consequences of automation are still not clear to
anyone. It is a subject which invariably stimulates a deluge of
controversial speculation. For now, though, we can note the one
element of automation which is not controversial at all—the fact
that we are going to have more and more of it.

Unfortunately, however, for those who would rather
deal with neat magnetic tapes and uniformly rectangular IBM
decks than with messy and variously shaped humans, some
number of the latter are bound to be around for a while. So
there also remains a collection of sticky and, for the personnel
men, difficult problems. Insecurity may shake employee morale,
depersonalization may turn his attitudes negative. Attitudes and
morale are the provinces of the personnel man, but his old
standard approaches do not seem quite adequate now, even to
himself.

The psychological problems arising from reduction in status
and security are beginning to be felt by professional and management personnel as well. Engineers, only a few years ago
considered the elite of the professionals, are among the victims
of the new disenchantment. The mass hirings and mass layoffs
of hundreds of engineers in response to the ebb and flow of
Government defense contracts are more and more coming to
resemble the old patterns for hiring and layoff of factory workers. The engineer today is seldom the special, broad expert who

in the past walked, essentially alone, along the production process, magically solving the critical technical problems that others could not solve. Rather, he is most often one specialist among many who labor at separate points along a great, complex chain. It would be grossly superficial to equate his labors to the single screw-turn of the production worker on the assembly line, but there is a degree of parallel.

And the engineers are feeling the change. In a study of over a thousand engineers and engineering supervisors, Eugene Raudsepp, a specialist in engineering attitude surveys, found that almost 30 per cent of the engineers registered "profound dissatisfaction" with the "prestige, status, and social esteem" accorded them by their companies and their communities. As one engineer complained, "Engineering is too often considered to be the least required function by nonengineering minded top management."[3]

Besides the threat of sheer technological displacement—the brute fact that a machine can do the jobs of many people better, faster, and cheaper than they can—there is also the more subtle peril of individual obsolescence.

The obsolescence problem applies to a wide variety of skills, but again, engineering provides a good illustrative example. Engineers begin to depreciate immediately after leaving school and continue to do so at an increasingly rapid rate. Dr. Thomas Stelson, head of Carnegie Tech's civil engineering department, reflects what has come to be a commonplace among both educators and industrial people. He says: "With modern technology advancing so rapidly . . . the decline in value, or obsolescence, of engineering personnel may likely become an increasingly serious problem in modern technology unless professional societies, employers, and educational institutions recognize its importance and develop suitable remedies." Dr. Stelson believes an experienced man may have to devote a third of his time to

[3] I have, incidentally, heard almost identical words pronounced many times by purchasing agents about purchasing, by research specialists about research, and especially by personnel men about personnel work.

self-education after he leaves school, just to keep up with his field. In the good old days five or ten hours a week of extra effort used to be a fairly sure-fire way of climbing past your fellow men on the ladder to success. Now, apparently, this won't even keep you on the ladder.

Eugene Raudsepp's examination of engineers' attitudes is not an unusual practice. Attitude surveys, a standard item in the personnel man's tool kit, are administered to all varieties of personnel, and in some corporations on an almost continuous schedule. They have been showing a high tide of dissatisfaction running among white-collar workers. It is not at all unusual to find 25 to 45 per cent of these employees responding unfavorably (and anonymously) to such questions as "How do you rate this company as a place to work?" or "How much concern does management in this company have for employees?"

The power of this negative thinking has been recognized even by the National Association of Manufacturers. In the introduction to an instructional booklet for management, NAM warns: ". . . while the salaried employee looks instinctively to his employer for both leadership and job satisfaction, recent developments have tended to undermine his traditional willingness to rely on management."

There was a time when there were two major advantages to being a salaried employee. First, it meant that, unless you fouled up pretty horribly somewhere along the line, you had real job security. Second, being "salaried" entitled you to an extra package of niceties which the hourly paid people in the shop did not get. This included more holidays, longer vacations, paid sick leave, more liberal pensions, company-paid insurance, and other benefits.

This second advantage has evaporated almost as completely as the first. The differences between fringe benefits offered salaried and hourly workers have grown much narrower. In fact, in some firms the benefit program improvements granted to salaried personnel *consistently* came from behind to match those already awarded in contract negotiations to union-represented employees. And this applies for professional and supervisory as well as for the nonprofessional white-collar workers.

This situation produces some interesting anomalies. One that I have noticed on several occasions finds the management people (including a goodly number of personnel men) virtuously telling each other during the negotiating period that the union people are already overpaid and should not be granted another cent. At the same time the management men are rooting—though usually *sotto voce*—for the union to win another holiday or two, full company payment of their medical insurance, or some other fringe delicacy.

A number of personnel men have noted anxiously the possibility that salaried employees may have begun to listen more attentively to the sounds made by union organizers. In the Industrial Relations Institute survey cited earlier, where "employee relations" surmounted "union relations" as a prime problem, the responding personnel executives also saw a drive to organize white-collar and technical groups as a probable main thrust of the unions. And the National Association of Manufacturers makes the point more clearly in *Satisfying the Salaried Employee—A Practical Manual for Building Better Relations with All Categories of White Collar People:* "The salaried employee today is being wooed by both unions and management. This contest for his support will be won by the one which recognizes the real needs and desires of the salaried group and provides the answers which will bring satisfaction. The outcome of this contest may very well rest on management's action at this critical juncture."

In cooler perspective there may be some question about just how critical this critical juncture really is. In the contest referred to by the NAM, management, it would appear, is still way ahead. While about 56 per cent of the blue-collar workers in the United States are unionized, less than 10 per cent of the office workers are. Only about 3.5 per cent of the engineers belong to unions, and this is a *decline* from a one-time peak of 5 per cent.[4]

Nevertheless, as many management men see it, the peril is still ahead. If the unions are to survive, the reasoning goes, they must grow. There are wise heads—or at least sharp eyes— among the union folk, and they too must recognize the consequences of the changing composition of the work force. The only way for unions to grow is through white-collar organization. There are some signs that the unions—especially the Teamsters—are stepping up the pace of their white-collar campaigns, and experimenting with some new "softer" approaches.

So, with the benefit of fervor, the juncture is critical now. Even without fervor it may get critical after a while. The question for the personnel man, and it is a difficult one, is what to do.

An old organization adage says: If you can't think of anything else to do, reorganize. Within the last five years or so personnel operations far and wide have been reorganizing. Ford Motor Company's 1963 decision to set up a special new personnel relations department for their salaried personnel is an example. According to the "Executive Communication" announcing the change, the purpose was to assist "in the development of personnel policies for salaried employees and for review and appropriate action regarding employment practices and conditions for such employees." The underlying concerns of Ford's top personnel executives emerge with even sharper clarity in a brochure used by the company in its instruction program for personnel department trainees. The brochure observes: "For the purposes of convenience in administration and because of differences in need, salaried employees are given special attention through the Salaried Personnel Office." And

---

[4] The major problem here for the unions has been, once again, people's status and image concerns. (How does it look for a professional to belong to a union, just like a common, ordinary laborer?) This, coupled with some exceptionally clumsy organizing efforts, has resulted in what union people themselves acknowledge to be a pretty miserable showing so far.

in an interesting aside, the brochure adds: "By and large, salaried employees at Ford do not belong to unions."

But reorganization is a structural thing, composed mostly of boxes and lines on large pieces of paper. What of more intangible matters? What, particularly, about the personnel man himself and his own interactions with the salaried employee?

In the ancient and classic days of their craft personnel men used to specialize in talking to people. In their modern era the majority specialize in their specialties. There are a number of distinct subfunctions of the personnel field. Most of them were born in the early systematization movements of the 1920's and 1930's. The catalogue includes: union (sometimes called labor) relations specialists, compensation (sometimes, wage and/or salary) administrators—including subspecies, from hourly wage specialists to executive-compensation analysts. There are employee-benefits administrators, health and safety specialists, and employment interviewers. Also technical recruiters, who hunt engineers, and placement specialists, who have charge of distributing those captured to the most appropriate places. There are testing specialists, who give tests to the ordinary run of job candidates, and personnel assessment specialists, who give tests and do other things psychological to the fancier runs. There are training specialists, called management development specialists in some organizations and personnel development specialists in others. And there are communications specialists and community relations specialists.

In the course of his organization life the average salaried employee will, from time to time, find himself in brief contact with the personnel specialist or a product of his specialization. He may, for example, be asked to fill out a job description form, or an attitude survey form, or a training-course rating form, or a readership survey form. Most often both request and form will come to him via the interoffice mail or from the hands of his supervisor, who, in turn, may have received them through the interoffice mail. Somewhat less frequently the form is accompanied by a brief, explanatory group lecture delivered by the salary administrator, personnel development specialist, or communications specialist. There may even be a sort of ritualistic question and answer period afterward, but there is usually little more.

The fact is that in most companies the contacts between employees and personnel men tend to be relatively few. When they do occur they are often limited to impersonal conversations on narrow bands of subject matter. Even in those relatively rare instances when they are more personally focused on the individual and his case the interactions may be quite arid. In his interview the placement specialist attempts to categorize and assess the skills of an employee who seeks to transfer from one organization unit to another. In his "audit" of the employee's job, the salary administration specialist tries to determine the *real* level of the job's responsibility and its *true* dollar worth to the organization. Ironically, in some organizations it is only in the initial employment interview and in those final bitter (or sweet, as the case may be) terminal conversations which personnel men call "exit interviews" that the average employee is encouraged by the personnel man's procedures to speak his mind. And usually there are prescribed formats even for these occasions.

The ethics of personnel work require that information given in confidence must be kept in confidence. The majority of personnel men observe this requirement quite scrupulously. But even so, when the basic relationship between employee and personnel man is so meager, few employees are inclined to place much trust in the personnel department. Thus, except under conditions which automatically guarantee anonymity, such as mass-administered attitude surveys—and some do not trust these either—the responses of employees to "sensitive" questions are often cautious. Many are reluctant to risk acquiring reputations as malcontents or insurgents. Even in the exit interview the candor which is expected from the departing employee, who presumably has nothing to lose, is often more theoretical than real. Few are inclined to scorch all the earth behind them. They may, after all, need a company reference someday.

But the pattern we have described is by no means a universal one. An increasing number of companies have recognized the problem of the personnel function's depersonalization through specialization. In response some companies have produced a new style of personnel "general practitioner." Less an expert in the subfunctions of his field, the generalist once more specializes in people contacts, and he tends to wander more among the troops.

At its best, this return to the classical traditions can serve a dual purpose. It can provide a transmission link for the employee who has a problem he cannot bring himself to discuss directly with his supervisor. If the personnel man is sufficiently competent he may be able to help resolve the issue and bring man and manager to closer understanding of each other's situations.[5] And secondly, the generalist approach, if properly designed, can help put the personnel department back in touch with what is happening beyond its own walls. What it does with its new intelligence is another matter.

At less than its best, however, the pattern of interaction between generalist and employee is little more than a superficial exchange of pleasantries. Or it may come to resemble the old counselor interviews in which the personnel man serves as a kind of catalyst for an old-style employee catharsis—resulting in lots of tension-relieving talk, but no substantive follow-up action.

The infrequency of contact and constrained style of communication which typically characterize relations between personnel men and white-collar employees comprise only one of the barriers which stand between them. There is another.

The personnel man encountered, even rarely and impersonally, is one thing—at least he is a creature of flesh and bone. But the

[5] A danger here is that some personnel men grow so fond of the position of middleman that they become permanent fixtures in the subordinate-supervisor relationship and therefore more of a barrier than an aid.

personnel man *heard about* is another thing entirely. The personnel man behind the scenes becomes the shadowy prince of the powers of darkness. He is the one who presses the red buttons and the black ones, who decides destinies and seals fates. There are tales of personnel men to fill a junior engineer's brain with indignation and a junior accountant's heart with fluttering. They are told by supervisors and they sound like this:

"Gee, Phil, I tried to get you a raise, but those guys in personnel stopped it cold."

Or, "George, I know it's tough on you and the wife and kids, but with this staffing cutback we're having and all, well, those personnel people are forcing me . . ."

Or, "I'd like to give you that six-month leave of absence with pay so that you could complete your master's thesis, Al, but you know how the personnel people would scream."

And so do the terrible tales go.

And, alas, with exceedingly few exceptions, they are naught but myths and fantasies. In reality, the chances are that Phil will get no raise this year, not because the personnel department stopped it, but because salary budgets are tighter than they were last year and the fewer dollars that are available just aren't going Phil's way this time.

As for George, the message from personnel may sound like the voice of doom, but the almost certain fact is that the voice is only an echo from elsewhere. Personnel men are not the ones who make the decisions to cut back employment. While some do make recommendations, there are very, very few who make decisions on who stays and who goes.

In Al's case, what needs to be said? His request, though it has the charm of novelty, is uneconomic and would make both auditors and stockholders frown fiercely. In some companies, as a matter of fact, the only place in which it might stand even the slightest chance of getting a sympathetic hearing would be in the office of the personnel development specialist.

The fact is that this behind-the-scenes personnel man is largely phantasmal, albeit very useful, created by first-line supervisors. Unloved decisions have to be made and unpleasant actions taken in all organizations. They are called for at all levels of the decision-making hierarchy—anyplace where a manager must make a choice between alternatives or select one man rather than another. They occur when a manager must say no to protect himself from censure or the risk of censure, or where a superior-level manager must consider a broader range of possibilities than a lower-level supervisor may even be aware of.

It is fairly obvious that the extent to which the effects of these unpopular decisions are felt tends to increase proportionately with the level in the hierarchy at which they occur—the higher the level, the wider the impact. It may be more surprising, though, that the extent to which individual managers tend to try to dissociate themselves from unpopular decisions seems to increase *inversely*—the lower the level of the managers in the hierarchy, the more inclination they seem to have to disown unpleasantness.

At the same time, however, while the lower-level manager may try to get as far as possible downwind of the unhappy act, he still usually subscribes to a kind of good-soldierism that is a key element of the management code. The commandment says that one does not criticize or blame one's boss, no matter what. It does not, however, say a thing against blaming personnel men.

Life, then, is not altogether generous to the personnel man. He is called upon to play the unenviable part of scapegoat, and he does so. Many times he does so purposefully and with grace. It is no mean feat to be a graceful scapegoat, and I say that without irony. The function of absorbing punishment for others is an old, honorable, and useful one.

Part Two

THE
SPECIALTIES

6

The Body Snatchers

UNLESS YOU ARE very rich, very young, or very, very poor, you once got a job. There are different ways of getting jobs. Most people go out and look for them. Some people don't have to. If you are very good at what you do—or, if you are an engineer, even fairly good at it—the chances are that one or more companies will send someone out to look for you instead. If you play your cards moderately well, you will probably not only get a job offer, but also at least a couple of good lunches, a dinner for yourself and your wife, and an airplane ticket to somewhere and back, whether you decide to take the job or not.

Special people called recruiters are put in charge of these pleasant interludes in other people's lives, as a regular part of their job responsibilities. Recruiters are the most colorful kind of personnel man and they are called by the most colorful names—body snatchers, headhunters, flesh-peddlers, and pirates. Few recruiters I know mind these epithets at all. Most, in fact, are proud of them.

Somewhere there is undoubtedly a recruiter who is dour and a worrier, but I have not yet met him. The recruiting heart is characteristically light and its spirit optimistic. And why not? All in all, no one in the personnel business has a more comfortable grip on job security than he does. Essentially, the recruiter is a salesman. His task is to sell his company to prospective employees, but, if he should one day find himself detached from that company, he can reorient without much strain, and turn his hand to recruiting his ex-company's employees for other companies. Most moderately competent recruiters have standing offers of a desk, a telephone, and a commission arrangement from one or more of the executive-search and other employment agencies with which they have continuous dealings. There is a maxim which says: Firing a recruiter is like throwing away a boomerang. Sometime soon you will feel his return —unpleasantly.

The life of the recruiter is a luxurious one. Expense-account pound for expense-account pound, there is probably no one below the corporate officer level who lives better. The mission of the recruiter is to make people happy, and in the process he can make himself happy too.

Recruiters seldom decide who will or won't be hired. Operating managers inside the corporation usually make such decisions. The recruiter's mission is merely to court, not consummate, and since he can rarely be sure which of his candidates will find favor with the managers, he plays the game as though all will.

There are various recruiting procedures, but the first step is usually the accumulation of possible candidates for a specific job opening. When he has an idea of the kind of man the company needs, the recruiter begins reviewing résumés. The more attractive ones win for their authors an invitation to the first of what could turn out to be a series of all-expenses-paid encounters with the company. After a preliminary interview with the recruiter may come interviews with one or more operating managers. Where applicant and job opening are judged incompatible that may be all. There will have been a casual lunch or two, reimbursement of travel expenses, and a few parting handshakes. These will be followed some days later by a letter which tells the applicant what a pleasure it was to meet and chat with him, how favorably impressed the organization was by his background and manner, but how, unfortunately, current requirements do not quite match his abilities. Many times the impression one gets from the really smooth write-offs is that this is more the organization's deficiency than the applicant's.

But if the candidate looks good, the recruiter is unleashed; and if the prospect seems reluctant or uncertain, the courting begins in earnest. The candidate, now quarry, is invited for a second visit and is asked to bring his wife along so that she too can see the advantages of the corporate locale—living in its community, worshipping in its churches, sending her children to its schools, and so on. During their visit, both the candidate and his spouse are, of course, sheltered, fed, and entertained well. From there on it is all a matter of continuing pursuit until the quarry is captured or breaks away entirely. By telephone, mail, and visit the struggle may go on for weeks, or even months.

From time to time there are for the recruiter intriguing departures from the ordinary. For example, in a major manufacturing firm several years ago, a strong-willed and even more strongly talented production manager decided that he wanted to reorganize his division by establishing a new department. The young executive's superior was opposed to the change, but he was completely unsuccessful in changing the production manager's opinion, and while it never came to so many words, the younger man made it clear that if he did not get his way on the issue he would probably quit. The senior executive seemingly capitulated. He agreed to allow the new department to be set up, and in their new spirit of cooperation both executives agreed that the first step ought to be to find a top-notch man to head up the new operation.

Thus the production manager prepared, and his boss cheerfully approved, the necessary paperwork authorizing the new position. The young division head specified his requirements to the firm's chief recruiter and sat back to await the flow of candidates. The candidates did begin to come, though in less of a flow than a trickle. And, somehow, each of the applicants was just a shade less than adequate. In time, the young executive gave up his original plan for reorganization and accepted an alternative format more in keeping with the traditional structure of the firm. He never learned of the arrangement made between his boss and the company personnel director or of the resultant "special instructions" which had been passed down to the recruiter.

There are other forms of Machiavellian maneuvering. I know of elaborately staged arrangements between internal company recruiters, acting on behalf of high-level executives, and outside executive-search consultants that seem the ultimate in incongruity. The outside manpower hunters are invited and sometimes even paid to lure away a particular company's executive in order to avoid the unpleasantness and discomfort which might result from having to fire him. The charade involves the full treatment, including, apparently, elaborate precautions to avoid the possibility that the company might learn about the negotiations.

But these twisted tales are the exception and not the rule. Basically, the objective is to get, not to give. Since the end of World War II, there has been a great organizational appetite for both technical and managerial manpower.[1] Recruiting is expensive, so expensive that some people do not even like to talk about it. Deutsch and Shea, one of the leading recruiting-advertising firms, tried to conduct a national cost-per-hire study in 1962, but found a number of companies refused to release such information, and a number of others would not even bother to compute the figures. Determining recruiting costs is indeed a complicated chore. A larger number of factors can be either included in or excluded from the computation. It all depends on the point the recruiter is trying to make—whether he is trying to prove how efficiently he operates, or how important (big-budgeted) his function is.

---

[1] As noted earlier, the quest for some kinds of managers—those whose specialties are subject to absorption within computer technology—has actually declined in recent years. At the same time, however, there has been a marked increase in the need for younger men trained in the new technologies, particularly computer programming.

Some good estimates on cost-per-hire have been made, however. *Not including* expenses for posthiring relocation or agency fees, they range from about $1,500 to $3,000 per hire. On average again, for every professional hired, the company makes offers to three or four. For every offer made, the recruiter interviews five to eight, and for every interview, the recruiter has screened from ten to twenty résumés. If one ponders the costs of advertising, airplane rides, restaurants, bars, hotel rooms, and related items—remember, not just for the hiree, but also for those candidates who do not pan out (plus the recruiter himself)—it is easy to see how the process gets expensive.

Recruiting for big business is a pretty substantial business in its own right. There are about 4,000 privately operated agencies in the United States, and another 3,800 Government-financed United States Employment Service offices. In the true American anticommunal but pro-associative spirit, there are even brotherhoods of personnel recruiters—for example, the 700-member National Employment Association in Detroit, and the 450-member California Employment Agencies Association. And, again in true American spirit, the private folks are not happy about the Government folks.

The United States Employment Service, one must admit, is quite impressive. Perhaps having caught the enterprise élan of those organizations it services, USES has been venturing after the glamour trade in a fairly significant way. Special federally financed, state-operated USES offices catering exclusively to managerial, professional, and technical personnel are now functioning in more than a hundred cities. One job featured by an Ohio USES office paid $23,754 a year.

Such goings-on aggravate the United States Chamber of Commerce. Said President Edwin P. Neilan passionately: "While millions go jobless, and many of them needy, the USES seeks better-paying jobs for employed scientists, technicians, doctors, lawyers and other skilled persons whose services are always in demand . . . USES recruits on college campuses . . . and even operates at conventions—a service useful to an employer who wants to pirate somebody else's valuable employees." The last part of Mr. Neilan's statement is especially interesting and would indicate that USES recruiters have indeed learned from their "private sector" counterparts.

Roughly speaking, there are three classes of recruiting. They are, in ascending order, college recruiting, middle technical and managerial, and high managerial. As you ascend the treatment gets richer.

College recruiting usually starts six or more months before graduation. It is, in fact, a bumbling sort of student indeed who has not had a half dozen interviews and two or three offers before he has been handed his diploma—the passport to the money country. The aspiring graduates seldom even need to leave their campuses for their first pleasant contact with their industrial futures. The college recruiters come to them, and at recruiting time the campus scene may take on many of the aspects of a medieval market place, with various company stalls standing side by side while the college seniors, like so many casual shoppers, move leisurely from one to another to sample the offerings.

The offerings at some market places are distinctly better than at others. Fathers who admire dollars should send their sons to technical schools. Reflecting our times (it was not always so), technical-college graduates average fifty to a hundred dollars more a month than nontechnical graduates at the beginning of their careers. After ten years, the difference is even greater, $2,000 or more a year. Social science degrees bring least among the nontechnical recruits (about $485 a month in 1964–65) and accounting degrees most (about $550 a month). Engineering graduates, by way of contrast, averaged about $630 a month for the same period.[2]

A master's degree in either a technical or nontechnical

<hr />

[2] Data are from the 1965 Endicott Report, which includes 200 companies, and from College Placement Council statistics, based on recruiting at 108 colleges.

specialty will usually raise the offer to the new graduate by $1,200 to $1,500 per year, and a Ph.D. will bring him $2,000 to $3,000 more than the bachelor's degree. Curiously, the Ph.D. salary advantage does not seem to last permanently. Ten years later, the Ph.D.'s average only about $1,200 or so more than their less-educated brethren. After fifteen years, if one looks at the top-paid people—say the highest-salaried 10 per cent of all degree-holders—pay differentials have all but disappeared.

But if the bidding is higher for some graduates than others, it is also true that the bidding for *all graduates* has been going up year after year. And this makes for an in-house personnel problem. Between recruiters and salary administrators, as between cats and dogs, Nature has produced an innate antipathy. The job of the salary administrator is to maintain order in the company pay plan. As he sees it, there ought to be a reasonable relationship between salaries paid to newly hired men and those paid to more senior employees. But there are difficulties here. The trend of average salary offers to new graduates has for many years been rising on a significantly steeper curve than the trend of pay for the rest of the employed population. One reason for this can undoubtedly be found in the natural inclinations of the recruiter. The recruiter's effectiveness is usually measured by one key criterion—his success in capturing talent. Generous salary offers can, of course, help in the process. Thus, in a kind of running battle, salary administrators press to keep salary offers down, while recruiters push to get them up.

College recruiting is not just a matter of pursuing and capturing graduates. There are important side duties. The most critical of these is the establishment of good relations with college faculties, especially with the deans of departments that nourish the kinds of students in which your company is interested. Directly or indirectly, deans determine who will be allowed to set up shop on their campuses, as well as schedules and facilities. Faculty members also can and do play a major part in determining recruiting success or failure on the campus.

A word here and there during the academic year by a revered professor about his own impressions of the worthiness of this firm or that can have considerable effect on the impressionable young collegian.

College relations are treated by most large companies with loving tenderness, and not just during the hunting season. In a number of leading corporations special personnel, often ex-academicians themselves, are assigned to give year-round care to the universities. Special seminars on new industrial developments in their fields are periodically arranged for faculty members, sometimes with a major share of their expenses paid. Summer jobs at good salaries, for both students and teachers, are held open within the company or, if necessary, even invented. Special grants and gifts of money or laboratory equipment are arranged. Deans and professors are sought out for consultation and to speak before company audiences, with, of course, appropriate honoraria.

Particular care is taken not to offend administrations, and here some interesting dilemmas arise. I have, for instance, known cases where a particularly bright young professor, after serving a summer assignment with a company, has been attracted by the larger material rewards available in servicing products rather than young minds. So, just before his autumn return to campus he may hint to his supervisor that he would be willing to consider an offer. But no matter how appealing the professor's qualifications may be, the situation is likely to produce anxiety rather than joy for the company recruiter. The last thing he wants to do is to pirate one of the dean's stars and face the consequent wrath of the dean the next semester, and probably for years to come. There is no happy solution, either, for if the professor does not get an offer, he is likely to feel that he has been rejected by the company. And for the recruiter to try to explain the circumstances of the apparent jilt might well be the worst of all possible moves.

One of the most striking recent developments in college recruiting has been the discovery of the Negro colleges. The recruiters have arrived in a great and sudden rush. According to *The New York Times* of May 23, 1965, at Hampton Institute in Virginia, the number of companies represented by recruiters increased over the last five years from six to 150. W. P. Malone of North Carolina College reported companies had sent some 350 recruiters to the Durham campus in 1965, an increase of fifty over the previous year. The pattern is similar at most other leading Negro colleges, though the picture is still bleak among the smaller, deep-South schools. Tougaloo Southern Christian College, in Mississippi, for example, placed only two graduates in one senior class outside its local community.

For the Negro there is still another encouraging sign. As a spokesman for Fisk University put it: "Businesses and industries are beginning to look a little beyond the 'instant Negro,' for whom they used to go. For some reason, they used to expect to find a Negro who was instantly prepared and had everything. Now they are starting to survey them more carefully and in addition to grades, are looking for personality and other qualities. They are beginning to treat them just as they treat any other students."

The total picture of Negro employment can only be seen (unless you have that special vision of the zealot—of either persuasion) as a confused, ironic, tragic, difficult, and hopeful one. One of its most surprising aspects is the feverish intensity of competition for Negro graduates. One veteran recruiter told me that many of his colleagues would now rather land a good Howard B.S. than a top Ph.D. from MIT.

This is not difficult for the cynic, or even the realist, to understand. The pressure has been strong, first from the Kennedy, then from the Johnson administration. Symbolic observation, at the very least, has become a necessity for the major corporations. The mechanics for symbolic observation are fairly simple: the notation "An Equal Opportunity Employer" at the bottom of their recruiting advertising; the hiring of a "certain number" of the "*best*" Negroes they can find in the shortest possible time; a company "policy statement" firmly against discrimination; and finally, a concerted effort to forget the whole subject just as soon as it can be done. There are, however, a number of companies that are quite serious about their equal-opportunity programs.

Within corporations the programs which succeed best and fastest are those which are blessed by the continuing concentration of top-level people. In some companies the equal-opportunity programs have this blessing. Specific high-status personnel have been named to represent the corporation's executive offices, and have been given specific charters clearly authorizing them not only to promote and encourage fair employment practices, but also to *monitor and report back* on the progress made by each of the firm's divisions.[3] This practice can be remarkably effective.

The second variety of recruiting on our ascending ladder centers on middle-level personnel. "Middle level" covers a broad scope—anything above the college level on up into manager ranks. In terms of money, the range is probably from about $8,000 or $10,000 to about $18,000 or $20,000 a year. Overall, the heaviest volume of recruiting effort goes into this area, since it represents the largest bulk of industry's technical and administrative personnel.

The recruiter may pursue middle-level quarry in several ways, depending on the number he needs. In these days of mega-million-dollar contracts, the award (or more often the *potential* award) of an Army, Navy, Air Force, Department of Defense, or NASA contract may escalate the recruiting campaigns to multimillion-dollar sizes. In deciding on a contractor the military or space agencies take into account the

---

[3] One example of effort beyond the routine is a widely distributed booklet put out by General Electric called "At Work in Industry Today." The booklet, a top-notch effort, tells the stories of fifty Negro employees of the firm, at levels from semiskilled through management. It is used in recruiting efforts at all levels, as one means of assuring Negroes that the company *means what it is saying,* one of the hardest tasks of all. Since the booklet speaks in personal and specific terms about people, rather than in the abstract generalizations of company policy, it has, I understand, been substantially persuasive to Negroes themselves.

capacity of the contractor to handle the task. In many defense programs the critical element that will determine capacity is neither facilities nor machines, but technical manpower. If a contending contractor is already involved in other defense design or production efforts, as most are, the Government customer wants to feel assured that the earlier program will not be weakened by the company's diverting too many people from it to work on the new program. Consequently, companies frequently try to gather as much technical manpower as possible *before* a contract award is made. What this means to the recruiter is more bodies, and fast—perhaps as many as several hundred or more engineers, mathematicians and scientists.

In such cases, newspapers and journal advertising, employment agencies, manpower-search consultants, field trips, and any other device, technique, or scheme that occurs to anyone is worth a try. But for the big winner of a big contract there is one best place to look, and that is toward the loser of yet another big contract. The recruiter's avocation is keeping up with the state of the business of his company's competitors and with other firms in related technologies.

The happiest of all coincidences occurs when his company wins a contract at about the same time that another company begins to phase out a major program. The simplest and most common way to capitalize on such an opportunity is through advertising in area newspapers. Sometimes, though, openly advertising for your competitor's people can be bad form. When it is, the recruiter may use blind ads instead. The blind ad does not, of course, actually safeguard the invader's identity, if the local firm really wants to learn it. It is simply a sign of good manners.

When the quality and volume of responses to the recruiting advertising are high, the recruiter will frequently go where the applicants are, rather than have them come to him. Sometimes he will be accompanied by one or more technical managers who are empowered to make job offers right on the spot. Other things being equal, this stockyards setting is not the most desirable one in which to be looking for a new job. Aside from the obvious deprivation of all the savory frills—the trips, dinners, drinks, and so forth—chances are that in the push and shove of mass hiring, the personal touch will be lost. With so many prospects among whom he must divide his attention, the recruiter is less likely to think of any one as a unique prize. And, if he does not, the rewards are not likely to be as rich as if he had.

Recruiting in the environment of a contract cancellation or program phase-out is *sad* recruiting. But there is still another kind. Until recently the grandest, gayest, and gaudiest recruiting of all was done at technical society conventions. Within walking distance of any convention center, hospitality suites, as they were called, proliferated like mushrooms. A prospect could spend his entire conference stay circulating from one company's suite to another's, testing his approximate market value, and sampling the best food and beverages. In the accommodations of some of the most liberal-minded firms, there were even pretty girls, seldom for any really immoderate purpose, but nevertheless considerably more titillating than lectures on cryogenics or fluid mechanics.

Lamentably, the hospitality suite is on its way out, a victim of the serious-minded. Convention trips are paid for by employers, and many of them take a dark view of hospitality suite activities. It is not so much that the companies objected to occasional hookey-playing from the working sessions, but rather that there was a certain abrasive irony when they found themselves paying for some other company's convenience in pirating their own best men. Some corporations simply stopped sending people to the conventions. Neither the professional societies nor the employees were very happy at that. Complaints were made, followed by negotiations, a truce, and gradually the closing of the suites. A joyous era had thereby come to an end.

For the higher managers and a relatively few very superior specialists, the recruiting process can be a very rich experience, and the longer it is drawn out, the richer it usually gets. If at the senior level one can get two firms bidding at the same time, wonderful things may happen. There could be two, three, or even more rounds of offer and counteroffer, and at each one dollars, titles, job designs, office decor, and stock options are all fair coin. Men who have been with particular companies for a score or more years, with salary increases of perhaps 20 per cent over the last five, have awakened suddenly to find themselves in the midst of such wild contests. And when it was all over, they dazedly walked away with an annual pay package 30 or 40 per cent higher than they had only a week before. The bidding game can even get itself spinning within a company, with the competition waxing as wildly between divisions as it ever runs between opposing corporations.

Less spectacular versions of the sport can be learned, and some men are apt students. There are, for instance, the gypsy engineers, who stay about a year or two per company and move at 10 to 20 per cent increases each time. The practice is not recommended for overeager juniors, though, for it produces a spotty employment record and suspicious recruiters. There are prerequisites for this game. You have to be a varsity man, and preferably a star. Your story then is simple—you have not found the work at your present company "sufficiently challenging." It is a salable theme almost everywhere.

For those who don't like traveling, there have also been ways of doing almost as well without moving. Even for one completely happy in his present job, the distribution of some well-prepared résumés, a meeting or two with another company's recruiter, and some well-timed conversations, with provisions for "leaks" to the right people, have often resulted in a 10 per cent increase from his present firm—just to make sure that he stays happy where he is.

In the real Arabian Nights adventures in recruiting, there are some special additions to the cast of characters—the executive searchers, and the best ones are silky and effective.

Their fees generally range between 20 and 25 per cent of the first year's salary of the executive they have searched out, plus expenses. *But the company pays.*

There is, of course, only one way to get a new executive into your firm, and that is to get him out of someone else's. This can be very awkward for intercorporate relationships, if you try to pry him out directly. For example, if you send your own recruiter around to work on what you suppose to be a ripe prospect, and he turns out not to be, he may very likely report the contact to his superiors, and your firm will automatically have been identified as on the hunt. If the reason you are looking for a new man is that you want to replace one of your present executives, you also face the risk of word leaking back to him prematurely.

There are other minor embarrassments in directly recruiting other companies' executives. For one thing, you may be betraying a certain inadequacy, since you don't have someone available for promotion inside. That does not speak well for your management-development program. From another standpoint, the company's outside quest contains an unmistakably sour message for those inside who feel they ought to be eligible for the opening. No matter how the situation is handled this is, of course, an unavoidable problem. Sooner or later the new man does, after all, appear upon the scene. But recruiting executives can be a very extended process, and there is an advantage in avoiding the prolonged irritation of the hunting period in favor of the single sharp cut of the announcement of his arrival.

A good many companies do not even want to talk about executive recruiting, sometimes for reasons such as those above, and sometimes for other, even touchier reasons. Among some industries informal agreements have been made *not* to pirate. In 1961, *Fortune* quoted a Republic Steel Company executive to the effect that the hiring of a steel executive by another steel company has been almost unheard of for the last twenty years. "Top management in the steel industry realizes," said the Republic spokesman, "that raiding for executives doesn't accomplish anything but civil war and excessive salaries.[4] Once you start it, there's no end to raiding." Despite the statement, though, a study reported sometime later by *Fortune* indicated that steel executives were, in fact, fairly movable—45 per cent had worked for three or more companies, and 30 per cent for four or more; 44 per cent had changed companies after the age of forty.

There is another reason why the steel companies might have been happier if the Republic man had held his peace. While no one has yet tested the "no raiding" agreements, there may be some trouble with them if they are ever examined under the antitrust laws.

Anonymity is only one of the values that the outside search agency is prepared to provide for its clients. Most agencies also have their own stocks of eligible or potentially eligible targets available for those companies who have not yet fixed their sights on a particular man. A moderately well-known executive-search agency draws good executive names without even trying.

Executives are a mobile race, and as aware as anybody of the advantages of staying loose. Because of their positions, though, executives do not typically send out their résumés indiscriminately when they are restless. Their names tend to be too familiar, and there are definite hazards in being identified as on the market but not yet sold. The executive-search agency is the perfect answer for such executives. All they have to do is get into the searcher's file and sit back to wait for bids.

Even when the searcher's file is slim for a particular talent specialty, he has ways of expanding it. He may solicit suggestions from his wide circle of acquaintances. (Searchers in-

---

[4] As I mentioned earlier, the bidding method of acquiring talent frequently produces in its enthusiasm salaries for the newly hired executive that are difficult to reconcile sensibly with the going rates for his fellow managers who are already in place.

variably do have wide circles of acquaintances.) Or he may turn to one of the devices of his trade. For instance, the recommendation request letter. Let us say that the search agency has been asked by a client company to locate candidates for a marketing vice presidency. If it has an inadequate supply of qualified names on file, the agency will gather the names and locations of all the marketing vice presidents it can find (in the same or similar industries as its client). As sources it can use trade-association rosters, corporate-officer lists, and so on. The convenient thing about this is that the agency does not have to know anything more about the people than their names. This is because the letter that it sends is so beautifully delicate in design. It asks not if the addressee is interested in the client's job opening, but rather if he *knows of* anyone who might be. This avoids the potential embarrassment of soliciting interest in a $75,000 job from a man who is already earning $100,000. It also from time to time does produce worth-while recommendations.

For a company there are sometimes windfalls that go with the snaring of a high executive. Some top men are naturally charismatic, and whither they go, so goes their whole team. When this happens it is considered the depths of unsportsmanlike conduct, and the executive who indulges in carrying his subordinates off with him will find himself very unwelcome around his former homestead even on visiting days. Nor is the searcher who arranged the original move likely ever again to be smiled upon by the losing firm, even if he had no part in the subsequent kidnaps. It is very hard to think of any searcher as an innocent bystander under any circumstances.

Another peril to the searcher's reputation is the chance that he may be discovered trying to re-recruit executives he previously placed. There are probably a few hyperactive searchers who would resell a management man they had sold a year or two before, but not many. When this sort of quick switching does occur it was probably the eager executive who thought of it first.

There are differing reactions to the searchers and to the free-wheeling executive mobility their activities encourage. Some companies are indifferent. The gilded chains of deferred compensation, stock options, and thick pension arrangements with which they bind their executives to their bosoms make them practically immune. Other companies disapprove of "raiding" entirely, as we heard earlier from the Republic Steel man. For the most part, though, companies don't talk much about the subject, one way or the other. Except, that is, for President George Spatta of the Clark Equipment Company, who told a *Fortune* interviewer: "If I see a good man I go out and tag him and drag him in, no matter where he is. Maybe it's even better if he's with a competitor . . . We have no training program. I'd rather let the other companies train them, then take them on later."

You can't beat that for clarity.

7

The Alienated Science
of Picking Winners

In a June, 1963, interview, *Business Management* asked Victor Pomper, executive vice president of H. H. Scott and Company, how to spot a really bright young man—a man who has the potential for becoming company president, or at least vice president. In his response, Pomper first assured the interviewer that "we bat about .800 in picking bright young men," and then he indicated that the key to this unusual success was in checking back on the candidate to age fourteen. "If a man doesn't distinguish himself in his formative years," said Pomper, "chances are pretty good he won't do so in the future."

Other employers, less certain of Mr. Pomper's premise, have different approaches. Whatever the employer's underlying theory of personnel selection may be, however, the first hurdle for the job applicant is usually the interview, and in recent years that has been getting tougher. Interviewing, once a relatively casual art, has recently become in many cases a sticky bit of scientism. In the old days there were two basic interviewing styles: the sweet and the sour. Both aimed at finding out as much as possible about the candidate in the time available. Theoretically, the interviewer was as interested in the applicant's skills and strengths as he was in his weaknesses. Generally, though, it was considerably easier to find an applicant's virtues than it was to unearth his deficiencies, so in most cases the interviewer concentrated on trying to discover the weak spots: potential ineptitudes, insufficiencies of dedication, and temperamental incompatibilities.

In the sweet approach the idea was to establish a warm, friendly relationship between interviewer and interviewee as quickly as possible. The object then, after winning the applicant's confidence, was to get him to relax. Thereafter it was merely a matter of asking the right questions and listening closely for what might be revealed in the answers.

The sour style, more often called the stress approach, was less frequently used, at least by premeditation. Its premise was that since the candidate would likely be subject to stress situations in the course of his job, it was a good idea to test his reactions beforehand. (One early clue to whether the interview was to be sweet or sour was where the interviewer sat. If he came out from behind his desk and settled down beside you, the chances were good that you were to be approached sweetly. If he remained trenched behind his desk—unless he was an amateur or just lazy—it meant the battle lines were drawn.)

In the personnel man's own hierarchy of the personnel business, employment interviewers do not stand high. There are exceptions; for example, there are the Ph.D.'s who specialize in the analysis and assessment of the presence or absence of the deep compulsions, repressions, and constrictions of high-level executive applicants. And there are the field recruiters described in the previous chapter, who are different birds entirely. But the average interviewer is likely to be a tyro who probably sat on the uncomfortable side of the interviewing desk himself not very long ago. Or, if he is more balding than bushy-tailed, chances are he has some time ago passed the top of his own personal career curve and is now on the descent.

The employment interviewer, as a category of personnel man, is not blessed by a reputation for high competence. A number of organization insiders share the views of Robert N. McMurry, a very senior management consultant, who in 1944 wrote:

"Employment work often possesses a powerful attraction for those who have an urgent need for power and prestige. Interviewing provides even a $25-a-week clerk with a chance to be the master of others, sometimes of persons with far better qualifications than he. The authority which such work brings with it is often irresistible to those who feel inadequate. Not infrequently, coupled with a lust for authority are also certain sadistic tendencies. Since the employment man is in the superior position he has ample opportunity, if he wishes, to be extraordinarily cruel through the frustration, humiliation and even open mistreatment of applicants . . ."

The employment interview continues to be a competitive sport played between the interviewer and interviewee, but in the simpler days of the past it was played according to some fairly straightforward ground rules. The interviewer asked questions about such things as your education, work experience, and ambitions. If he was of a more sophisticated stamp, he might even want to know about your hobbies, the kind of work you most and least liked to do, and which of your previous bosses you were fond of, or hated, and why. Your answers to his questions were supposed to help him make a reasonable estimate of how smart you were and how well you "handled yourself," whether or not you knew your field, and whether in your career so far you had made acceptable progress in terms of salary and promotions. He also wanted to know whether you would be fitting company for your boss and fellow workers.

The interviewee, in turn, made his answers in shapes that he judged would be most pleasing, and the interviewer followed up by probing for detail, rooting out gaps in the story, and pursuing any inconsistencies he could spot. The nice thing about the whole process was that both parties knew who they were and what the business of the day was about.

It isn't like that any more. Technology has arrived upon the interviewing scene, and with it its devices.

I recently received a promotional leaflet on a new personnel-interviewing handbook. Among other things I was promised

"19 questions to ask the job applicant to quickly spot his strong and weak points . . . delicate subjects that bring out his true character . . . the LDG technique that tests out the attitudes, values and social skills of the applicant . . . [and] a simple gracious phrase that ends the most intimate interview in seconds." Nor was the sweep of this new marvel limited to employment interviewing. I could also learn "in clear, direct language . . . how to discover company rumors and 'impressions,' how to communicate with employees along the company 'grapevine,' how to deflate the troublemaker—and maintain dignity, what to tell a man you're going to fire, a 4-part orientation interview that instills company loyalty . . . and much, much more."

The *depth interview* is a general term which describes the newer "psychologically oriented" approach to personnel selection. One of its variants is called the nondirective or unstructured method. A casual observer crossing the interview scene during some nondirective interview sessions would know neither what was being done, nor who was doing it to whom. The nondirective plan is basically an invitation to the interviewee to sit around and free-associate for a while. What comes out has some resemblance to an evening with Sigmund Freud—though no one, so far as I know, has yet been daring enough to install a couch. It ought to be emphasized that I am *not* talking now about the probings of the professional psychologists employed by some companies, but rather about what has become in some firms the garden-variety approach to interviewing, practiced by an interviewer with no more psychological background than that which comes with a bachelor's degree in business administration and a couple of coaching sessions on technique.

Deep psychology is not the province of depth interviewing alone. It is, in fact, rampant through most modern interviewing styles. There is, for example, the "patterned interview." The patterned interview is conducted according to a guide form which provides a large number of often innocent-sounding questions for the interviewer to ask. *But in smaller print*—literally, between the lines—is the *real* stuff that counts. Following are some sample items from two patterned interview forms, one developed by McMurry, Hamstra and Company for general use, and the other by Swift and Company for salesman interviews. What is shown first is the actual question to be asked by the interviewer. Inside the parentheses is the "small print" which is the real point of the inquiry:

> Present address. (*Will this location affect his attendance? Is this a desirable neighborhood? Does it appear consistent with income?*)
>
> Part-time jobs during (your last or present) employment. (*Does this indicate industry? Ambition? Lack of loyalty? Lack of interest in duties or position?*)
>
> Have you been married previously? (*Any indications of impulsiveness? Incompatibility?*)
>
> To what extent are you dating? (*Any indications of lack of maturity? Pleasure-mindedness?*)
>
> What debts do you have? (*Is he solvent? Is he impulsive in spending?*)
>
> Is your wife employed? (*Will this offset his motivation? Does this indicate incompatibility?*)
>
> What serious illnesses, operations, or accidents did you have as a child? (*Were there conditions leading to overprotection? Has he any immature traits due to childhood illness?*)
>
> Occupations of your brothers. (*Will a Swift sales job give him sufficient prestige?*)
>
> What illnesses, operations, or accidents have you had in recent years? (*Is he mature in his attitude toward health?*)

And, my favorite:

> What do you and your wife do for recreation? (*Are these favorable to work with Swift? Any peculiarities?*)

In 1961 Milton M. Mandell did a comprehensive research study for the American Management Association on employment interviewing in American companies. His sample included 273 firms, from small to large. Mandell noted about a half dozen different interviewing approaches currently in use, and there are more.

About 20 per cent of the surveyed firms utilized the depth interview. The dangers of depth interviewing, as Mandell points out, are that some interviewers develop so great an enthrallment with the "psychological" interpretation of the applicant's childhood history that they give it as much or more weight than his recent work history. Nor is that very surprising, when one notes the kind of elements the depth interviewer is supposed to explore. For example, Mandell lists: The number of places in which the candidate lived before the age of fifteen; the number of his friends and his relations with them; his interests in sports —does he like the rough or sedentary kinds; his early organization memberships—was he a Boy Scout, did he go to Sunday school; at what ages did he learn to swim, begin to drive a car, go dancing, date girls, and so on.

When one considers, however, that depth interviewing calls for penetrating not only the candidate's childhood but his present life as well—the types of food he likes and does not like; his drinking and gambling habits; the personal characteristics, ages, and occupations of the people he prefers; and the means of transportation (auto, plane, train, or ship) he prefers—it is hard to see how any interviewer could resist playing amateur psychologist.

Some other high points of the Mandell study are worth noting. One is the time interviewers spend with applicants. As with many other phenomena of organization life, it varies according to one's place in the hierarchy. Among Mandell's sample companies the average time spent with plant employees was thirty minutes; with office employees, forty-five minutes; college seniors, ninety minutes; engineers and salesmen, two hours; and with supervisors and executives, three hours. These figures include total time spent by both personnel and operations people, usually in two or more separate sessions with the interviewee. On the average, the number of people who interview an applicant increases with his level. The range is from two interviewers for plant and office applicants up to four for supervisors and executives.

But it would be pretty risky to conclude that there is any particular advantage in longer interviews, either for the applicant or the company. As Mandell and others have pointed out, one of the major problems with interviewers is that too many tend to make up their minds about a candidate in the first few minutes of the interview anyway. What they do in the remainder of the scheduled time is merely ceremonial. A research study by Edward C. Webster in 1959 found that in a series of interviews scheduled for fifteen minutes, interviewers typically made their decisions within the first four. In Mandell's own study interviewers' "snap judgments" was ranked as their second "most frequent mistake." In first place was the belief that they talked too much, and didn't listen enough.

In the survey Mandell asked respondents to identify the factors given greatest weight by company interviewers. The answers were as follows (shown is the factor, and in parentheses the number of firms in which it was given "greatest weight"): Personality, temperament, and/or attitude (119); Experience (77); Appearance (69); Intelligence (21); Personal background (21); Ability to communicate (20); Adaptability and/or ambition (16); Motivation (12); Initiative (8); Performance (7); Poise (7).

He also asked for opinions as to the factors that could be measured well and those that could be measured only poorly in the interview. Unsurprisingly, appearance was a factor thought to be readily measurable. But while personality traits were felt to be well measured in 138 of the companies, in 51 others they were believed to be *most poorly* measured. Motivation, which Mandell calls one of the most fundamental of all factors, was judged about equally measurable or nonmeasurable.

Thus, about the only factor which was clearly judged to be both weighty and readily measurable was appearance. And since Mandell observes later in his study that interviewers, "without realizing it, in most cases," are inclined to make their too-quick judgments about candidates on such superficial factors as appearance, voice, and a brief review of the application blank, this all fits together.

One of the more jarring results of the Mandell study came in responses to his question: "Do you feel interviewers are unjustifiably biased toward certain types of applicants?" More than 40 per cent of the companies responded affirmatively. In further elaborations of their answers many went on to specify the biases they believed existed. In addition to the expected prejudices with regard to race, sex, education, socio-economic status, religion, and so on, the respondents noted interviewer tendencies "to approve those whose attitudes and philosophy resemble their own, [and] to lean toward similar types of applicants, regardless of job requirements." And, concluded one respondent brightly: "It is only natural for interviewers to be biased toward good-looking members of the opposite sex."

An equally shocking result of the Mandell study was that of the 273 companies surveyed only 16 per cent reported having made any recent changes in their interviewing practices, despite acknowledged defects. Mandell attributes the lack of change to company beliefs that what need to be improved are the skills of the interviewers rather than their methodologies. But alas, even if that is so, only a fifth of the companies had any training programs for their interviewers.[1]

Not all interviews are hand-to-hand and man-to-man affairs. Some are group contests. There is, for instance, the panel interview, a method borrowed from the military and civil services, in which an applicant is interrogated by a team of company

[1] One final sidelight before we leave the study findings. There is an old and rather dishonored practice of interviewing wives as well as candidates in some companies. Mandell found that the practice had declined somewhat. A 1954 AMA survey showed that about 26 per cent of the surveyed firms interviewed wives regularly, plus about 10 per cent more on an occasional basis. Only 13 per cent of Mandell's 1961 survey participants reported they interviewed applicant's wives.

representatives. One ostensible advantage of the method is that it allows panel members, other than the one asking the question, to observe more intensively the interviewee's reactions. Another advantage is that the group questioning and subsequent discussion of applicant qualities are supposed to minimize the effects of individual biases, since each interviewer's impressions and his reasons for them can be tested with his fellow panel members. An offsetting disadvantage cited by those who reject the panel approach is that group members may tend to cramp each other's styles. Interviewer man-hours required by the panel interview could better be spent in individual interviews with the applicant. (Nobody is very concerned about the interviewee's time, of course.)

A still more unusual multiple approach to interviewing in industry is the group oral performance test. Here interviewees are dealt with en masse. Candidates for the same position opening are brought together and presented with one or more multi-faceted problems, generally ones involving business situations. The applicants are supposed to discuss them with a view to their solution. For example, a group of candidates for an industrial relations director's job might be asked to deal with such questions as: What steps would you take first in assuming your new position? How would you approach establishing your relations with local union officials? What organization design do you prefer for the industrial relations function? As the candidates discuss, agree, and disagree with each other on the topics prescribed, their performance is judged by a panel of raters.

By far the most elaborate of group appraisal techniques are incorporated under a program called the Assessment Center method. This method has interesting antecedents. It was used by both the Office of Strategic Services (OSS) and the German officer corps during World War II. The approach is intensive, extensive, and expensive. AT&T and Standard Oil of Ohio are among the most devoted adherents of this selection method. AT&T has more than forty Assessment Centers in the United States, each staffed by an average of eight examiners. The company sends about twelve employees a week through each center, scrutinizing such items as their interpersonal skills; the degree of control they exercise over their feelings; their intellectual capacity; their passivity, dependency, and nonconformity; and their administrative skills. The candidates are judged by their performance in paper and pencil tests, business games, leaderless discussion groups, and brainstorming sessions. The program includes both competitive and "co-operative" exercises, but even in the latter the candidates are actually contending to see who can co-operate best.

The ultimate product of the AT&T Assessment Center is a rating for each candidate which designates him as "acceptable for promotion now," or "not acceptable now but possible of becoming so in the relatively near future," or "not acceptable now and unlikely to become acceptable." According to Douglas Bray, AT&T's director of personnel research, a candidate's nomination for center assessment is based upon his supervisor's opinion that he possesses the potential for early advancement into management. Bray reports: "It has come as somewhat of a shock, therefore, that well more than half of those assessed are rejected by the assessment staffs as *not* having abilities warranting immediate promotion. In fact, a substantial minority are deemed to have little potential for promotion even in the more distant future."

One advantage claimed for group assessment methods in general is that a large number of candidates can be considered simultaneously. Also, since much of each employee's time is indeed spent working in groups, the process is "realistic." According to its supporters, candidates become so involved in some of the exercises they forget they are being tested and react more naturally than in typical interview situations. Finally, the group process allows direct and immediate comparisons to be made between individuals faced by the same situation at the same time and under the same conditions.

On the other hand, however, one can wonder whether *too much* emphasis is being placed on the group situation. Does it give the smooth operator too great an advantage over the less socially adept but analytically or creatively superior candidate? There are also marked differences in the over-all quality of each group. An individual who might shine as the bright star of one assemblage of candidates could be a failure in another superior group, and it is difficult to calibrate judges' standards well enough for them to recognize over-all group differences. Bray reports that AT&T's managers were shocked at having more than half of their nominees rejected by the raters. But why should they be? The candidates were, after all, being judged not against the common run of their fellows, but against already preselected competitors. Besides, if the examiners passed all of them, or even a substantial majority, it would be hard to explain the need for Assessment Centers.

Psychological testing has been treated harshly by the newspapers and periodicals in the last several years; a fact that has produced considerable touchiness among the testing specialists. Objections have been raised against the psychological tests' intrusiveness, the seeming absurdity of some of their questions, and the cabalistic style of those who administer and interpret them. The validity of tests as effective predictors of success has also been challenged, even by some psychologists. These psychologists point out that not enough is yet known about which factors produce job success, particularly in the professional and administrative jobs. There is, for instance, a wry parable told about the testing of the chief executives of a hundred companies, and behold, all turned out to be suffering from psychological maladjustments. When later we discuss managers and their rises, we will note that some really do seem to ascend, not in spite of, but because of their "problems."

In June of 1965 the United States Civil Service Commission placed a ban on the use of personality tests by Federal agencies in determining who will be hired, fired, or promoted. The action was taken in response to a special House Government Operations subcommittee investigation into charges that the tests which had been used in some Federal agencies violated the private lives of employees and had no bearing on their jobs. Cornelius Gallagher, chairman of the subcommittee, congratulated the Commission and predicted "the rippling effect" of the decision would also influence private industry and "be very helpful to everyone who has to work for a living."

Not so far. While the use of psychological tests may be increasingly frowned upon outside corporate walls, it continues to expand within them. The growth is quieter but no less vigorous. There are more tests now than ever before, and more testing companies. In a number of corporations the time allotted to the testing cycle has been increasing as well. Administration of some test series, including interview evaluation by a staff psychologist, can extend for as long as several days. Even Wall Street, one of the last important pockets of resistance to the testing movement, appears to have been penetrated. Early in 1965 the *Wall Street Journal* announced that the New York Stock Exchange and the Psychological Corporation are now working on a test battery for customer's men.

Company psychologists are also used in the selection process for new employees, particularly at the higher levels, as well as in screening personnel who are being considered for promotion, foreign transfer, possible assignment to management training programs, or other special categories. Here again, in recent years there has been heavy criticism of the indignities and absurdities which often characterize the psychologist's process. There are those who feel that his primary mission is to search for and screen out all forms of deviation from the acceptable model of organization-man conformity.

A good deal of the criticism is warrantable. At the same time, however, I feel impelled to say a word or two on behalf of the psychologists themselves. I have known a number of them in the assessment business and, by and large, they are not a bad lot. Many do have considerable tolerance for diversity. At any rate, a session with the professional psychologist may be far preferable to the alternative we are about to discuss—the Evaluation Interview, in the hands of the amateur.[2]

Developed by the Psychological Corporation, the Evaluation Interview is probably one of the most "in" of all the interviewing systems currently extant. Dr. Richard Fear, a vice president of Psych Corp, as it is called by those who know, has written a book about the system. He has also, as the book jacket advertises, trained "hundreds of interviewers in a wide variety of companies." The Evaluation Interview as philosophy, as well as process, deserves particular attention.

Some of the ideas and instructions in the Fear book are sound. Fear points out the desirability of predefining job requirements before the interview. He notes and cautions against several of the common faults of the inadequately trained interviewer—tendencies to overgeneralize, to make premature judgments, to do too much talking, and so forth. The book also contains other general, elementary instruction of a useful sort.

But in its essence, in its fundamental view of the interview as a relationship between interviewer and interviewee, the Evaluation Interview is alienation on a rampage. It is a dehumanized encounter between manipulator and manipulated, in which *neither* manages to remain a person.

Nothing, however, speaks so eloquently of Dr. Fear's system as Dr. Fear's own words. First, what manner of man is the ideal interviewer? Fear answers early in the book, and clearly: "Since it is not always easy to elicit information of a somewhat delicate and personal nature, *the interviewer must be a good salesman.* [Italics are his, here and later.] This statement may be surprising to some, but it is nevertheless true. The interviewer must be able to sell the applicant on 'opening up and revealing his hand,' even though some of the information de-

---

[2] Here is some general advice which may be useful in dealing with the assessment psychologist: If you don't like a question he asks you, tell him so, politely but firmly, and ask him to go on to something else. Don't try to outwit him, or to convince him of the error of his ways, or to outphilosophize him.

veloped may be of an unfavorable nature. Hence, it is exceedingly important that the interviewer possess the type of personality that will enable him to do a good selling job. Only by successful use of indirection and other techniques for setting the stage will the interviewer be able to get the real story."

Fear does not leave it there, though. His advice on how-to techniques is specific and extensive. Some examples:

—The interviewer must be able to get information *without giving the applicant the slightest hint that his remarks are being interpreted.*

—In a sense, he [the interviewer] is like an actor performing a role on the stage. He consciously uses certain devices to get certain effects. In the beginning, these techniques may seem slightly artificial, but with constant usage and continued practice, they become almost second nature and, hence, adroit and polished.

—Anyone [who wants to be a good interviewer] can improve his facial expression by doing two things: (1) raising his eyebrows frequently and (2) smiling more often. Raising of the eyebrows, in particular, should be effected whenever questions are posed. The ensuing expression gives the person the appearance of being *receptive* and serves as a powerful tool in getting the subject to open up.

It is not expected, of course, that anyone can go through an entire interview with a smile on his face. At the same time, it is extremely important that a half-smile be permitted to play about the lips, particularly when asking somewhat personal or delicate questions. The edge is taken off a delicate or personal question when it is posed with a half-smile and with the eyebrows raised.

Dr. Fear encourages interviewer trainees "to practice some of their questions in front of a mirror, so that they may learn to use the full potential of their facial manipulation." He warns, however: "The brighter, the more alert, and the more sensitive the applicant is, moreover, the more the interviewer must try not to overdo."

—One of these techniques [for encouraging the applicant to speak freely] is concerned with *giving every appearance of agreeing with everything the man says.* This is done by frequent nodding of the head and by making such short comments as "I see," or "I can understand that," or "uh-huh." . . . Even a slight frown may be enough to alert the man to the fact that his remarks are not getting a favorable hearing. In such event, he may get the feeling that he may be damaging rather than helping his case and may therefore shut off information that might have provided valuable clues to his behavior.

—Whenever he [the applicant] does divulge unfavorable information, therefore, we *play down* the importance of that information by some casual, understanding remark. If, for example, the candidate tells about a difficulty he has experienced with some supervisor, we encourage him to describe the experience by such a remark as "I guess a good many people run across a boss like that somewhere along the line."

There are many more step-by-step instructions in this comprehensive primer in guile. There is advice on the wording of the questions themselves. Fear does not believe in a direct question when a "softer" way can be found, and it almost always can. For instance, instead of, "Why did you have trouble with your boss?" Fear suggests, *"To what do you attribute the little difficulties you experienced with your supervisor?"* And instead of, "Do you plan to get married?" he suggests, *"In connection with your social activities, have you found anyone with whom you would like to settle down, or is this decision being deferred?"*[3]

The fourth chapter of Dr. Fear's book is entitled "Interpreting Early Home Background." In it he lays out for his pupils a small set of mincing, clinical steps toward a deeper understanding of the candidate's psyche. Fear suggests excavation

---

[3] One can only ask: Is this all a lot of banal nonsense, or *do you apprehend that the quality of discourse might just conceivably touch on some lack of cogency?*

into such areas as the applicant's mother's and father's temperament (". . . it is important to list five or six of the father's traits"), which parent the applicant feels he is more like in his own personality makeup, and so on. If the interviewer has been particularly winning in establishing a friendly climate with the interviewee, Fear also advises that it might be interesting to ask at what age the applicant went through puberty.

I have known a number of men who have been conducted through Fear's five-day interviewer training courses. These have been reasonably intelligent but not clinically trained people (mostly business administration or industrial relations graduates). Frequently, the thing about the training which especially impressed them, sometimes awesomely, were the devices it provided for entry into just these childhood recollections. As one personnel manager told me, after having exercised his newly acquired skills on a man in his fifties who was applying for a manufacturing superintendent position: "It was amazing. Here I was listening to this tough old buzzard who has been running his shop like a top sergeant for years, and he was telling me how scared he used to be of his father." What earthly use this information would be to the personnel manager, unless he planned to undertake the superintendent's psychotherapy, was never made clear. But there it was, and based upon the obvious thrill the personnel manager enjoyed in having made the discovery, my guess would be that he will continue to hunt out such items in future interviews, at least until the novelty wears off.

Perhaps the most disturbing aspect of the Evaluation Interview is Fear's conception of "truth" and its uses. The first and crucial test is to "decide whether the applicant is telling the whole truth or whether he is coloring certain aspects of his story to make the best possible impression." Watch out for the man who talks about his accomplishments but avoids his shortcomings, and be careful of the man who pauses before answering key questions, because more often than not he is devising a reply which is intended to make him look good. Fear also cautions against the applicant who fences with the interviewer, and *especially* against "the extremely clever type of person who disarmingly admits the existence of certain minor shortcomings in order to give his over-all story more credulity." In advice that has the ring of a correspondence course for the aspiring private detective, Fear tells the interviewer to be alert to physical symptoms in the suspected evader—squirming in the seat, changes in facial expression, and so on.

If, in the interviewer's judgment, the applicant exhibits more than his allowable quota of these symptoms or danger signals, his information is rejected. But he will never know it. Evaluation Interview rules require no reciprocal straightforwardness on the part of the interviewer. On the contrary, as Fear explains: "At the risk of redundancy, it should be pointed out again that the interviewer must mask his reactions completely whenever he encounters a man who does not 'come clean,' thus giving no inkling of the fact that he is not going along with the individual's story."

To me there is a terrible distortion of values here, something worse than the endless warp of deception which twists through the system, and that is the essential demand for submission. No, for more than submission—for the submissive personality. By the peculiar ethics of the Evaluation Interview, the interviewer is trained in, and called upon to use, a whole arsenal of assorted trickeries. But if in their encounter the applicant attempts any defensive tactics of his own, he is silently disqualified. To be heard at all he must approach the interview not as applicant but as supplicant. He must eschew any inclination he may have to affect his own future, and instead passively surrender his fate into the hands of the interviewer.

It is an odd irony. In the fundamental traditions of business, the ideal enterprise man is competitive, alert, and aggressive. He is called upon to present both his company and himself in appealing images. But here, at the outset of their careers, potential employees are condemned for these very same instincts.

An employment interview is for most people an anxious time.

Applicants try to "look good," most often by emphasizing their "strengths" and de-emphasizing their weaknesses. Some, however, *overemphasize* their strengths and try to hide their weaknesses completely. This is a poor choice in tactics. It is a naïve approach, but it alone does *not* mark its user as an incorrigible liar, unsuited to polite corporate society. Nor, in my belief, does it mean that his interviewer has either the duty or the right covertly to reject him without notice.

There is a more human alternative. When the interviewer believes he has detected significant inconsistencies or important exaggerations in an applicant's presentation, he does not have to pretend he has been "taken in." If the interviewer suspects what he is being told, he can confront the applicant with his doubt. He does not need either to badger or to insult the interviewee, but he should make it clear that the interviewee's statement does not seem consistent with other information he has given. This provides the applicant with the opportunity to explain the apparent disparity, or to modify or withdraw the claim. Of course, if after repeated confrontations, the interviewee continues to present himself, his work history, and his achievements in a way that the interviewer cannot accept as credible, the interviewer can—and probably must—reject his candidacy.[4]

To those interviewers who are concerned that an "alerted" interviewee will be better able to fool them, some reassurance: If he is not clever enough to avoid the loopholes in his story to begin with, it is unlikely that he will be clever enough to close them successfully under the pressure of the interview situation, unless, of course, his claim is valid.

Judgments have to be made about applicants for employment. A bad selection can be expensive for a company, and it can be harmful for the employee as well if he is misplaced and therefore predestined for failure. The employment interview has traditionally been the primary means for obtaining

---

[4] And he should, in most cases, do so gently but explicitly.

information required in selecting employees, and it is likely to continue to be for the foreseeable future. The interview can and should be designed and conducted, not as a dabbler's journey into the applicant's psyche, but as one part of an open effort to estimate how well the person is likely to meet the *requirements of the particular job opening* for which he is being considered. This means that the interviewer must have a clear picture of what those requirements are. Too often he does not. Too often the acceptance or rejection of a candidate is not an outcome of the evaluation of the applicability and adequacy of his background and ability vis-à-vis the job for which he is being considered. It is rather a judgment, *according to the interviewer's criteria and biases,* of how well the candidate performed in the particular series of person-to-person interactions which comprised the interview encounter.

As one psychologist told me, "Many interviewers have been evaluating people for twenty years without changing their criteria, even though the requirements of the jobs for which they interview have changed drastically." And, he continued, "Damned few interviewers ever bother to verify their standards even in the most basic way—by going back six months, or a year, or two years later to find out how well the people they selected are performing on the jobs."

The employment interview can be used as an opportunity not only to obtain information and impressions, but also to test out those impressions. Contrary to Dr. Fear's injunction, it is both useful and practicable for the interviewer to *exchange* with the applicant. In the course of the interview the interviewee can be informed of the tentative hypotheses the interviewer is developing about his abilities and shortcomings with respect to the job for which he is applying. The interviewer can say, for example: "I get the impression that you prefer to concentrate on implementing established programs, rather than on planning or development work. How do you react to that?" Or: "I get the impression that you do well in supervising shop operations, but that you have had some difficulties in supervising professional people. Do you think that's right or not?"

The candidate can confirm these hypotheses or deny them. Where he chooses to do the latter, he should be given the opportunity to provide information from his background and prior experience to support his case. It is up to the interviewer, through the exercise of his own skill, knowledge, and intuition, to assess the additional information and to determine whether or not a change in his original hypothesis is warranted.

For some critics the "ethical issue" of the employee selection process revolves around a single-dimensioned question about the right of the interviewer to invade the applicant's privacy. In my view that is not a very functional way to frame the issue. For some people *any* question asked may be, if not an invasion, then at least an intrusion into their privacy, while for others privacy encompasses a much smaller domain. The key determinant of good practice in the interview is not, for me, the matter of privacy, per se, but whether or not the interviewer has carefully considered the relevance of the information he has the power to elicit, whether or not he has tested in his own mind his real *need* to know. And most important, whether he has willingly exercised his responsibility for establishing a climate in which both he and the interviewee can maintain their dignity and integrity.

8

Dollars[1]

MONEY IS FUNNY. Most people like it a lot. Wise men, who speak with the voice of enterprise, say that money provides The Incentive, and that men's hands and brains work best only when they see a clear and immediate relationship between how hard they strive and how much money they get.

Other people say that money is not really much in itself, but rather, that its real importance comes from the fact that it is a symbol of grander or deeper things, like power, prestige, and security. The truly wondrous aspect of money, they believe, is that it can be made to represent almost anything people want it to represent.

There are also those who do not like money at all. Karl Marx, for example, in his early days, even before he had gotten around to such matters as *Das Kapital* and the *Communist Manifesto,* said that money was a source of man's "alienated consciousness." Money, said Marx, brings out man's greed, aggression, and acquisitiveness, and thus causes the displacement of his genuine human needs for love and affiliation. The urge for money leaves only economic man, a dehumanized abstraction. Erich Fromm tends to agree with Marx, and also finds a galling

[1] Frankly, this will be, in places, a rather more difficult chapter than most of the others in this book. He or she who labors in the big and methodical establishments and is paid according to their systems may, however, find it worth the strain. Everyone else please skim.

injustice in money and its uses. Fromm points out that money may be acquired in a number of ways: by one's own efforts, by exploiting others, by inheritance, by luck, or by fraud. But no matter how acquired, its mere possession allows one to exchange it for almost anything he wants.

There are more global views of money and its meaning too. Some see a profound connection between money and our whole twentieth-century system of rationality. In his modern classic of psychoanalytical interpretation, *Life Against Death,* Norman O. Brown comments: "The connection between money thinking and rational thinking is so deeply ingrained in our practical lives that it seems impossible to question it . . . At a more philosophic level, sociology correctly says that money reflects and promotes a style of thinking which is abstract, impersonal, objective, and quantitative, that is to say, the style of thinking of modern science—and what can be more rational than that?"

These are some of the ways in which philosophers think about money. The thoughts are relevant even to the more mundane discussion to follow. People who work in business organizations get paid. They get paid different amounts, and someone has to figure out, at least approximately, what these amounts should be. The people who specialize in this complicated task are called wage and/or salary administrators. They are still another kind of personnel men, except in a few old-fashioned establishments where they may be finance men.[2]

"In free countries," an elder statesman of the personnel field has said, "employees, for the most part, are paid according to their contribution." And from this pronouncement and its amplified echoes have grown the majority of the dilemmas, in-

[2] Emphasis in this chapter will be on the administration of salaries rather than wages. In general, "wages" are rates per hour paid to hourly employees. "Salaries" are usually determined on a weekly or monthly, sometimes even an annual basis, and are paid to professional and clerical personnel. A great deal more has been written on wage than on salary administration, and current practice in the wage area is less incongruent, though some of its underlying theory has also recently been opened to question.

congruities, and overstretched rationalizations of the salary administration specialty.

The main trouble is that salary administrators keep trying to prove the point, mostly ex post facto, and the results are very untidy. The trouble begins when you try to decide what "contribution" means, and it gets worse after you make the decision. How, for instance, do you compare the contribution of the teacher versus the television announcer, the fireman versus the fashion model, or the President of the United States versus the chairman of the board of General Motors? And then, how do you explain the differences in their pay?[3] How do you resolve one of the more bitter bits of irony: that a college-educated Negro could, until recently, expect lifetime earnings of about $185,000, while an eighth-grade-educated white could look forward to $191,000?

Of course, it can be argued that these examples are the dramatic anomalies—the extremes. Well, then, let us look again. In 1933 certified public accountants had an average annual net income of $3,968, while engineers averaged $2,900. But in 1950, the CPA average had only increased to $4,002, while the engineer's had jumped to $4,700. In 1963, the average offer by public accounting firms to new college graduates had risen to $5,928, but the base salary for beginning engineers had moved up to $6,708. Did the contribution of engineers actually change from being significantly less than to markedly more than that of CPA's? And if so, in whose judgment? During the period from 1939 to 1950 semiskilled factory workers increased their earnings by 172 per cent, while professional and managerial incomes increased by only 96 per cent. From 1950 to 1961, though, professional and managerial earnings advanced by 75 per cent, while those of the factory workers rose by only 59 per cent.

The contribution hypothesis just does not hold up very well.

---

[3] The President of the United States earns $100,000 per year, plus $50,000 for expenses. In 1964, GM's board chairman's pay was over $800,000, not including expenses.

The quest for a neat correlation between worth and reward is a natural one which fits nicely with most people's idea of the way things ought to be. But the fact that they ought to be does not mean they are. Money value determinations are not the products of fine, dispassionate measurements made in the dust-free, dehumidified atmosphere of a laboratory. Rather, they are continually buffeted and rebuffeted in the turbulent environment of the messy outside world, and not merely on a supply and demand basis, either. The answers do not just tumble off those rugged but accurate free-competition scales. In itself, the market theory of labor pricing is no more adequate than the contribution theory. A great many factors—supply and demand, subjective and sometimes arbitrary judgments, agreements negotiated from positions of strength (or weakness), Government legislation, and even the ephemeral whims of social conscience —all influence the amounts of money people get paid.

The point is that there are some things that salary administration can be expected to do and other things that it cannot. It can help establish a *limited* and *transient* orderliness in the way people get paid. It cannot structure a sublime and everlasting order where everybody's pay is self-evidently equitable and proper in comparison to everybody else's pay.

When you talk about salary administration in most companies, you have to begin talking about something called the salary structure. To those who like symmetry, the salary structure is a necessary framework for rational action. For those who take a looser approach to life, it is a collection of constraining boxes. In fact, a company's salary structure is comprised of a series of contiguous salary ranges within which its employees are paid. Each of the ranges has a specified minimum and maximum, usually called the salary range, but sometimes designated by terms like salary group, grade, level, class, or code.

The average difference between the minimum and the maximum of each salary range is about 30 to 40 per cent at the lower end of the structure, and it frequently grows to more than a 60-per-cent spread for high-level management personnel. Thus, for the lesser positions in the organization, a typical range might start with a salary of $600 a month and go to a maximum of $780. On the other hand, a senior management job might start at $2,000 and top out at $3,200. The justification for this kind of distinction—or discrimination, as some might feel it— usually is that the potential difference *between the minimum and maximum* "value of contribution" possible among higher-level executives is significantly greater than for employees at lower levels.

In general, the difference between the minimum of one salary range and the minimum of the next-higher range is about 10 per cent. As you move up the ladder, the differences between the minimums of the ranges tend to increase. The explanation for this generally is that as you evaluate the higher-level jobs it becomes more difficult to make fine distinctions; therefore, greater distinctions are recognized by greater dollar differentials.

In a study of the salary structure of seventy major firms, the National Industrial Conference Board found that the number of ranges in a company structure ran from five in one organization to over ninety (essentially no structure at all) in some others. The median number was nineteen. Only about a third of the companies used their salary structure through the chief executive level, and less than half included *any* corporate officers. For the unincluded, of course, there are no prescribed limits.[4]

So, the salary structure is a series of salary ranges, some low and some very high. But how is it decided who gets what? Obviously, the chief executive ought to be in the highest range, but from that point down the answers become less clear. As one textbook writer unblushingly puts it, the way in which order is brought from chaos is through the process of *job evaluation*.

[4] Even where the structure does include officers, it does not tell the story of their real earning potentials. Stock options, deferred compensation, and other kinds of bonuses are over and above the base salary rates encompassed by the structure ranges.

There are a large number of job-evaluation systems in existence. Estimates run into the scores, and if you include minor variations the number would probably reach the hundreds. Fortunately, however, they fall into three basic classes; perhaps four, if you include the classification system used extensively in the Federal Government but seldom in industry. The three most frequently used industrial systems are: job ranking, the point method, and the factor-comparison method. At times, combinations of these systems are used simultaneously.

The objective of the job-evaluation system, whichever one is used, is to measure the value of each job in relation to all other jobs in the organization. The ultimate results are translated into one of the salary ranges of the company's salary structure.

The job-ranking method is the simplest approach to evaluation, but for sophisticated salary administrators it carries the aura of the kindergarten, and so it is considered only slightly better than no system at all. Basically, job ranking is just that. Jobs are arrayed in a descending order from the most to least important. This is usually done by a committee. After the jobs are ranked, each is assigned to one of the salary ranges of the company salary structure.

The point and the factor-comparison methods of job evaluation provide opposite examples of Norman Brown's observation that there is a close parallel between "money thinking" and the style of thinking prevalent in modern science. In the salary administrator's quest for scientism he invokes through these systems all of the elements of the spirit Brown has high-lighted: abstraction, impersonality, objectivity, and quantification. These are the revered and advertised features of both systems.

The point method of evaluating jobs starts not with the jobs but with a collection of preselected factors which have been determined to be important for the jobs to be evaluated. Studies of evaluation plans have compiled literally hundreds of "names" for the various factors used. A fairly representative sample follows:

Analytical requirements
Decision-making
requirements
Initiative
Complexity
Supervisory responsibility
Ingenuity
Quality
Adaptability
Personal appearance

Working conditions
Communication responsibility
Risk-taking
Judgment
Co-operation requirements
Capacity for self-expression
Persuasive requirements
Work pressure
Responsibility for money

There can be from three to twenty or more factors in a particular system. After their selection a rating scale is constructed for each factor. The scale consists of a series of verbal descriptions, with each description representing a higher level of requirement than the preceding one. These descriptions are generally called "degrees," and each is accompanied by a range of point values. For example:

Factor:	*Capacity for self-expression (requirement to transmit ideas and convey opinions to others)*	Point Values
1st Degree	Work of mostly mechanical nature, with not much opportunity for self-expression.	0–10
2nd Degree	Few chances for self-expression. Must determine salient points of things on occasional instances.	11–20
3rd Degree	Ideas are given, but they must be transmitted to customers, public, or superiors in adaptable manner.	21–30
4th Degree	Must convey ideas to customers and public with basis for presentation. Must know significant facts.	31–40
5th Degree	Must convey ideas to large groups through writing, speaking, or graphic presentation.	41–50

Thus, the job to be evaluated is measured against each factor in the evaluation plan, with points being assigned to it in accordance with the appropriate degrees. It should be emphasized that it is the requirements of the job and not the qualifications of the incumbent that are supposed to be measured. In salary administration classicism each job is evaluated just as though it were brand new and unoccupied. After a point rating is given to the job on each factor the points are added up, and on the basis of this total the position is assigned to one of the ranges of the company salary structure. Of course, the higher the point total, the higher the range it gets.

There are a number of highly complex versions of the factor-comparison method of evaluating jobs. Essentially, these approaches attempt to "measure" jobs in about the same way as the point plans. Positions are compared with one another, again on a variable number of factors, except that the factor-comparison method does not use predefined degrees such as those shown above. Rather, comparisons are made directly between existing jobs on each of the factors used.

This is a simplified description of how some of the systems work, or are supposed to work. The objectives and principles really look quite good. They do seem to aim for impartial equity. Problems do not arise out of the objectives of the systems, but rather from their premises and application.

The main stream of job-evaluation technology has been running toward the quantitative systems. In the Industrial Conference Board's study of company evaluation plans, more than 80 per cent of the firms surveyed used some kind of quantitative approach. D. W. Belcher, author of one of the classic handbooks of wage and salary administration, high-lights the supposed advantages of the quantitative approaches over the more simple, less quantified methods such as ranking. Says Belcher: These methods "break the job down into parts for consideration, instead of dealing with the whole job. Thus, in the quantitative methods of job comparison, separate judgments are made on each factor . . . Making several separate judgments with respect to each job and attaching numerical values to these judgments make the results of job evaluation more precise."

What are the rules for selecting and developing the factors to be used in the quantitative plans? J. L. Otis and R. H.

Leukart, two more standard authorities in the job-evaluation business, cite them as follows:

> The factors chosen must be ratable. The amount of each factor required must vary from small to large among the different jobs.
>
> The factors chosen must be ones which are judged to be important—only those factors should be included which, when evaluated, will determine accurately the rate of pay or the relative worth of the job.
>
> The factors must not overlap in meaning. Each one should be a measure of one and only one aspect of the job.
>
> The factors must meet both employer and worker standards.
>
> The factors must be universal in application or be applicable to the type of jobs for which the system was constructed.

In addition to these by Otis and Leukart, there are two other points that are usually included by evaluation plan designers:

> The factors should lend themselves to as clear and definite description as possible in order to facilitate understanding and application.
>
> The job evaluator must carefully avoid being influenced by the qualifications or abilities of the incumbent. He must limit his considerations solely to the requirements of the job itself.

Quantitative job-evaluation systems started around 1920. The systems were originally applied to production jobs in factories. They were found to be helpful in developing pay-rate differentials for various kinds of production work, and they still are. Thus, for a long time the standard text writings on job evaluation were oriented toward the factory context—the evaluation of production jobs. But what seemed to be a good approach for valuing one kind of work was too readily accepted as a sound way for evaluating very different kinds of work. And that is the key. The difference between work done in professional and managerial jobs and the work done in production jobs is not just a matter of degree (the pun is intentional), it is a matter of kind.

To begin with, let's look at the supposed advantage of breaking the job down into its component parts so that "several separate judgments" may be made with respect to each job. In the first place, the isolation, definition, and valuation of factory job factors such as physical demands, responsibility for tools and equipment, responsibility for material and products, safety hazards, and so on, is one thing. The isolation, definition, and valuation of the factors commonly included in professional and managerial jobs, such as planning requirements, analytical requirements, communication and contact requirements, decision-making requirements, and so forth, is quite another.

Second, aside from the difficulties involved, the "breaking down" process is simply *not* a valid approach for examining jobs involving complex, intangible, intellectual activities (as opposed to the relatively tangible and discrete processes of factory work). In reality, the very process of fragmentation obscures rather than clarifies the meaning of the professional job—a meaning that can only be understood by recognizing the *operational interrelationships* of most aspects of the professional's work.

The Otis and Leukart premise, that factors must be ratable and must vary among different jobs, seems sound. Without variations, no distinctions can be made and measurement would serve no purpose. Where the question does arise, though, is in application. How meaningful are many of the variations commonly high-lighted by the quantitative plans, and what real impact do they have on the worth of the jobs to which they are applied?

Once upon a time, the factors of *"education and experience required"* were almost inevitably prime criteria in the general run of evaluation plans. But after a while the futility of trying to pin-point a specifically required "number of years" of either factor, even though they can be expressed in neat quantitative terms, was recognized. So in many evaluation plans these factors were dropped or, less fortunately, attempts were made to couple the number of years with some further qualification. For example: "Must be able to understand general instructions/high school graduation" versus "Must be able to understand broad, undetailed instructions/two years of college."

Aside from the artificiality of such verbal tail-chasing, there are other flaws in overemphasizing ratability as a criterion, particularly in evaluating professional jobs. Why bother to measure distinctions between jobs that really do not matter? These kinds of measurements actually distort rather than contribute to appropriate job-value relationships.

To illustrate the point, let us say there are two research chemists, Mr. A and Mr. B. The job of Mr. A requires him to spend essentially all his working time in investigating highly complex physical phenomena. When his job is evaluated on the Analytical Requirements factor, it is, therefore, credited with the maximum possible points for this factor, let us say 150. Chemist A's duties, though, do not require any extensive outside contacts. His relationships are almost entirely with people within his own work unit and are fairly straightforward. On the Relationships factor, then, he gets 10 points. He supervises no one and therefore he gets no points on the supervision factor. Thus, his total on the three factors is 160 points.

On the other hand, we have the job of research chemist Mr. B, which requires pretty much the same kind and level of analytical work—150 points again. However, Mr. B spends only 75 per cent of his time at it. He happens to have been assigned the task of helping to train new junior laboratory technicians. For this he gets 20 points on the Relationships factor. And because his particular project involves a good deal of report preparation, he has been assigned two typist-clerks. This gives him another 20 points for Supervision. His total on the three factors is 190 points.

Thus, Chemist B's job rates 30 points higher than Chemist

A's, and this may be enough to land it in the next-higher range of the company's salary structure. Yet, the really important function—the critical element each chemist is *actually being paid for*—is his analytical work. The other factors, in reality, are extraneous.

We might well say here that Chemist B's job is poorly designed, that someone else could better be spared to train the technicians, and that the typists could more advantageously be placed in a pool and supervised by a clerical supervisor. In fact, as Otis and Leukart point out, "Only those factors should be included which . . . will determine . . . the relative worth of the job." The complication, though, is that in any one plan there will be some factors which are *quite* significant for some jobs but not at all significant for others. Yet, as the plans are used, all jobs are evaluated against all factors.

In traditional job-evaluation technology there is an almost holy principle which commands the cleavage between *the job* and *the individual* who occupies the job. The assumptions are these: A job is an organizational block. It is a specific set of those duties and responsibilities which the organization requires in order to accomplish a predefined and limited purpose. A job, according to the classical rites of organization theory, is *not* put together to utilize the particular set of talents and skills of the man who happens to fill it, but to meet the organization's needs as efficiently and economically as possible. Again, perhaps a fairly reasonable concept when one thinks about production work, but a formidable barrier against any realistic understanding of the dynamics involved in shaping professional and managerial jobs. Especially at the middle and higher levels, these jobs just are not standard slots into which standard, interchangeable pegs can be pushed in and pulled out. The professional, if he is indeed a professional, more often than not *brings* something unique to his job, and thereby *does* something unique to it.

The potential result or "product" of the work of the research or design man or the manager ought not be equated with that of the production worker. The quality and quantity standards for production workers are almost invariably preset within a narrow range, i.e., in terms of number of units and quality control criteria. But the acceptable product of the researcher's efforts cannot be predefined except in the broadest and most general terms. The same research, engineering, marketing, financial, or operations problem, assigned to different people, may well result in solutions of vastly different quality, produced in significantly different lengths of time. And the term "quality" here is more than single-dimensioned. It may encompass not only a better answer, but also a wider answer, with salutary effects which were not even contemplated beforehand.

Most of the job-evaluation systems currently in use are unrealistic and inappropriate for their purposes. But large organizations do require a systematic methodology for determining how people are to be paid. There are, I believe, alternative approaches which would more adequately serve this purpose.

Chances are that apples are best judged by size, flavor, and resistance to worms and bruises. Now, girls could be judged by those criteria too, but if they were, some pretty irrelevant elements would be getting more attention than they deserve, while other important ones would be overlooked. One of the first steps in the development of any job-evaluation approach should be the systematic identification of the *essential* elements of each "occupational family" within which evaluations are to be made. In other words, for each specialized field—engineering, sales, accounting, and so on—the evaluators should identify clearly and realistically *what it is that is really being paid for;* those aspects of the work that actually characterize its nature and that provide a scale along which specific differences in level of responsibility or skill may be distinguished. These are the only factors that should be considered in the evaluation process, and they will probably differ markedly in different occupational groups.

At the same time, those responsible for evaluation should recognize explicitly that while worth and value can and should be treated in certain set terms—responsibility, required skill level, rarity in a given occupational population, and so forth— the treatment must always be specific and limited. Thus, rational and effective judgments may be made of the relative value of different jobs in the same field, and even for different jobs in related though not identical fields, but not for different jobs in fields that are totally unrelated. Accountants, for example, may be compared to auditors, but there is little use in attempting to rationalize the measurement of their "contribution" on the same scale that is used for engineers.

An evaluation system should not attempt to atomize jobs into their smallest possible parts and then to treat each factor in isolation. Rather, the systems should seek to recognize integral *combinations of job elements* based on the natural dynamics of the jobs. These combinations should be thought of in terms of a whole, a "system," rather than an isolated or solitary component. For example: scope, kind, and depth of subject matter dealt with; and processing, treatment, and result requirements are all interrelated elements which should and can be considered as a whole by the job evaluator.

And, finally, the essentially inseparable relationship between man and job, particularly in the evaluation of the more senior professional, technical, and managerial jobs, should be recognized and provisions should be made to treat this relationship systematically.

Employees advance from the minimum to the maximum rate of their particular salary range by means of a salary administration concept called the merit review. The dollar limits of the salary range are ostensibly based upon the evaluated value of the job, *without regard to how well or poorly the job is being performed.* But the actual pay an individual gets within the range is supposed to be determined by *how well he is performing*—by his merit.

In the good old days people asked for raises. The employee weighed in his mind such factors as his current bargaining position, the mood of his boss, and the state of the business, then plunged or tiptoed into the mahogany-paneled chamber to take his chance. As often as not the larger and more frequent raises went to those with the bold or persistent styles, whether or not they were also the more proficient performers in their day-to-day duties. But such scenes are seldom played in corporations today. Salary increases have become a good deal more ritualized, and, as a matter of fact, probably a good deal more equitable as well.

In most major American companies a merit review is scheduled once a year for each professional and managerial employee. Most often the review of the employee's pay is accompanied by a review of his performance during the preceding year. This is usually presented with some degree of formality and involves the use of a document called a performance appraisal or performance review form. The performance appraisal is usually filled out in advance by the employee's supervisor and subsequently "discussed" with the employee in a private meeting between the two. Most appraisal forms contain anywhere from several to dozens of items against which the employee's performance is to be judged—for example, quality of work, initiative, and potential—with each item rated along a continuum or graded alphabetically or numerically. Finally, there is a total or summary rating, and from this the manager decides what, if any, salary change ought to be made. In some appraisal systems the salary administrator's passion for dispassionate quantification takes over again, so that the various items are differentially weighted and a numerical summary rating is directly translated to a corresponding dollar in the salary range.[5]

The explanation of the salary change to the employee, or the

---

[5] Though I have no direct evidence, I am quite sure that somewhere, at this very moment, there sits a salary administrator who is working out a system which includes the intercession of a computer and eliminates entirely the need for manager, man, or words between the two.

reason for no change, is only one of the purposes of the performance appraisal discussion. Two others in most systems, ostensibly at least equally important, are: First, to provide a regularly scheduled opportunity for the manager to inform the employee of how well or how poorly he is performing his job; and secondly, to provide an opportunity for the manager to advise and coach the employee and so to help him grow and develop.

Until the late forties or so the great majority of performance appraisal programs centered on the assessment and rating of traits—that is, individual personality characteristics or qualities that were allegedly the determinants of the employee's on-the-job performance. After consideration of the individual's rating on key items such as aggressiveness, dependability, perseverance, and so on, the manager provided his counsel and advice to the employee in remarks like: "You're a good man, Fred, but you don't have self-confidence. You ought to be more aggressive in selling your ideas."

Trait-rating is still moderately popular among appraisers, but it is definitely on the way out in the more discriminating personnel departments. A number of faults go with trait-rating that are difficult to ignore. First of all, in a corporate environment which values hard specificity, the trait-rating approach is too softly general, too speculative. Who is to say exactly which and how much of any particular personality characteristics ensure successful task performance? Further, among tough-minded, results-oriented line managers, the discussion of subtle characterological complexes is not a comfortable task. It can get particularly uncomfortable when the manager finds himself suddenly and unexpectedly counterconfronted by the threatened psyche of the subordinate who has been told he lacks self-confidence.

The movement away from trait-rating has been toward such approaches as the American Management Association's Standards of Performance. In these systems, the emphasis is upon *results* rather than characteristics. Says AMA: "Standards of performance should be: statements of basic results required of the operation; worded to include references to accurate means of measurements . . . a quantity and/or quality; worded to prevent misinterpretations; [and] set up in officially approved form . . ." The idea is appealing, and conceptually, there would seem to be a good deal more validity in judging and paying for the results of effort rather than for the psychological style of the performance.

In introducing the system, Lawrence Appley of AMA begins: "In this development of standards of performance, the objective is to use finally *only* those standards which can be measured definitely by facts or figures." But Appley, a reasonable man, goes on to say that, though this is desirable, it is not always possible.

For many personnel men, though, qualifiers just don't count. Any employee's performance, from the district salesman's through that of the marketing vice president, is assumed to be measureable. When the circumstances do not fit, the salary administrator, striving mightily for the necessary "facts or figures," like Procrustes chops or stretches them until they do. And once again, as in the fragment-quantification methods of job evaluation, the system breaks down.

The problem is not in the approach as an approach. On the contrary, with the exercise of reasonable judgment, the performance standards system and others of its kind provide a decently logical method of assessing work performance, as well as a way for the manager to communicate his expectations to his subordinates. The problems arise when a good idea is rigidified into an immutable law. It is not just that the standards themselves can become disfunctional and nonsensical. What is worse is that the system may be taken seriously and become *in fact* the basis upon which salary determinations are made. Under the circumstances, the individual employee adapts to the rules of the game, and concentrates his efforts in those areas that will make him look good on the scoreboard. For instance, I have seen times in the personnel department itself when the heaviest effort was being devoted to peripheral *but quantifiable* programs.

Campaigns to get higher percentages of employee participation in extracurricular bowling teams and employee clubs became all important. Writing and rewriting an ever-increasing number of job descriptions was given top priority. Meanwhile, more significant but less measurable areas were neglected.

Another fundamental flaw in the typical performance appraisal process stems from the basic assumption that the average manager can *simultaneously* sit in judgment on his subordinate's performance, decide whether or not he will get a pay raise, and provide helpful advice and guidance. In the setting required by most salary review–performance appraisal procedures, the manager thus finds himself in the curious position of playing prosecutor, judge, and friendly counselor all at the same time. In trying to meet the requirements of all three roles, the manager, at the very least, faces a mechanical dilemma. Should he inform the employee at the beginning of the discussion session what the salary action is going to be, and then proceed to the background and the counseling? Or should he take the more dramatic route of building his case first, and save the dollar news for last? If he does the former, the likelihood is that once he has announced the climax of the drama, his subordinate's attention to what follows may be minimal indeed. The employee will probably withdraw to reflect contentedly on his good fortune, or to brood over his resentment, depending on the amount of the raise. On the other hand, saving the denouement for last may be no better. A state of suspense is certainly not conducive to the cool contemplation of information about one's performance.[6]

The designers of most performance appraisal programs have aimed for precision. Precision in the measurement of performance, and precision in relating the amount of pay to the quality of performance. The objective has been to promote greater dis-

[6] The inappropriateness and ineffectiveness inherent in most current performance appraisal practices were demonstrated in the early 1960's by a study conducted by the Behavioral Research Service of the General Electric Company, which will be discussed in a later chapter.

crimination in paying people "what they deserve," or as one personnel vice president I know said it: "We want to pay our best people very well. They are the most important resources of our organization, the ones who will ultimately determine its progress. We want them to stay with us and we want to motivate them. When it comes to the run-of-the-mill kind, we aren't that concerned. If I have a choice to make, I'd rather overpay the top ones even if I have to underpay the others."

But that is the way vice presidents talk.[7] There is evidence both within individual companies and in the salary survey results that it is not happening that way. Rather, year after year the data collected in salary surveys show not an increasing but a slowly decreasing pay differential between the highest-paid and lowest-paid personnel who do similar kinds of work. Perhaps this is because reality comes in a more practical shape for the lower-level manager. To him, after all, falls the responsibility for the product which day after day must be sent out the back door. Quality levels are kept adequate, paperwork is completed on time, and shipping schedules are met through the efforts of others besides the brilliant. And for this reason and other bits of human frailty, or perversity, or good sense, it seems wise to remember the run-of-the-mill kind too.

---

[7] When they are talking about those people down there. As we shall see later, though, when we discuss executive pay, the conversation usually gets mellower as it gets closer to home.

9

⟡══════⟡

Even More Dollars

"CERTAINLY MOST IMPORTANT from the standpoint of the shareholders," said GM's president in 1959, "is the General Motors incentive program. This consists of, first, the bonus plan, for which a substantial number of executives are eligible, and, second, the stock option plan, in which about 250 of the principal executives participate.[1] Details of these plans have been explained many times, but the point I want to make here is that it is largely this incentive program which is responsible for the fact that in General Motors so many executives are—to borrow a term from the diplomatic service—career executives. It is also this program, with its incentives and rewards made proportional to contributions, which has caused our executives to give the business that something extra that is so necessary to success."

And so we come to the subject of "that something extra"— executive compensation—how they pay the really grand figures on the corporate landscape. GM's president John Gordon's affection for the General Motors incentive program was hardly a surprise. In 1962 Mr. Gordon earned $589,850, of which $408,750 resulted from its application to him. The compensation of big business executives is a big story in a number of ways. Even the job of keeping track of who gets how much, when, and which way the trends are going gets a large share of attention. There are probably a score or more organizations de-

---

[1] At that time, about 0.04 per cent of GM's total employees.

voted to collecting and analyzing the number on executive pay checks. Besides the Securities and Exchange Commission, which officially includes this chore under its charter, some of the better known include *Fortune,* the National Industrial Conference Board, *Business Week, Nation's Business,* and McKinsey and Company. Perhaps the most exquisite collection of all belongs to the American Management Association, which AMA advertised as follows in a special *New York Times* supplement in September, 1963:

> In the world of modern management, there is perhaps no area in which information is more avidly sought or more difficult to come by than the problem of executive compensation. AMA has established an Executive Compensation Service that is available to members on a separate subscription basis. The service is truly unique. It not only offers authoritative information on prevailing compensation levels for top management, but also includes over 200 secondary management positions on which data are otherwise almost impossible to obtain.

Elaborating further, AMA explains that its data come from 5,000 companies representing 85 per cent of the industrial corporate business in the United States and Canada, that it has compensation reports on some 150,000 individuals, and, reassuringly, that these are kept under lock and key at all times.

In 1962 the National Industrial Conference Board reported on a study it had made of extra-compensation plans—the magic word is "extra"—in 405 leading manufacturing concerns. The board's findings, unsurprisingly, confirmed that, financially, it is nice to be an executive. While two thirds of the manufacturers had some form of bonus arrangement for some or all of their managers, only 15 per cent included their professional and technical personnel under such plans. Less than 4 per cent provided anything "extra" for their first-line supervisors. In contrast, 65 per cent of the plans included middle management, major executives were covered in about 90 per cent, and corporate officers were included in almost all the plans. But the Conference

Board report doesn't tell the whole story, for there are extra-compensation plans and there are *extra*-compensation plans. There are literally hundreds of combinations and variations, which range from simple incentive bonus arrangements, through special management fringe benefits[2] (no-interest home loans, free tax and legal counseling, scholarships for executive offspring, use of company-owned cars and hunting lodges, paneled offices with original Renoirs on the walls, and so on), and ultimately peak at the stock-option and esoteric deferred-compensation approaches.[3]

Not including the free services and assorted merchandise, extra compensation sweetens the pot for those who get it by estimated averages of 25 to 45 per cent of base salaries. But that's *average*. At the middle-management levels 10 per cent is about par—not much more than a taste—while at the really high echelons, more than 100 per cent is not unusual. For Mr. Gordon, as we have seen, it was 225 per cent—sweet indeed.

For those at and near the very top, the "principal executives," as Mr. Gordon called them, there are stock options. When one begins to talk about principal executives, incidentally, the salary administrator and his job-evaluation expertise fade out and the compensation specialist and his tax-accounting expertise fade in. McKinsey and Company's Arch Patton, a long-time compensation expert, thinks this ever-increasing complexity is a good thing for personnel, "perhaps, just what is needed to make the personnel function the really important top-management job it should be by 1970."

[2] Surprisingly, fringe benefits are not really fringy any more. While their exact costs to the individual corporations are seldom disclosed, estimates by those who should know (for instance the United States Chamber of Commerce and McKinsey and Company) indicate an average cost of 30 per cent of payroll, and as much as 40 per cent in some companies. These costs, of course, cover the benefits of all employees, not just those of executives.

[3] When we say peak we are not taking into account the superpeaks—those really special arrangements such as *The New York Times* reported (April 10, 1960) for Alfred Perlman, president of the New York Central. Mr. Perlman signed an agreement with himself arranging for $50,000 per year to be paid to him as consultant after his retirement.

More than four fifths of the firms listed on the New York Stock Exchange have some form of stock options for their executives, and according to *Business Week*'s estimate, options account for an average—note, *average*—of 25 to 35 per cent of the executive's total compensation. The current number of firms providing options represents a phenomenal increase. In 1953 only about 30 per cent of the major companies in the United States offered them.

A variation of the stock option that first appeared in the mid-forties is worth a special citation for creativity. It was called the phantom stock plan, and it provided its fortunate participants with the best financial part of stock ownership without requiring them to own stock—in fact, without even requiring that there be any stock.

Under this arrangement, each selected executive was granted a specified number of make-believe "units," each with a stated dollar value equal to the current market price of real stock at the time of the issuance. From that point on, every time the company paid a dividend on its real stock, the holder of the phantom stock received an equal amount, just as though his units were real. If there was a stock split later, the owner of the phantom stock had his unit credits increased proportionately. And best of all at some still later time, often after retirement, the company paid him the difference between the theoretical value of the originally issued units and the then-current market value of the real stock.

Management Record found the phantom approach particularly appealing and explained it this way: "What, one might ask, are the advantages of owning 'dividend units' [phantom shares] rather than actual shares? One, of course, is that the individual takes no risk; he may gain substantially but he cannot lose . . . From the company's point of view, by paying a bonus in dividend units instead of in cash or stock, more money is retained in the business. And, if profitably employed, this money may earn enough to cover the cost of the cash 'dividends' on the phantom stock. So everybody should be happy."

Sadly, everybody was not happy. Some stockholders were quite unhappy, so they brought the matter to court in 1958. And while the court was not entirely unsympathetic to management's case, it nevertheless enjoined any further issuance of the phantom stock.

Still another flash of inspired compensation thinking resulted in what has been called, fittingly, the "fairy godmother" clause. But this fairy godmother is even better than Cinderella's. For while she switched off her magic at twelve o'clock, very nearly causing Cinderella a good deal of embarrassment, the fairy godmother clause really times its magic to make sure that for its wards there are no embarrassments.

The clause provides the very essence of flexibility. If for some reason the market price of the company's stock should decline instead of rise after the issuance of a batch of options, the company merely terminates the now-unappealing package and reissues an alternate set pegged at a lower price. For instance, in 1958 Aluminum Company of America called back its 1956 options priced at $117.25 a share and reissued new ones at the more attractive figure of $68.50.

Aside from its "philosophical" basis, which we will be discussing soon, the principal rationale for stock options—including those touched by neither phantom nor fairy—is usually set forth pretty straightforwardly. The options, say their supporters, play a major part in attracting and retaining top management talent for a company. Several years ago, Gwylim Price, chairman of the board of Westinghouse, made this point in testimony before the Securities and Exchange Commission. Price stated that he personally knew three top Westinghouse executives who had turned down offers of the presidencies of other well-known companies because of the hold of their Westinghouse options. But for some critics of the options plans, that is one of their major disservices to the economy as a whole. Tennessee's Senator Gore, an especially captious voice on the subject of options, has called them "cut-rate bargain purchases for highly compensated executives." He believes that if the options did not have such a tight clutch on the executives, some of them might go out and start up their own companies. And that would mean new competition, with accompanying benefits to the consumer.[4]

The complaints against the big, quick windfalls produced by the stock-option plans have had some effect on Washington. A 1964 revision of the tax laws eliminated a tax advantage that many feel was one of the most attractive features of the programs. Before the 1964 change an executive could sell his stock after only six months and his profits would be taxed as capital gains, at a maximum rate of 25 per cent. He could then use the remainder to exercise his option on the next accumulation of stock which had been set aside for him. Senator Gore estimated that what he calls this "tax loophole" cost the Government as much as $100 million a year in revenue. The loophole, however, has been inexorably pulled into a hard knot. The executive must now hold his stock for at least three years before the capital-gains provision can be applied. If the stock is sold before that time its dollar gains are taxed at the much higher rate of ordinary income. Two other harsh facts have also emerged from the tax law changes: new option programs must now be offered at a full 100 per cent of market price, and the maximum number of years allowable from the time the option is offered to the time it must be exercised has been cut from ten to five years.

Theoretically, however, the tax changes ought not make any difference. In late 1964, *Business Week* reported that a good many companies were quite concerned about the demise of the six-month capital-gains provision, and were actively searching for new ways to get more ready cash to their top men quickly. But *Business Week* also observed that "wholesale scrapping of

[4] Other senators too have been unfriendly to stock options. In 1957 the Senate Subcommittee on Antitrust and Monopoly reported its view that stock options have the practical effect of feeding inflation. Since price increases tend to raise stock prices, and since the value of the executive's holdings is contingent on the market price of his company's stock, his financial interests are best served by raising the prices of his company's products, or so concluded the subcommittee.

executive stock-option programs was not in the cards. Too many companies feel that options are the only way to compensate top executives effectively." To support the point, the magazine quoted the no-nonsense classicism of a major steel company comptroller: "Stock options give the executive an opportunity to buy stock with the presumption that he isn't going to run out and sell it. We offer stock options to assist management in attaining proprietary interest in the company."

The hazards of high taxation are not new to the compensation specialist. Some time ago they stimulated the creation of "deferred compensation," a work-now-get-paid-later approach which has become increasingly popular among major corporations. A 1963 survey by the ubiquitous Industrial Conference Board reported that deferred-compensation plans were in effect in about 40 per cent of the larger companies. Unlike stock options, however, deferral arrangements have brought forth hardly a whisper of criticism. This may be because they bear a cousinlike resemblance to pensions, and there is a certain sanctity about pensions which makes them hard for anyone to knock.

Again, there are many variations, but essentially a deferred-compensation arrangement is one in which a company agrees, usually by contract, to pay a particular executive certain amounts of money for certain lengths of time *after he retires*. Usually these agreements place some requirements on the executive too. For example, in most cases the executive must remain with the firm until retirement age, and after retirement he must not go to work for a competitor. Many of the deferred-compensation arrangements also include provisions for payments to be made to the executive's beneficiaries in case of his death. The tax advantage of this plan is, obviously, that the executive pays no taxes on the income credited to his deferral account until he actually receives the money, after his retirement. At that time, presumably, he will be in a lower tax bracket.

One of the major advantages of the deferral arrangement for the company is that it provides an even longer and stronger leash on key men than does the option arrangement. An offer by a competitor firm of an immediate salary increase—currently taxable—becomes less tempting to an executive who would thus have to forfeit his postretirement nest egg.

George H. Foote, another McKinsey and Company expert on compensation, describes the attraction of the plans this way: "Obviously, the appeal of the deferral plans to companies and their executives—an appeal that stems from the promise of personal income tax savings—is a potent one.[5] Moreover, the periodic attacks by advocates of tax reforms on the 'privileged' tax status of executive stock options are likely to impel companies to look harder than ever for other, less vulnerable methods of easing the impact of personal income taxes on their key executives. And what alternative offers more valid and compelling attractions than do these deferred compensation agreements?"

Various people have tried in a number of ways to explain the whys and how much's of executive compensation. The explanations range a continuum that flows from hard realism to almost mystical lyricism.

In 1957 the General Dynamics Corporation sponsored the University of Virginia Graduate School of Business Administration in a study of executive compensation. Among other things, the study reported that the executive acts in a unique role in the economy, a role not envisaged in classical economic theory —that of making possible the effective working of organized groups. Determining the form of the executive's compensation, said the researchers, then becomes a delicate matter. It should be

[5] As Foote points out, though, it is not a simple matter. Applying deferral plans in a manner that will be of *real* advantage to the executive can be complicated. For example, an $82,000-a-year company president twelve years from retirement, in electing to defer $15,000 a year of his current income would effect a $2,100 tax saving on his planned $45,000 after-retirement income. *But* if he had taken what was left of the $15,000 even after taxes (about $5,000) and invested it in sound growth stocks at, say, 4.5 per cent net growth factor, compounded over twelve years, he would actually wind up better off at retirement time by about $3,000. The problems of the rich are deep, very deep.

looked upon, not as a reward for services rendered, but rather as an inducement to perform. Thus, the study concluded, "As a form of compensation . . . if the executive were paid only a straight salary it would suggest that the payee is primarily a hired man, not a part owner or even a professional manager." And that would never do.

On the other hand, Ralph Cordiner, former board chairman of General Electric, seems less concerned about damage to the sensitive executive's self-image than are the Virginia academicians. Mr. Cordiner's reasoning is simple and direct: "The relatively few people who are financially successful in attaining top level positions in competitive industry and are effective in carrying out these responsibilities for the common good, are the highly competent survivors of a competitive struggle that is all the more intense because of the potential rewards."

Another interesting piece of reasoning for high-executive pay levels runs along altruistic lines: Without a very high salary for the top executive, the salaries of those in the numerous managerial layers below him would be unduly compressed. Or, to quote a 1962 issue of *Management Review:* "If the president receives the same as or little more than the vice-president, who would want to be president?" And so on down the line. Explains the writer patiently: "If the first-line supervisor gets $8,000 a year, and there are nine levels of management above him, an average spread of 33 per cent between each level of management would, in itself, require that the chief executive be paid more than $100,000." As any but the most obtuse can see, it is all just simple arithmetic.

The key word that justifies the varied and elaborate shapes of executive compensation is "incentive," a term often applied to executive pay programs. The purpose of incentive systems is to motivate, to get the executive to maximize his effort. It is the same theory, deep down, that applies to the hourly production worker working under a piecework plan. But if money is to be an effective motivator, it has to come at the right times, and only at the right times—when the executive is performing in a superior manner.

How can one tell when the executive is performing in a superior manner? In many incentive systems no one even tries. A formula, based on the executive's organizational level, base pay, and so on, determines the percentage share. And from there on the matter becomes automatic, according to total company earnings and the going price of its stock. Some observers do not think this approach produces much motivation. James W. Tower of Industrial Relations Counselors, Inc., a New York-based consulting firm, says: "Stock options are the extreme example of incentive in which the yield to the individual bears little relationship to his effort. The advantage to the individual depends, among other things, on a rise in the price of the stock . . . no one would deny that forces unrelated to good management may have even greater impact on the price of the stock to the advantage of the lucky executive who has been given an option, has exercised it, and has not yet sold his stock."

Acknowledging the weakness in too-automatic distributions of extra compensation, some companies have been trying to be selective. They have attempted to make incentive plans more discriminating by tying rewards more directly to the results of individual executive performance. Too often, though, the attempt is again accompanied by the fetish for *measurement*. Predetermined goals are set, usually in the form of numbers or dollar bogeys which the executive must meet to be eligible for extra compensation. The further he surpasses his goals, the greater his bonus or stock options. The theory here is the same one we encountered earlier when we discussed the quantitative approaches to performance appraisals and salary determinations for the more common citizens of the corporations. The faults of the systems are similar too. They can encourage concentration on a limited number of short-range payoff items at the expense of equally important or sometimes more important areas that were either overlooked in setting the goals or neglected because they were too subtle or long-range to be readily quantifiable.

Interestingly, one of the major criticisms by some United States commentators on the Russian system of rewarding top managers—who also get incentive pay—is the shortsightedness of the Soviet approach. For example, according to the October, 1963, issue of *News Front*—"management's news magazine"— "The Soviet incentive pay system places the manager under great pressure. He has not only to fulfill the plan but to over-fulfill it in order to reap the rich rewards. For this reason the Soviet executive tends to concentrate only on short-range goals, almost completely ignoring long-term productive capacity of his plant."

Which would seem to say that, communist or capitalist, most of all, an executive is an executive.

10

━━━━➤

How to Make a Manager

AS ANY NUMBER of people can tell you, those who own American businesses do not run them, nor have they for many years now. American businesses are run by managers. And when we say "run by," we do not merely mean that these managers implement stockholders' instructions or respond to their implicit desires. We mean that managers *determine* and *control,* in the fullest sense of those words. In a way, this fact is quite remarkable. For it to hold true, enormous numbers of United States citizens have had to be willing to turn their money over to small groups of people, most of whom they have never seen, to be used in ways few of them understand. Obviously, Americans were and are willing to do this. The reason they are is that they have something called "confidence in management." What this really means is "confidence in the management way."

For the most part, their confidence has been very well placed. The management way is probably the best way of running things—big things—that anyone has thought of so far. It works. It works so well, in fact, that almost every type of large organization has adopted the system—universities, endowment funds, the armed services, private charities, and even the production organizations of the Soviet Union. The increase in numbers and influence of management men in the Soviet Union, where the industrial manager class now ranks just under the party official class in the hierarchy of that "classless society," is especially good news to the American business community. Managers tend to feel a natural kinship with other managers, a warm enough feeling to radiate right through the Iron Curtain. To a large number of American executives, the rise of their Soviet counterparts is the one indisputable sign that better East-West relations are on the way.

So, the rise of managerialism is a good thing. But, good as it is, managerialism's image is even better. And no wonder, for its public relations men are its own sons, and in large measure so are its customers. A hundred years ago, the king of the Vulcans, as Andrew Carnegie liked to be called, pronounced a truly Vulcanian tribute to the system. "Take away our factories, take away our trade, our avenues of transportation, our money," said Carnegie. "Leave us nothing but our organization, and in four years, we shall have re-established ourselves." In today's environment, it is bad form to be so extravagant, and there is always a chance that the Federal Government might accept the challenge. But while the style has become more moderate, the essential message is still enthusiastic. For instance, Ralph Cordiner, General Electric's former chief executive, states: "Not customers, not products, not plants, not money, but managers may be the limit of General Electric's growth."

And from Champion Paper and Fiber's Karl Bendetsen: ". . . good, well-developed and well-rounded managers are always in short supply. They are surely one of industry's greatest assets. They are too often left to develop or not develop by happenstance."

The supply of such tributes is almost limitless. They are typical prologues to sessions of the chamber of commerce and the American Management Association. No less a personage than President Kennedy joined in the adulation of managership in his 1963 message to the AMA. "The role of management in our society," said the President of the United States, "is critical in human progress. It serves to identify a great need of our time: to improve the standards of living of all peoples through effective utilization of human and material resources."

But not only are managers important, they have also been scarce. The most frequent cry, particularly in the fifties, was, like Mr. Cordiner's, that there might not be enough of them to go around.[1] Industry's response to this worry came in two ways. First, the mushrooming growth of the executive-recruiting business. For a while the competition for managers preoccupied the corporate chiefs as much as did the competition for customers. The second response to the shortage was a profuse blossoming of something called "management development." Precursors of management development—for example, foreman training—originated in the early 1900's. By 1923 the American Management Association had been formed, and it began to sponsor management conferences on manufacturing, sales and personnel problems. But the full flowering of management development did not come until after World War II. The first serious attempt to impart management theory as well as practice began in 1952 with the AMA's Management Course. This four-week program is still thriving today. It has produced more than nine thousand graduates and AMA modestly describes it as probably "the most influential management theory program in the world."

The purpose of management development is to make managers—not just new managers out of nonmanagers, but also big managers out of small ones and good ones out of mediocre ones. To understand the process involved we ought to have some idea about the successful finished product. There have been some extraordinary specifications developed. One of the most complete lists comes from Lemuel M. Boulware, a former personnel vice president for GE. Boulware is most celebrated as the father of GE's union relations approach, but he was also a student of management. Under the heading "These Are Traits in

---

[1] We have been hearing just a little less of this recently, as speculation increases about the computerization of middle management function. See Chapter 5.

Common to Outstanding Leaders I Have Personally Known," he includes fourteen points. Among them:

—Leaders find in their work not only a means of earning but also a reason for living.

—Most leaders have hides as thick as a rhinoceros as far as their own personal pride is concerned, but they are extremely sensitive to the pride of others—and always on guard against hurting others needlessly.

—Having faith in the ability of their work to speak for itself, they are not afraid of their jobs or of anyone who threatens their jobs. Thus, they are always free from self-consciousness and are always themselves, whether with top executives or the men on the job.

—Most leaders are not naturally inclined to invent, or become authors, or create new systems, or demonstrate their own personal talents or accomplishments publicly. Neither do they spend much time selling themselves.

—All leaders control their tempers to a marked degree—do not give way to uncontrolled enthusiasm or despair—but move from day to day, from week to week, on an even keel.

—Most leaders have the faculty of gaining confidence without becoming intimate with individuals. This avoids personal entanglements and the obligations they impose. Most leaders are, therefore, in a position to deal fairly, squarely, and impartially with their men on the sole basis of their individual merits.

—All leaders suggest, rather than order.

Boulware also provides a short course for spotting leaders at first glance. Under the heading "Signs of Leadership," he lists such sure signals as: "A low voice and, frequently, slow and thoughtful speech; Rarely in a hurry; Easy gait and moderate pace; Does not show all he feels and thinks; Looks you squarely in the eye without staring; Bored with too much logic; Is not usually a heavy reader."

Is it funny? That depends. Mr. Boulware, I am told, was a great salesman both before and after he became an industrial relations vice president. He had a salesman's flamboyance which was—and still is—the envy of a good many personnel executives. One can imagine that he wrote his list with tongue in cheek. The trouble is that there are those who do not chuckle easily. They take this sort of thing very seriously. For example, in the August, 1964, issue of the "Newsletter" of the National Society of Professional Engineers is an article titled "How to Climb the Executive Ladder." In it is an extensive message from the head of the department of mechanical engineering of a New York college. Among the "rules the successful executive must follow," this senior educator includes: "There must be built into a man poise and a certain air of aloofness . . . a sense of separation from those in the ranks below him. As a man climbs the ladder and moves from one social stratum to another . . . he must change his mannerisms and characteristics and must fit that particular group as though he were born and raised to that status he has acquired, and it must be done quickly . . . It is expected that an executive will live up to his income and travel with the proper people when he joins the corporate way of life . . . When a man is promoted, he is expected to leave old friends behind . . . a wife who insists on retaining friendships with wives of her husband's subordinates is downright dangerous." No tongue in cheek here, and no flamboyance. Only minor tragedy that such pathetic meanderings could find their way onto the page.

Not all that has been written about managers has been so fanciful. In the fifties, sociologists W. Lloyd Warner and James Abegglen studied 8,300 executives via statistical collection, interview, and personality test. Executives, according to Warner's later report, are most often sons of executives. A little over half of these major managers in American industry were the offspring of a prior generation of managers or owners of business. This was almost five times as many as would be the case if the distribution were proportionate to their numbers in the general population. By contrast, 15 per cent of the executives were the sons of laborers, which was about one third the expected number, based on the proportion of laborers in the population.[2] Interestingly, this points to still another similarity of pattern between the managers of East and West. Soviet industry expert G. O. Granick, author of *The Red Executive,* reports that today's young Russian manager is also very likely to have come into his managerial berth from a managerial family. Occupational mobility in the USSR, according to Granick, seems to be about the same as it is in the United States, though Soviet mythology still tells of the hero's rise from the proletariat.

As a matter of fact, a growing number of proletarians have been rising in the United States. A 1929 study of executives by Taussig and Joslyn showed that the number of managers-descended-from-managers was then closer to *ten times,* rather than five times, their proportional number in the American population. And a more recent (1964) study by Market Statistics, Inc., in collaboration with Dr. Mabel Newcomer, indicates that fewer than half of today's business leaders now come from families sired by business owners or top managers. Further, only about 11 per cent are the sons of wealthy parents.

What accounts mainly for the changing picture, according to sociologist Warner, is the increase in the number and importance of giant corporations. In smaller companies, more frequently family owned or controlled, the call to high leadership has apparently remained quite muted for the lowly born. But in the great corporate complexes, the lesser intimacy of relationships, coupled with the high volume demands for young managers, has made prior socio-economic status a less important element in the selection process.

But the key factor in this recent widening of the high road to management can be found in the managing job itself—the requirements for *technological competence.* And the increased availability of higher education to a broader spectrum of the

---

[2] Other "under-represented" groups in the managerial array were sons of white-collar fathers, with about four fifths of their proportional share, and farmer's sons, with a little less than three quarters of their share.

population has enabled a great many more people to acquire technological competence. Operating vocationally at almost any level of life in the middle of the twentieth century is, to some degree, a technical problem. Even to the low-skilled laborer, the fork-lift truck is now as familiar an implement as the pick and shovel used to be. But nowhere has the requirement for technical know-how become as much the *sine qua non* as in the big multi-technologied corporation. And when we talk about technology we ought not limit our thinking to techniques for the application of the physical sciences. Even the manager whose function is least connected with research, development, or engineering has his own technology to master. Tax accounting, operations research, market forecasting, information processing, wage and salary administration, among others, have all become technologies. All, with ever-increasing necessity, call for the educated or at least the trained performer.

And it shows. In 1928 only three of ten corporate executives were college graduates; in 1955 six of ten were. Since 1955 the trend has further accelerated. While there are no statistics available using precisely the same base as that used in the 1928 and 1955 figures, later researches indicate that the current figure is probably above 70 per cent.[3] A further indication of the increasing technological requirements, even in what used to be the most intuitive function of industry, has been a sharp rise in the number of Masters of Business Administration at all levels of the managerial hierarchy, including the top. A recent study of newly selected company presidents shows that MBA degrees among them had increased fivefold in the last ten years.

Russian managers too are becoming better educated, especially in heavy industry. The Soviet manager, however, is almost invariably trained in engineering, while law and business ad-

---

[3] According to a 1964 report of the Council for Financial Aid to Education, 75 per cent of the two highest officers in the hundred top United States corporations are college graduates. The Ivy League's performance in producing corporate top brass was spectacular—48 with undergraduate and 30 with graduate degrees. Harvard was individual champ, producing 24 of the top men.

ministration specialization are about equally common in the United States. Some anti-establishment critics are scornful of the American trend. The Russian manager, they say, because of his training both in school and afterward, is a man dedicated to the real and meaningful work of producing goods, while the American manager tends to be a dawdler, preoccupied with the peripheries of numbers manipulation and paper shuffling. In the USSR, however, there has been a mounting complaint about the lack of such dawdlers. Writing in the *Ekonomisheskaya Gazeta* of September 29, 1962, a Moscow official says too many Russian factories are run by executives who "are unable to use the methods of bookkeeping analysis, who are not conversant with the subjects of financial policy, Soviet legislation, and the organization and economics of labor . . . The facts show that some heads of enterprises and institutions, while having the proper knowledge of purely technical matters, exhibit an absence of rudimentary knowledge and skills when it comes to administrative work."

What is the executive like? What are his personal characteristics, and how well do Mr. Boulware's rendition and the 1952 AMA view hold up? Not very well. Unfortunately, at least from the standpoint of the executive recruiter and others responsible for separating the stars from the utility-grade players, there do not seem to be many measurable personality traits that serve as valid predictors of managerial success. Psychological researchers report that their reviews of more than a hundred different studies aimed at identifying such traits has shown only 5 per cent of the traits repeated in four or more of the studies. The September, 1958, issue of *Nation's Business* reported at length on the results of some research on this subject undertaken in the General Electric Company, this time under the auspices of another GE vice president, Harold F. Smiddy, a contemporary of Boulware's. The GE research "shows there is no standard pattern of personality traits for a good manager." Says *Nation's Business:* "The GE Management

Consultation Service [Smiddy's organization] collected a list of traits, abilities, characteristics, and attributes for leaders and managers found in writings on the subject; many were contradictory and often absurd." (One can't help wondering if Mr. Smiddy had Mr. Boulware's writings in mind.)

But the speculation continues, especially with respect to the manager's underlying character. Says Warner: The manager is autonomous—that is his single outstanding characteristic. He is a decision-maker, unencumbered by doubts or the anxieties which come from considering too many alternatives. Warner explains the source of the executive's autonomy in terms of his family relationships. "A close inspection of the private worlds of the more successful executives . . . reveals more about these men. Perhaps their most dominant psychic characteristic is a feeling that they are on their own and capable of independent action. More deeply stated, their emotional identifications with their parents have been sufficiently loosened for them to be free and act in the present in terms of the immediate future . . . They have left home not only in fact; they have left home also in spirit."

In "A Profile of What Makes for a Good Manager," published eleven years after *The Development of Executive Talent,* a more sophisticated American Management Association admits that "One manager may be as different from another as reserved Frederic G. Donner, head of General Motors, is from gregarious, dynamic Sherwood Egbert, leader of Studebaker-Packard." But, continues AMA: "Despite differences in personality: the men who rise to the top in management do have certain qualities in common—notable among them a capacity for continuing growth." AMA catalogues a number of additional managerlike qualities. Most are less than startling —a mature personality, intelligence, diligence (managers, says AMA, work almost thirteen hours overtime each week), and activity in church and community affairs, usually in leadership positions. A few items in the catalogue do stand out; one, that executives, according to a University of Minnesota study, "appear to have fewer neurotic or psychotic tendencies than would be found in the general population" (one wonders who began to worry about that), and two, despite Mr. Boulware's personal observations to the contrary, AMA says "almost all are avid readers."

The autonomy, energy, intelligence, mental health, and spiritual involvement of the manager type presented in Warner's and AMA's views are appealing, and it would be comforting to think that our economic affairs nestled securely in the hands of such stalwart men.

There are some other views, however. James Abegglen, Warner's co-researcher, was not entirely satisfied with autonomy as the explanation for managerial self-selection. In a subsequent research program Abegglen conducted a depth study of twenty Chicago executives who had risen from poor, or at best modest, beginnings to high places in the corporate structures. Abegglen too concentrated on their family lives, but he came away with a considerably less felicitous impression. Fifteen of Abegglen's twenty successful executives had experienced severe strain in their early relationships with their fathers. Some form of chronic or acute unpleasantness—divorce, illness, death, financial problems—characterized the family situation. And, perhaps most important, the son who would one day be a corporate leader believed that the family's difficulties stemmed from his father's inadequacies as a protector and provider.[4]

The connection to be drawn between this early experience and its influence on the later character formation of the executive is in what psychologists call reaction formation. Simply put, the executives as youngsters, rather than identifying with their fathers in the way boys usually do, reacted against their fathers and strove with as much energy as they could muster to be as different from them as possible.

The big critique of the manager as organization man and the

[4] On the other hand, the son saw his mother as a stronger character than his father, though he did not experience her as a warm or protective person in the motherly sense.

man in the gray flannel suit has been so widely broadcast that it hardly needs detailing here. For the corporation critics like Mills and Whyte and others, the manager is Midwestern dull, Ivy League haberdashed, Republican, other-directed, insensitive to art, sexually repressed, and invariably conformist. He is hand-picked by the preceding generation of managers in a "self-per-petuating oligarchy" based upon his "conformity with the criteria of those who have already succeeded." Those criteria, according to the critics, include race, nationality, faith, politics, sectional antecedents, manners, speech, personal appearance, and the public relations aptitudes of his wife. If he comes through on these, all else he needs is a true devotion to managing as a way of occupational life, and he is set.

One criticism of the manager is worth a momentary digression. That is his alleged conformity. There is conformity, or rather, there are *conformities* within the corporate organization, but I think they are inadequately understood by many of those outside the structure. First, there is, of course, a visible kind of conformity: the dark suit, white shirt, and clean-shaven look. With exceedingly few exceptions, the manager is a conformist on this account, but I do not believe that is of any particular consequence.

Second, there is a deeper conformity of more consequence: the conformity born of the need for acceptance. It can be restrictive and if extreme it can prevent the development of an individual sense of identity. This conformity runs through our whole society, and managers are about as subject to it as the rest of us. But there are some effects produced by this conformity that are not altogether bad. "Corporate statesman" is a more fashionable image than "robber baron" for managers today, and most favor it. Conforming to the corporate statesman image has an effect on overt behavior, at least on overt behavior that can be seen by those outside the organization. It can inhibit raw brutality and temper ruthlessness.

There is a certain kind of intellectual skimmer who takes the measure of the organization and its inhabitants at one quick look. What he often sees, though he does not realize it, is the manager practicing his image. The reaction of the skimmer has sometimes been to sneer at the genteel smoothness of present-day executivedom, and to register a curious kind of grieving for the old iron men of yesteryear. It is not that most of these skimmers approved of either yesteryear or the old iron men, rather that they miss their "color and vitality." But there are those also who miss the color and vitality of the saber-toothed tiger. That is because they never saw him in action—close up.

There is a third conformity, and it is the most important from the standpoint of our discussion. It is conformity to the objectives and style of those who hold power. But there are significant though subtle differences here. This is obedience to recognized power, not a bowing down to what Erich Fromm calls *"anonymous, invisible, alienated authority."* Not for all, but for more managers than one might suspect, this is a *calculated* conformity. To be sure, sometimes it is so well practiced that the manager can do it instinctively, responding not only to the overt orders of his superior but even to inferred hints. Further, it can be and sometimes is expressed in nervous or even obsequious style, and with a commitment that is feigned rather than real. But the point is that whether you admire the strategy or despise it, it is *strategy,* not unknowing, involuntary submission. I have seen managers who are good at it rise high, assume power, and then, with no qualm at all, reverse entirely the policy or direction of the boss they had previously supported. This may not be an admirable way of operating, but neither is it blind conformity.

We have wandered some from our search for the root of the managerial urge. Returning to it, perhaps the best we can say in summary is that there is not one but many roots, and at many depths. Some poor boys from the wrong side of the tracks do rise, probably for reasons not dissimilar to the reasons for the rise of the poor boys of old—the Carnegies, Fisks, and Fords: they possess drive, devotion, and talent. Rich boys may succeed more easily, and it is a fact that a good many more of them do. Men strive to be managers in reaction against inadequate fathers, and men strive to be managers through strong identification with and encouragement by adequate fathers. Men become managers because they are well-integrated personalities and are internally self-confident, and men become managers because they are insecure and driven to overcompensate for the inferiority feelings which ride them. Men succeed as managers by performing tension-easing reconciliation functions, and men succeed as managers by being inexorably tough.

Whatever the managerial temperament, the managerial—and premanagerial—mind must be nourished and the managerial spirit honed to become most effective. That is the current way of corporate life. Or so it seems. Actually, the management development mode is not universal in its appeal. Some still believe in the old rough-and-tumble of intra-organizational competition as the best practical approach to the selection and nurture of the novice manager. The cream, say the advocates of the old style, will rise to the top on its own, and better, not worse, for having been churned up some in the process. A 1961 study by industry-serving Opinion Research Corporation revealed that despite the ringing endorsements of their highest company executives on the subject of manager development, when plant managers were asked in the privacy of their own office, and with a guarantee of anonymity, what they thought were their major responsibilities, the development and training of managers was near the bottom of their lists.[5] Coincidentally, formal managerial training has so far engendered little enthusiasm among the Soviets either. Professor Granick finds the most prevalent Soviet theory is that "some men are born administrators, some ripen on the vine through the process of living, but none can be manufactured in the classroom."

---

[5] Near the top were production scheduling and cost and budget control. Recollecting our earlier discussion of the big measurement push, this is not surprising. Production scheduling and cost and budget control are quantifiable as can be, but how would you measure and put incentive bonus points on the development of one or two, or half a dozen future managers?

In most cases, the combination of a natural lack of enthusiasm for systematic manager education and the press of more immediate profit-oriented concerns by the middle levels of the corporate structure would, if left unchecked, ultimately kill off the majority of management development throughout the country. Except for two things—the intermittent clarion calls of top management, and the enthusiasm of yet another variety of personnel man known as the training director, the personnel development specialist, or some similar title.

No one, so far as I know, has even been ambitious, curious, or persistent enough to figure out how much is spent each year in the United States on the training of managers, but there is no doubt that it runs into the tens of millions of dollars. We are talking now about what the corporations spend. That does not include the additional dollars invested by those less fortunate souls who are not bright, personable, or lucky enough to get the company to pay their educational bill. Manager training goes on both inside and outside the company walls. Within the walls, there is hardly a self-respecting company anywhere that does not offer at least a few courses in the management specialities. The courses are taught either during or after working hours by business administration professors borrowed from nearby colleges, or by special training personnel, permanently assigned to the training director's staff.

The biggest and most elaborate management training, though, as one might expect, is carried on by the biggest and most elaborate companies. IBM has a nice old converted mansion at Sands Point, Long Island, to which it sends its elite group for about a month of concentrated instruction. General Electric has its upper-Hudson facility at Crotonville, New York, probably the most extensive American effort from both the physical standpoint (a thirty-two-acre campus, with high-comfort, live-in facilities, bar, dining room, and so on) and the program (more than three months of instruction and discussion utilizing the top names of both the academic and practical business worlds).

Another standout is the Nestlé Company, which conducts an eight-month program at a special campus in Lausanne, Switzerland. This course concentrates on international management complexities, and in a gesture of broad-minded—and economically sound—generosity, Nestlé has opened up the program to participants from other companies as well as to its own people. The income from outside tuition helps to defray the not-inconsiderable expense of running the establishment. A number of other corporate major leaguers also run programs but have chosen not to maintain a permanent facility, finding it more convenient to hire facilities on an as-needed basis, and in some cases to hire too the consulting services of specialists such as the Industrial Conference Board and the American Management Association to run the training operations for them.

By its own admission, AMA is the undisputed champ in this area, and it has the accessories to prove it, including a twenty-three-story building in New York's Rockefeller Center. AMA draws more than seventy-five thousand people and nearly $9 million a year by setting up about forty courses for management personnel, plus countless seminars and conferences. The variety of subject matter is impressive. AMA distributes seminar and course catalogues thick enough to be the envy of any number of medium-sized state universities for their printing and layout quality. Subjects run from "Fundamentals of Finance and Accounting for Non-Financial Executives" through "Personnel Administration—Measuring the Dollars-and-Cents Value of the Personnel Function" to "The AMA Course in Anti-Trust and Trade Practice Regulations."

There are smaller operators too. They include the low overhead but legitimate consultant who will hire a hotel suite in midtown New York and run a management practices conference any time he can gather a dozen or so applicants together. The charges to the participants' firms range from about $150 to over $1,000, depending on conference length and the prestige of the consultant. Also among the smaller operators are the how-to-get-to-be-president-quick offerings of the quacks. Companies themselves seldom pay the toll for these shady pedants, who draw their victims from the vast pool of the corporate-ambitious but unappreciated would-bes.

   Though AMA is big, and getting bigger, the principal locale for educating executives is still the college campus. The symbiotic relationship between the academic and business cultures started with the Harvard University program in 1943 and expanded through the mid-fifties. There are now close to fifty special programs for management training offered by major universities[6] in the United States and Canada. This does not include the regular on-campus undergraduate and graduate business school curricula. (In the United States alone there are more than six hundred college business schools and departments of business administration.) The campus-located management-development courses run from two to thirteen weeks in duration and cover subject matter as specialized as the manufacturing process involved in producing a specific product, or as broad as the liberal arts. There are even courses in poetry and music.

   How do managers like the courses? For the most part, they like them very well, once they get used to being back on campus. Harvard's Professor Kenneth R. Andrews surveyed more than six thousand back-to-school executives on their reactions to a wide variety of programs in which they had participated. More than four fifths of them had positive feelings about their experiences. Such reactions have been read, especially by training directors, as evidence of the sound design, excellent instruction, and over-all worthiness of the programs. It is likely, though, that there are less obvious conditions which also help the popularity score. The great majority of managers approach their campus stay with a considerable pre-established glow. As Professor Andrews discovered, the fact that they have been asked to attend the program is almost invariably interpreted by man-

   [6] Some of the top schools: Harvard, Stanford, MIT, Case Institute, University of Southern California, UCLA, Michigan State, University of Michigan, Northwestern, Penn State.

agement students as a "harbinger of advancement, a recognition of achievement, and an opportunity for development."

Campus life is pleasant, no doubt about it, especially as a break away from the high-pressure routine of the manager's workaday life, and this undoubtedly contributed to the managers' favorable reactions. But lest one get the impression that enjoyment of the educational program was somehow connected with an away-from-home opportunity for executive frivolity, Andrews's study reassures us to the contrary. Professor Andrews asked the manager-students: "What per cent of men were considered to be 'party boys'?" and "To what extent did the social activities of others interfere with their own studies or sleep?" The proportion of negative responses—negative this time meaning lots of party boys and too little study or sleep—was quite moderate.

Without wanting to dim the light of virtue that shines through these responses, I cannot help but add a word or two about them. Recollecting some of my own experiences at such sessions, there was, indeed, a good deal of concentration on the work to be done, but there was also a fair amount of after-hours activity, with pretty general participation. There were, to be sure, light partyers and heavy partyers, but the former were usually pretty tolerant toward their weaker-fleshed brethren. And on the reciprocal side, the heavier indulgers were usually considerate enough to hold their late-evening congregations in a nearby bar or in the room of one of their more jovial and convivial number. Thus, their revelry seldom disturbed the more sober and studious. I find it hard to believe that any member of either group would be so unsportsmanlike as to call any of his mates—except a roaring, bad-mannered alcoholic—a "party boy."

One interesting finding of the Andrews study came from the way managers answered questions about the value of the courses to them, and their potential value for others in their companies. The managers indicated that while they felt the programs had been extremely valuable to them and that they would also help "top management" and "personnel most likely to be promoted in the firm," it would not be worth-while to send "lower-level management" or people who had problems.

Finally, in a triumph of pure faith, Professor Andrews asked these hard-bitten economic men: "Using hindsight again, if you had it to do over, which of the following alternatives would you have selected if the company had given you an unprejudiced choice between the two, and if the program carried no promotion implication—a university-sponsored executive development program or the amount of money (tax-free) which the program would have cost the company (including tuition, travel, meals, and lodging)?" *And 89 per cent, reports the professor, said they would choose the program!*[7]

Being picked to attend a development program is an honor and an opportunity, but not, alas, always an unadulterated joy. While few see their selection for the program as a signal that they need remedial attention, there are those who nevertheless do feel some discomfort in being "sent away" from the plant or office for several weeks, or even months. For almost any decently sensitive management man it must come as a small blow to learn that his boss feels he can be spared from the job for that length of time. Then too, there can be another unhappy thought—that while the manager is gone someone at home has to mind the store. For the anxiety-prone manager, the honor of selection for a lengthy instructional program can produce some pain. I have known executives away on extended programs who called their offices long distance twice a day, every day, to inquire in that agonizingly casual tone about how things were going. And it is not always an imaginary dragon causing their worry. A bright young subordinate does indeed have his opportunity to shine during the old master's absence.

There can be other dampers on the pleasure of the training

---

[7] I get the impression that in retrospect even Professor Andrews blushes a little at how far he pushed this one. Says Andrews: "The question itself was criticized by some. One man said this was like asking a soldier whether he would be a coward under fire; it would be difficult to know without a test."

program. Management men have wives as well as bosses, and children as well as organizations. The domestic difficulties that sometimes rise out of a prolonged absence can be considerable. Picture the setting as the well-rested and intellectually stimulated manager returns home to the wife who, without the aid of a firm fatherly hand, has been trying to hold up against three or four executive offspring. The reunion scene, as he tells her blithely about what a great time he had and how swell the meals were, could turn out to be a disaster.

One more worry, though usually a temporary one, is felt especially by the middle-aged and older managers when they return after long absence to the land of books and lectures and studying. Many wonder how well they will do, whether or not they can readapt to an academic environment, how good a showing they can make, and what kind of report will go back to their companies. In the majority of programs these worries are unfounded. The academicians generally treat the executives quite gently and in most programs there are neither tests nor grades.[8] On the positive side, there is another aspect of program participation which frequently turns out to be a nice extra for the alert younger manager. The programs, especially those catering to intercompany groups, provide a good setting to meet and be met. Consequently, there are opportunities to make contacts which subsequently lead to new job offers.

What are managers being taught? Setting aside the subject matter that deals with particular company policies and procedures, and the courses which instruct in the vocational specialties, we can generalize two main answers. They are being taught "how to handle people." And an attempt is being made to broaden their appreciation of the world within which they have to do business. To be sure some qualifiers must be added.

[8] The internal IBM program is a special, and from the executive's point of view, a rather threatening exception. At Sands Point, not only are managers instructed, they are also assessed and psychologically tested. How well they do plays a significant part in determining their future careers with the company.

For one thing, the picture of the world that is being conveyed is often a somewhat restricted and value-laden one, and for another, there are many different views on how to handle people.

In broadening the manager's appreciation of the big world that exists outside the corporation, one of the richest phrasings of intent I have heard came from AT&T. For an especially ambitious ten-month program for the development of Bell System managers at the University of Pennsylvania,[9] the company outlined the objectives of its "Institute of Humanistic Studies" this way:

1. To enable a potential future executive to understand and interpret the social, political, and economic changes —both national and world wide—which will influence the problems of corporate management to an increasingly greater degree in the future. This might be defined as developing a breadth of outlook, looking towards future "statesmanship" in business.

2. To indicate the importance, impact, and use of history, science, philosophy, and the arts in the world today, particularly as they influence large groups of people, such as employees, customers, and stockholders.

3. To motivate the participants in the program to accept the concept of intellectual activity as a never-ending process to be continued throughout their lives.

4. To balance with a humanistic background the almost complete attention generally given by younger men to the business of acquiring technical knowledge and competence as a result of working in an atmosphere of intense competition with other individuals.

5. To offset a tendency to overconformity, which is bound to occur in a business which is highly specialized and which promotes almost entirely from within the organization.

More briefly, Western Electric Company describes its program objective this way: "The program is basically oriented

[9] The length of the program has since been shortened drastically.

to the management of the business but it has sufficient scope to encourage the men to assess their goals in life and to become more effective not only as managers but as family men and citizens of a free society."

Some may be tempted to write off both statements as no more than the sweet typewriter work of personnel men—particularly the communications specialists. That is far too simple. There is operational reality here too. The rapid expansion of American business ventures into international marketing precludes the possibility of ignoring the outside world. Even parochially inclined top managements are forced to recognize the need to maintain a decent level of awareness of the economic, social, and political systems of those foreign nations within which they will do business. The potential cost of ignorance is too high. If in their initial contacts the corporations' men are dull to the sensitivities of a foreign culture, the company faces a high likelihood of rejection. And in some places, if those responsible for maintaining an already established foreign operation become too clumsy, there is even the possibility of confiscation. A primary response of American business to these new requirements has been the formation of large numbers of special international-marketing organizations within the corporations. Accompanying this, incidentally, has been a heavy demand and premium salaries for sales and technical personnel who are familiar with the languages and customs of other countries. The second response has been the development program efforts toward familiarizing domestically oriented managers with international business facts of life.

But that is not the full explanation. Much has been heard lately about the social responsibilities of business. What this means is hard to determine. Whether it indicates a dawning realization on the part of the corporation of its responsibility within the society, or merely a dawning recognition that it is a good idea for the corporation to *look* as though it is concerned about its responsibility, is an arguable topic. The fact is, however, that even if the corporation's concern were solely with its public relations projection and not at all with substance, a better philosophical party line is still required. The good name of private enterprise is under attack, if not siege. A decade or so ago the corporation's critics could be and were dismissed as pinks, liberals, or fuzzy thinkers, and that took care of them. No further defense of the business way was required, and it was seldom offered. But the climate has changed, and now, by the corporation's own assessment, a better case for the enterprise system must be made. And since the posture of defense is itself an unaccustomed and uncomfortable one, a counterattack in the cause of right thinking must be mounted as soon as possible.

In the call to arms each manager is supposed to do his bit. At the strategic level, managers have been exhorted to participate in political affairs. At the tactical level they have been urged to speak out more loudly and more frequently—and not just to each other. They have tried, but it has been difficult. The anticorporation men have been talking to the public for a long time; the procorporation men have only recently begun. Thus, the management development program is, among other things, a place for regrouping and reindoctrination, where new verbal ammunition can be distributed and where the management troops can practice using it.

But what do these men really gain from the management development programs? According to reports from those who have attended them, the volume of reading is heavy, the subject matter wide-ranging, and the immediate learning experience stimulating. The sad fact is, however, that the long-range effect in most cases seems to be negligible. Back home there is too little hospitality to sustain the new outlook. Before their exposure to the development programs, phrases such as the Bell System's "intellectual activity" and concepts such as Western Electric's "assessment of life goals" were unfamiliar and discomforting to most of the management men. For some they remain so right through the program. But even those who are reached often find the task of transplanting and sustaining their new perspectives from the program to the organization too difficult.

In 1964 Walter Guzzardi, Jr., of *Fortune* studied at length

"The Young Executives" in 150 American businesses. These were *the* young executives, those already marked and on their way to the upper reaches of their organizations, those most likely to have participated in the best management development programs their companies could make available. By any standards, one would have to judge that the series of *Fortune* articles which resulted from Guzzardi's study was not unsympathetic to its subjects. The young executives were seen as intelligent, aggressive, action-oriented, and certainly not conformists. But Guzzardi also had to conclude that "To the young executive, speculative thought is as foreign as the game of *bocce:* it belongs to another culture, which he neither understands nor has any curiosity about . . . He is interested neither in the economics of the society outside his corporation, nor in its 'great issues.' Cultural and political freedom engage his interest very seldom, and he rarely feels called upon to speak in their behalf."

It is an awesome fact that managers really are vital to the society. It is another awesome fact that not many of them ever give society a serious thought.

11

<del><==></del>

All the News That Fits
We Print[1]

WITH ITS SPECIAL GIFT for recognizing the truly tran-
scendent values, the National Association of Manufacturers de-
fines the mission. "The task of communication," says the NAM
handbook *Satisfying the Salaried Employee,* "[is] to achieve
an understanding and appreciation of employees' wants and desires on the one hand, and of management's efforts to 'do right
voluntarily' in providing these material and spiritual benefits
to the fullest possible degree on the other."

Changing the emphasis from piety to digestion, James F.
Stiles, Jr., former chairman of the board of Abbot Laboratories,
tells how. "One need never fear to give his employees facts,"
explains Mr. Stiles, "the real problem is to *know what facts to
give them.* At home, I have a boxer dog. It seems as though he
is always hungry; yet, however hungry, he will not eat merely
any old thing I put before him. Certain things he will consume
with relish; others he will ignore, with an air of offended dignity. Knowing what my boxer dog likes and wants, and respect-
ing his judgment in these matters, I would be foolish to feed
him otherwise."

In fact, though, some new diets have been devised for the
feeding of employees, if not boxers, and the point now is not

[1] An old communicator's motto, courtesy of Roger Hebert.

just what they like, but what is most nutritious—served up, of course, as appetizingly as possible. The reason for the change stems primarily from the difference in purpose between the old communications and the new. Employee communications as a distinct organization craft began about the time that business firms got too big for the chief to know all his personnel by their first names. The size and dispersion of the company's work force also began to make it impractical to continue the regular annual or semiannual company dinner meetings. In a 1960 speech on employee-relations history at Westinghouse, Howard S. Kaltenborn, vice president and assistant to the president, recalled the period ninety years earlier, during which George Westinghouse invited his whole work force of fifteen employees to dine with him at one of Pittsburgh's hotels. The dinner, said Kaltenborn, was "in the interest of sociability and mutual understanding," and it was held annually for some years after.[2]

A number of the corporate giants tried during their growing stages to maintain the sociability and understanding by other means. When personal contacts became impossible, they turned to the mechanism of communications. First among these was the company newspaper. Its theme, as the professional communicators now deprecatingly describe it, was "The three B's": Brides, Babies, and Bowling. The company news sheet was originally intended to keep all the company folks up on family news, and thereby maintain the family feeling. The idea was to keep the news personal, folksy, and benign. Controversial issues were avoided, except perhaps for an occasional fatherly scolding on such matters as abuses of coffee-break time.

Some of the techniques of the early communications efforts and how they grew are nicely illustrated by more of Mr. Stiles's words in an article called "What Your Employees Want to

---

[2] When the number of Westinghouse employees got too large to fit into Pittsburgh's largest hotel dining room, Mr. Westinghouse gave away turkeys at Thanksgiving instead. By the time the practice was abandoned in favor of another benefit program, the company was spending about $10,000 a year on turkeys.

Know," which he wrote for the American Management Association. Though the article was written in 1957, it has an older sound. Stiles tells of speaking at an annual company banquet in which "little cards" were given to employees upon which they could write questions. Says Stiles: "I had thirty-five silver dollars with me and for each such question received, I offered one silver dollar." He received eighty-six questions one night, and since there wasn't time to answer them all, he began a column in the company newspaper. At the time of the AMA article, he had received 3,650 written questions, with names signed to them, and he was continuing to pay out a dollar per question. Stiles admits there were occasional problems with the method. For instance, three employees sent in twenty-two questions apiece, "but a little personal conference cleared that up." And at a company mass meeting an employee sometimes asked an irrelevant question. But in these cases, said Stiles, "I just give the employee the dollar and ask him in the future to frame his question for the purpose of getting information, not a dollar. I do this with a smile, of course, which makes it all right."[3]

For better or worse, there are not many executives left who use the James Stiles approach. Current employee communication programs are no longer reckoned in silver dollars. *Nation's Business,* in February, 1960, spoke of "the billion-dollar employee communication programs."[4] And the orientation has become tougher-minded and more aggressive. Brides, Babies, and Bowling have been spurned forever, and in their place have come the three P's—Productivity, Profits, and Principles. The "family maintenance" function of communication has been swept aside by the concept of communications as a "marketing strategy." As J. S. Parker, General Electric personnel vice

---

[3] In his summary, "Guides to Effective Communication," Stiles, who says he is "honored when a man calls me 'Uncle Jim' or 'Mr. Jim,' " advises, among other things, that in communicating with employees, one should "try to be personal but never paternalistic."

[4] Other estimates run from a couple of hundred million on up.

president, told the NAM Industrial Relations Institute in 1961: "Success in marketing today will seldom be achieved (even if the product is good) unless aggressive advertising and merchandising occur." Management, continued Parker, has had to undergo an "agonizing reappraisal" of the ineffectiveness of its employee communications. The time for folksy gossip columns, cooking recipes, and pictures of live babies and dead fish has passed. And further, its replacement by a mixture of employee-benefits news, messages from the president, and the bland "free enterprise crusade" wasn't much better. The time has come, said Parker, for the "*era of interpretation and persuasion.*"

GE and a great many other major corporations have taken Parker's words very seriously and have gone into interpreting and persuading with vigor.[5] The range of topics open and amenable to the new hard-hitting communications effort is as wide as all outdoors. There are, however, some favorite themes. These include the threat of growing union power, the threat of inflation, the threat of the shorter work week, the threat of foreign competition, the threat of increasing Federal Government control, and the *lack of threat* of automation. Though these topics are not our subjects here, by examining a few of them briefly we can get a more concrete idea of the brightness, and sometimes even the virtuosity, with which they are handled by the corporate communicators.

One would have to have been far away for a long time to have missed hearing of the evils of the wage-price spiral, its pernicious effects on pensioners, widows, and orphans, and the staunch corporate battles to "hold the line." Standard Oil Company of California, in a twenty-three-page employee booklet called *What We Believe,* outlines its philosophies on such subjects as working conditions, job security, benefits, pay, and labor relations. It spends about half a page on each. It gives five pages, though, to the heading "Governmental Affairs," a sub-

---

[5] GE, as will become evident in this chapter, is one of the leaders, if not *the* leader, in "communications technology" and its application.

heading of which is "Inflation." Standard recommends five "vigorous steps" to prevent "the evils of inflation." They include, of course, preventing Federal spending from exceeding income except during recession or war, and opposing general wage increases that claim too great a share of any increases in output.

On the threat of foreign competition, the warnings have become increasingly dire. The usual pivot for the communicator's case here is the disparity between wages in the United States and those in Europe or Japan. In response to a recent union counterthrust, which pointed out that wage levels were rising more rapidly in other countries than in the United States, the communicators reply that our levels are so much higher that it will be years and years before the foreigners catch up. Other points made by the corporate side include such items as the tax advantages that Europeans have and the trade barriers that some countries have set up to prevent American sales within their borders; while at the same time, as P. F. Bauer, senior vice president of Allis-Chalmers, says, "European competitors are 'hanging at every corner' hoping to invade U.S. markets."

Some of the heaviest output of the communications mills recently have been reassurances on the topic "Automation is really your friend." The primary theme has been that automation is nothing new, it is just the same old process of modernization which has been going on since the day of the steam engine's introduction. In the long run it will produce more goods, services, and purchasing power for us all. It is also our one hope in meeting the threat of foreign competition. That's the story, and it is loud and clear.

Why all the concern, then? Ellison L. Hazard, president of Continental Can Company, explained it this way in a 1964 speech to the Executive Club in Chicago:

We in industry have been inarticulate. This must change! We have been our own worst enemies. Improving our technology and productive power, trying to keep our industries competitive with the rapidly automating industries of other nations is not enough. We have permitted the "free riders" on private enterprise to sabotage our objectives with a flood of propaganda based on half-truths and worse. These myth-makers have been talking to the public while we have been talking to ourselves . . . We must convince our employees that automation is simply a continuation of the process that has taken the housewife from the wash tub to the push-button washing machine. We must convince our employees of the truth that automation means progress for all people—not just for management or for the owners of business.

In the recent employee-communications campaigns, Government—Federal, that is—has become a prime focus. Not that the corporate view is an unpatriotic one. Actually, no one has more affection for our founding fathers than the corporation men. The trouble is with those people who are in Washington *now*. The flavor of the communications line on government is captured by looking once again at Standard of California's *What We Believe:* "[Founded on] a firm belief in individual liberty and the private enterprise system, we favor government action at the local or state level, wherever possible, in preference to increasing centralization at the national level because we feel decentralized government is generally closer to the problems of the people and more responsive to their will . . . we believe that, fundamentally, government spending should be limited to providing those necessary services which private enterprise cannot supply better and more efficiently . . ."

Early in this book we observed that while there is a kind of general anxiety among personnel men about their roles and purposes on the corporate scene, there is one area in which they operate with the warm assurance of feeling needed and useful, namely, the labor relations field. For the communications specialists, no less than for the contract negotiators and grievance handlers, this is also true. In fact, with the modern corporate reverence for the power of words, the lion's share of credit for a successful (no union) representation election, or a decertification election, goes as often to the bright young communicators as to the grizzled old labor relations men.

Styles of address on the topic of union relations vary according to time and place. On one end of the continuum is a bone-crusher approach such as this one, quoted from Central Virginia Industries' pamphlet "The Office Worker, the Employer and the Union." The section entitled "A Sample Talk to Employees by an Employer" concludes like this:

> Remember, if you vote for the union, you are voting away your rights, privileges and freedom. You are subjecting yourself to paying of dues, fines, assessments and initiation fees, which are very expensive and could put you out of a job if you couldn't or weren't able to pay them. You are subjecting yourself to a situation where the union can tell you when to work and when not to work, or to call you on strike as they did in Iowa, Michigan and Montana. You are subjecting yourself to the control of someone connected with the International Union—a complete stranger to you and your problems, who has the right to refuse something you have accepted and to order you on strike.
>
> In view of the foregoing, it is our opinion that you don't need an outsider who is a stranger to your and our problems to come between us. Our door has always been open to any employee individually or to any employee committee, and it will continue to be open for you as in the past. We are sure that the union can't get anything for you that you couldn't get for yourself; however, they can needlessly call you on strike and cause you and the other employees to lose your pay. We think you can judge for yourselves what is best for you and trust that none of you will want to vote for the union.

This sample represents an extreme. Few major firms would choose to use so roughhewn a battering ram. Aside from considerations of taste, the sample speech comes awfully close to leaving its enunciator open to an unfair labor practices charge of threat or intimidation.

By way of alternative, there is the much gentler mode of Standard of California. In its employee booklet *You and Your Company,* under the heading "What About Unions?" Standard first reminds its personnel of the "many policies and programs developed by your Company's management to assure you fair treatment and to provide a rewarding career." It then continues: "We sincerely believe that good employee relations can be maintained and essential employee needs fulfilled through sound management administration, without the necessity of union organization and representation. Your Company's wages, hours, and working conditions are among the best in industry, and its employee relations policies are designed to promote fair play and mutual respect . . . As for union membership, it is your Company's belief that representation by an outside organization is not necessary in order for employees to enjoy fair treatment and good working conditions. However, this is something that all employees should decide for themselves after careful consideration of all the facts . . ."

In a down-to-cases assessment of their efforts by the real industrial communications pros, the chances are that neither Central Virginia nor Standard of California would win a prize. Central is too crude and Standard is too wishy-washy.

There are prize winners, though, and among the foremost is General Electric. The company won the 1963 International Council of Industrial Editors' Clement E. Trout Memorial Award as Communicator of the Year. General Electric's communications style in the labor relations area has been widely admired by its fellow companies, though it is somewhat less widely imitated. The GE method is generally known as Boulwarism,[6] after the same Boulware whose leadership requisites we quoted from in Chapter 10. Boulware became vice president of employee and community relations for the company in 1946, at a time of low spirits within the company's executive office. The United Electrical, Radio and Machine Workers (UE), then a "red-tinged" union, had just won what was acknowledged as quite a decisive victory in simultaneous strikes against General Electric, General Motors, and Westinghouse. Boulware, formerly in the marketing field and a colorful man by all standards, approached his new job with his old sales philosophy. To him, the company's failure in its labor relations was a failure in marketing. Recalling his prescription, GE's *Employee Relations News Letter* of December 31, 1954, said, "General Electric management [had to] set out with a firm resolve, first to begin to do whatever was necessary to achieve ultimately the same success in job marketing that we had accomplished in product marketing. In other words, we wanted good job customers and satisfied job customers."

Substantively, the Boulware methodology goes like this: First, in preparation for contract negotiations, the company studies intensively all information it deems relevant to the formulation of the new contract—wage trends, productivity rates, benefits, contract terms, and so on. According to Philip Moore, the company's chief negotiator, GE spent eighteen months in this kind of preparation for its 1960 negotiations.

After its studies are completed, GE decides what it will offer at the bargaining table. As Professor H. R. Northrup, a longtime admirer of Boulwarism, put it: "Instead of offering less than it intends to give, then permitting the union to force (or often *appear* to force) it to grant more, G.E., after its careful research, puts what it believes is proper on the table and changes this only on the basis of what it considers 'new information.' "

From the company's point of view, this spurning of the

[6] Actually, communications is only one aspect, though a most important one, of the over-all labor relations approach called Boulwarism.

"horse-trading" or "ask-and-bid" school of collective bargaining represents a higher form of morality. As Moore put it: "We do not feel that we should be a party to deliberately deceiving either employees or the public by making it appear that only a union show of belligerence can produce a fair offer from the Company, or that force is required to make the Company treat employees as they want and deserve to be treated. How could either employees or the public have any real respect for General Electric if this were the case?"

From the union's standpoint, however, successful implementation of Boulwarism means for union negotiators the end of any really dynamic role in the bargaining process. It is frustration incarnate. If a union cannot "win concessions" from a company, if it cannot see itself, and be seen by its members, as an effective contender in the competition, with power to shape at least a part of the outcome, it is well on its way to being superfluous.

The indispensable tactic in General Electric's labor relations strategy, like the indispensable tactic in a successful island invasion, is saturation bombardment. GE maintains a relatively high level of communications firepower throughout the year, but it gradually rises even higher with the approach of negotiations. And coincident with the company's announcement of its offer, the word barrage reaches an apogee which is sustained until ultimate victory.

The aim is there, and the ordnance is impressive. In a post-strike compendium of its 1960 communications,[7] the company's headquarters communications experts recollected special éclats and noteworthy techniques of the period. Dozens of media and methods are cited. Among them are: news specials, source books, management staff meetings, special staff meetings, briefing sessions for supervisors, round-table conferences, management newsletters and bulletins, feedback reports, employee attitude surveys, daily news digests, letters to employee homes,

---

[7] A three-volume set, assembled, no doubt with an eye to history, as a permanent record of a well-waged communications campaign.

the *Negotiation News,* the *Relations News Letter,* and, of course, the regular employee newspapers.

And not only is GE's arsenal extensive, it is also versatile. It had the capacity, for example, to range from an eight-page *Relations News Letter* on "The Complex Problem of Employment Security" (August 12, 1960)—which covered such erudite topics as "Fluctuations in Business Investment Expenditures," "Research and Development Expenditure," "Geographic Dispersal of Industry," and "Population Changes"—all the way to colorful descriptions of the behavior of James Carey, IUE president, during negotiations sessions. For example, from the September 1, 1960, *Negotiations News:* "He [Carey] flew into a rage that for a while looked like one of those planned affairs he went into way back in July. But, as he continued screaming that he was 'no liar' and then went into a wild series of threats of all kinds of physical violence to Mr. Moore [GE's chief negotiator], it was easy to see that Mr. Carey had lost all control of himself. He started around the end of the table screaming threats and headed for Moore when his own associates called for a caucus. This prevented successfully any further wildness in front of us, but it went on so loud that everybody on the tenth floor of the building must have heard it."

While, for some, Boulwarism is a beacon, for others the GE technique is arbitrary and arrogant. In fact, GE's process has been found illegal by the National Labor Relations Board, and the company has been ordered to desist. At the conclusion of its unsuccessful 1960 strike against GE, the International Union of Electrical Workers brought a case before the NLRB and asked that the company be cited for refusal to bargain in good faith. The trial examiner, later supported by a split decision of the full board, held that General Electric's communications campaign had been aimed at derogating the union.[8] According

---

[8] Hearings on the case lasted six months and produced ten thousand pages of testimony as well as thousands of exhibits. The board's decision ultimately rested not on any single instance or particular combination of instances, but rather on GE's "entire course of conduct" during the negotiations.

to the trial examiner, the "very massiveness [of the communications effort] showed that GE was trying to undermine the union by dealing with the union through the employees instead of the employees through the union." Further, claimed the NLRB, the company's communications to employees were aimed at disparaging and discrediting the IUE as bargaining representative.

But, perhaps most significant, the examiners also concluded that the nature of the company's campaign was such that any change it made in its position, in actual negotiations with the union officials, would have to be seen by the company's employees as inconsistency, or weakness, or expediency. Thus GE could not engage in a legitimate bargaining process.

The reaction to the NLRB decision, not only from General Electric but from a major segment of the business community, was strident. Almost immediately after the board's announcement, GE announced that it would appeal to the courts.[9] At issue, as the company saw it, was the basic right of free speech. Worse yet, many felt that though the company's right to speak had been truncated, the union's right had been maintained. Said David Lawrence in the *New York Herald Tribune:* "Equal rights and freedom of speech—which have been proclaimed as symbols of democracy—have a hollow sound today as the country is asked to accept a ruling just issued by the NLRB denying to an employer the right to express his views to his employees except through union representatives at the bargaining table." Referring to future litigation, the *Wall Street Journal* commented: "Unless [the board findings] are overturned, frankness and fair play certainly will have little legal standing in collective bargaining."

When examined under a cooler light than that which heats the air between the antagonists in the case, the rightness or

---

[9] The case is currently being considered by a circuit court and eventually may go to the Supreme Court.

wrongness of GE's exercise of Boulwarism is not a simple issue. There is, undoubtedly, a good deal of truth in the contention that the company's approach to its employees was meant to persuade them that acceptance of the company's offer was in their best interests, and that they would do well to press their union leaders to go along with it. It is also true that GE's daily communication bulletins on the progress of negotiations presented the IUE leadership, especially its president, James Carey, in an unflattering light, though so far as I know there has been no claim by any party that the descriptions of Carey's behavior were untrue.

Further, there is a high probability that in its elevated pronouncements of its "fair but firm" position, GE does assume a posture from which, theoretically, it would be very difficult to bend.[1] And, finally, GE's claimed straightforwardness may satisfy its own high morality, but in their insistence on keeping sole possession of the initiative, GE's negotiators do, in effect, deprive their union counterparts of any share in the most dynamic part of the bargaining process. Since few people or institutions take kindly to the prospect of emasculation, the company ought not be surprised when it encounters something less than the union's warm co-operation in the process.

But, what is the effect—what is the real, the practical impact of Boulwarism in terms of its power to determine the outcome of the negotiations contest? In my opinion, GE's "victory" in its 1960 negotiations was not won because of applied Boulwarism. It was not a result of the company's overwhelming communications, nor inordinately the product of its bargaining tactics. Rather, GE won because its over-all position—eco-

[1] But theory is one thing and practice often another. In actual fact, GE did make almost two dozen changes (many admittedly minor) in its initial offer during the negotiating sessions. My theory is that had the IUE position been powerful enough to win them, any number of other changes could have been made, with GE's face easily savable under the "new information" clause.

nomic, strategic, and in the actual substance of its contract proposals—was stronger than the union's[2]

It is possible to accept the alternative hypothesis, that it was indeed GE's word volume and maneuvers which won the battle. But to do so, and then to attempt to specify and impose means for redressing the balance, involves considerable risk. There are a few limitations on freedom of speech in our society which have been found necessary. Restrictions against libel, slander, and inciting to riot do exist. In the labor relations area, there are prohibitions against the use of threats of reprisal, or the use of force, or the promise of benefits as inducements. It would, however, be extremely difficult to go much further in the restricting process without serious jeopardy to some fairly fundamental democratic values.

To cut off a company's opportunity to try to influence its employees, while leaving a union's opportunity intact, is, on the face of it, unfair. To try to devise a system which "measures" and "equalizes" the volume or impact of communication by the two parties is impractical. To try to prescribe content specifications (beyond the already established laws against coercion and bribery) is both impractical and censorial. None of these courses is attractive to me. The "threat," if there is one, of GE's or any firm's communications effectiveness in indoctrinating its employees can, I think, best be met by counter-communications, not by legal restraints.

At any rate, in the long run, it is my guess that, on the testing grounds of future negotiations, the awesome power currently ascribed to Boulwarism will be found to have been exaggerated.

Communications specialists, by and large, are most enchanted by technique. If you ask them, as I have, what the

---

[2] There are also those, including members of the internally feuding IUE itself, who believe that union president Carey was a particularly inept tactician in the GE negotiations and the subsequent strike. He was subsequently defeated for re-election.

outstanding accomplishments have been in their field over the last ten or fifteen years, most are likely to answer by citing the introduction of one or more of their favorite devices—closed circuit TV, animated films, or some other kind of audio-visual aid. They are least likely to respond in terms of the dynamics of the sending and receiving of information *between people*.

This process is known broadly as "interpersonal communication" or, in its various parts, under such headings as "manager-man communication," "two-way communication," and "up-down-horizontal communication." Interpersonal communication is an area which has lately received very serious attention from a number of corporate and academic behavioral scientists, but it is one within which few corporate communications specialists move with any comfort. For most communicators, in fact, it is a totally joyless precinct. It offers neither the clear-cut battle mission of the labor relations campaign, nor the ballyhoo of the cost reduction campaign. And it promises neither the victory of a successful decertification election nor any readily apparent impact on the rising curves of company production graphs. It has instead been an intangible, confusing, and often frustrating body of speculation, even for the few who have been curious enough to explore it.

But whether the devotee of campaign-style communications likes to think about it or not, for some time now those who run organizations have recognized that all does not course freely, easily, and purely through the organizations' message channels. There are, in fact, blockages, obfuscations, and distortions which trouble the flow, and they can be inconvenient or even downright harmful at times.

For example, there is the "screening phenomenon." A number of years ago corporation leaders reached the inescapable conclusion that sheer volume of activity was imposing upon them and their highest lieutenants unmanageable burdens. In responding to this threat of inundation, many companies decentralized decision-making responsibilities. In a correlated pattern, attempts were also made to replace the old rigidities of "rule of official channels" with a new, more flexible "rule of functional channels." The mood of this new philosophy was liberal; its aim, to encourage direct communication between those whose functional responsibilities involved interrelationships, often even when they were at different levels of the organizational hierarchy. Elimination of the requirement that individuals transmit the substance of their operating plans and problems up through the management chain of command allowed personnel to work things out among themselves. In this way situations could be dealt with knowledgeably and effectively by the lower-level personnel who were directly involved, and executive-level management would be freer to deal with the larger, more important issues.

In some ways the new communications concept seemed to work. But in others it did not. While the rule of official channels may have slowed down corporate operations to some extent, it also ensured senior management's awareness of what was going on, while it was going on. The new system provided no such insurance. Instead, it produced intermittent status reports of what had already happened. And the senior manager became an audience, rather than one of the links in the action chain.

The problems lay in the composition of the stories. They were often written not only with an optimistic eye for the happy ending, but with a compulsive need for happy middles and beginnings as well. For many of their authors it was a matter of emulation. Down would come the messages about how well things were going at the corporate top, and up would go the messages about how well they were going below. Until suddenly it was discovered that they weren't going well at all, in fact, that problems had reached crisis proportions. And in the inevitable post-mortem, it was found that the situation had been bad and getting worse for a long time, but no one had wanted to say so.

A second place where the flow of the communications stream

turns muddy is where it runs neither up nor down, but over the flat lands between supposedly interdependent suboperations of the enterprise. The company tableau, as portrayed by word and picture in the annual shareholders' report, is a vision of the company crew, shoulder-to-shoulder, and bolder-and-bolder, pulling together toward one big goal—success of the business. Closer up, however, those who actually walk the scene can hardly avoid bumping into the iron curtains which stretch between engineering departments and manufacturing departments; manufacturing departments and marketing organizations; between the line operations and the staff operations. As any but the most guarded general manager in the world will admit, there are embarrassing blemishes on the smooth face of the company teamwork epic. Restrictions on interdepartmental cooperation and information exchange could indeed be considered *the rule* of organization life, but for the fact that it is so hard to find an exception that proves it.

The lower and the upper levels of the corporation are separated by distance. The suboperations of the business are separated by organizational structure. One may be tempted to explain the communication breakdowns, therefore, in terms of separation. If this were so, there would seem to be one place at which the communication process should run with considerably more ease and efficiency, and that is between the manager and his immediate subordinate.

There are few inscriptions carved so large and deep on the "good" manager's tablet as the personnel department commandment: "Measure your subordinates' performance regularly, and communicate your judgments to them." For a quarter century or so, the performance appraisal has been growing in usage and acceptance as *the method,* until it now stands like an inviolable rock in the foundations of almost all extant personnel programs. The theory behind the process looks pretty good: It is a framework within which objective measurements of the employee's work can be made by his supervisor, and reported to the employee in a systematic and dispassionate manner. It is an assured way for the employee to learn how he stands with the boss—where his performance has been seen as bright and shining, and where it needs further buffing.[3] By finding out how he needs to improve, the employee is better able to concentrate his efforts on his weakness. Thus, assuming that he has the native capacity, he can upgrade the level of his performance—which ought to make him happier, his boss happier, and ultimately, the organization more effective.

With its obvious appeal to everyone concerned, a few behavioral scientists have lately begun to wonder why so many supervisors seem so reluctant to use the performance appraisal process. Why, indeed, personnel departments in company after company have to patrol the system to make sure that managers do not slip their scheduled commitments, or even skip them entirely. Among the curious have been two General Electric psychologists, E. T. Huse and Emanuel Kay. In examining the situation further, Huse and Kay not only found supervisory reluctance, but also learned that "employees often approached the [appraisal] interviews with more dread than enthusiasm or even curiosity." In a study of supervisor-subordinate pairs, the GE researchers reported that most of the subordinates saw their own performance in a better light than did their supervisors, and their reactions to their supervisors' criticism, even when phrased in the euphemisms of "improvement needs," were negative. "The more criticism . . . the manager cited in appraisal discussions, the more likely the subordinate was to be defensive and to reject the manager's help." Nor did it do any good to use the traditionally recommended technique of sandwiching the sour words between sweet ones. "The use of praise," said Huse and Kay, "had no measurable effect on employee reactions to criticism or on subsequent job performance." All of which came as one very jarring blow to the personnel department's theories of managership. But more blows were forthcoming.

In 1961 the AMA reported on a research study headed

[3] Other purposes which the performance appraisal typically serves were described in Chapter 8.

Superior-Subordinate Communication in Management.[4] The study examined "high-middle management" personnel—typically, just under the vice president level—to determine how much common understanding there was between superior and subordinate on various aspects of the subordinate's job, supposedly as clear-cut and central a topic as one could hope to find. Except that in testing managers and subordinates independently, the researchers found that only 46 per cent of the pairs agreed on more than half the elements which composed the subordinates' job duties. On the subject of "Job Requirements—skills, experience, formal training, and personal characteristics needed to perform the work successfully," only 23 per cent agreed on more than half the topics.

In the somewhat more abstract area which dealt with possible changes in the subordinate's job within the next few years, there was even less agreement. And the results were similar when the researchers tested for mutual recognition of the major obstacles or problems the subordinate faced in performing his job. On these last two subjects *more than a third of the superior-subordinate pairs registered "almost no agreement on the topics."*

So, while one may be *tempted* to explain the communications breakdowns in terms of separation, it would seem best to resist the temptation. The relationship between the manager and his subordinate may be a less separated one than many others in the organization structure, but it does not seem to produce any noticeably better communication flow.

Even before the industrial psychologists and sociologists turned their attention to the problems of communication inside organizations, the management systems men had noticed that something was wrong and had set out to fix it. As they saw the problem, somewhere in the design of the information flow sys-

[4] Conducted, under a grant from the Foundation for Research on Human Behavior, by N. R. F. Maier, L. R. Hoffman, J. J. Hooven, and W. H. Read.

tem there were flaws which, despite everyone's best intentions, had caused its failures. The flaws were usually presumed to be mechanical, so the systems mechanics concentrated on the mechanisms of the process. New reports were devised, progress charts were developed, and extra carbon copies were made of nearly everything and routed to nearly everybody. To some of the systems specialists it occurred that the people, as well as the formats, might need some repair, so communications manuals for supervisors were written, effective communications courses were given, and company-wide campaigns were started for the encouragement of more frequent staff meetings.

One of the most intriguing offshoots of the systems men's efforts to improve organization communications has been a sort of "omnipotent semantics" approach. Fundamentally, its aim is to make words—usually, written words—exact tools. The omnipotent semantics designers start with the "problem" that identical words mean different things to different people, and they set out to correct it—that is, to make identical words mean identical things to all people, at least, within the corporation. Once this is done[5] the new exact language can be put to use in everything from job descriptions to company charters.

A few other major medications are prescribed for the ills of intraorganizational information flow. For the most part they come under the heading of enhancing the two-way communications spirit. To a greater or lesser extent, those who promote these remedies acknowledge that communication problems are more a matter of people dynamics than of faulty mechanisms or inexact words. At the simplest level the remedies proposed usually involve the training of supervisors to be "better listeners." At more erudite planes the solutions call for substantive changes in the basic relationships between people in the organization—elimination of anxieties and defensiveness between organization members, encouragement of joint goal setting by

---

[5] It usually involves the issuance of some sort of new company dictionary, in which quite often the words defining the word have to be defined, too.

supervisors and subordinates, and the opening-up of channels for emotional as well as intellectual expression by all.

But this is a very tall order, and for some it seems unlikely to be filled. To the doubters, communication problems are less a cause than a by-product of organization troubles. William H. Read, associate professor of psychology at McGill University, draws this conclusion from his research in management communication: "Information is, among other things, a weapon and a defense. It can be shaped, changed, and in myriad ways utilized by an organization member to achieve his ends, maximize his gain and to weaken the position of his competitors within the same organization."[6] And Read believes that so long as conflict and competition for limited rewards remain intrinsic facts of the corporate life, efforts to reform either the systems or the people in them are not going to be successful.

Another way of thinking about Read's point is that in most organizations people do not trust each other. And that, as much as any other, is the reason why information is withheld, distorted, or otherwise bruised. The climate is not safe enough for a free and open flow. How many present-day organizations could really tolerate having it any other way? How many supervisors could handle open communication, even if they could get it? Two-way talk takes time, a great deal of time, and there are other things many supervisors would rather be doing. Furthermore, once he opens the channels, the supervisor faces risky possibilities. His subordinate may eventually want to pick not only the time for the conversation, but also the topic, and that could be dangerous.[7]

The good communications man is in on practically everything. He is the packager of a wide variety of products for

[6] One of Read's most interesting research findings was that in the large corporations he studied, managers were less well informed about their subordinates' daily work problems when the subordinates were highly ambitious than when they were only moderately ambitious.

[7] As we will discuss in the next section, there are possibilities for reducing distrust within organizations, but they require much more than a change in mechanics.

employee consumption, from big, broad banquets of words on "company principles" and labor relations issues, to smaller, bulk-cooked but individually wrapped items like orientation handbooks.

In the majority of modern companies, the likelihood is high that somewhere in the course of his initiation rites—sometime after he has been through the trials of interview, aptitude-testing, and reference-checking, and has landed the job offer—the new employee will be presented with an assortment of printed matter. In addition to such paraphernalia as insurance sign-up cards, patent-release agreements, and security questionnaires, the package will also include a booklet. The booklet may be fifty or sixty pages long, will be printed on durable, high-grade stock, usually in at least three colors, and will be cogently titled *You and Your Company, Working with General Motors, Going Places with Ford,* or something of the sort.

This is called an orientation handbook, and it is the product of the personnel department. Probably, a number of personnel men contributed its ingredients, but the communications specialist was master chef. Communications is *the word* of modern personnel. As we will continually rediscover in the pages to come, communications is what makes just about every progressive personnel effort tasty as well as nourishing.

An employee-orientation handbook is supposed to do a number of things. For one, it is supposed to inform. But not too much. Except on those subjects which are simple, nontroubling, or unavoidable, it usually tries to be general and noncommittal. Most of all, like any sales brochure, the orientation handbook is supposed to be appealing. And it usually is—exquisitely so.

For instance, there is *You and Your Company,* which takes YOU—in capital letters—from initial employment all the way to retirement in the first sixteen of its profusely illustrated pages.[8] Along the route of this short and happy career cycle,

---

[8] As we noted earlier, the Your Company in this case is Standard Oil of California. Seven of these sixteen pages are taken up by introduction, table of contents, and quite good line drawings. Net remainder: nine pages.

Your Company tells YOU about your pay, holidays, vacations, sick pay, medical insurance, leaves of absence, company insurance, group insurance, and finally about your social security benefits.

There are only two mildly sour notes in this workingman's *dolce vita.* One is an entry entitled "If you are hurt on the job," which begins with the reassurance, "Chances are it will never happen," then proceeds to make you almost sorry that it won't by informing you of the generosity of the company's benefit program. The other intruder onto the idyllic scene is a brief passage following "If you enter active military service." There is not much your company can do to shelter you from this particular peril, but it will do its best "to make parting easy and return pleasant." Interestingly, the section consistently refers to your being "called" into military service. It doesn't say a thing about one who departs for the soldier's life by choice (but then, under the circumstances, how could anyone?).

You and Your Company lilts along for another thirty-five or so pages and concludes with a final section on the gentle beginnings and growth of Standard of California, all attributable to "Two or three generations of people—people like you—[who] have built, patiently and faithfully, everything that the name Standard Oil Company of California means today." Not a word of credit is given to Mr. Rockefeller, Sr.—and there is, incidentally, only one sentence on a certain 1911 Sherman Act decision by the United States Supreme Court.

There are other communications missions which ought to be noticed. In 1960, for example, the Thilmany Pulp and Paper Company of Kaukauna, Wisconsin, embarked on what was for it a new adventure. It was called "Hits, Runs, and Errors," and it was a cost-reduction campaign. Cost-reduction campaigns and their cousins, quality-improvement campaigns, have been around for a while. Like labor relations communications, they provide a special sense of worth to the communications specialist, for here again he is "contributing to business profitability."

Theoretically, the basic task of the communicator in these campaigns is to make employees *aware*—to motivate them and to sustain their involvement in the program. Practically, there is another basic task as well, and that is to make the program look like a roaring success—no matter how it turns out.

For the communicators, the process begins with the naming of the new baby. Thilmany's "Hits, Runs, and Errors" is a fairly representative outcome of the deliberations. It could have been "Quality High," or "Target—Zero Defects," or (three years later) "Error-Free in '63." After that, usually varying only in sequence, designing and printing posters; writing a kick-off speech for the company president; sending sincere-sounding (or peppy) "personal" letters to all employees, stressing the "vital need"; producing pictures, charts, graphs, and display-boards recording day-by-day "progress toward our goal"; holding an awards program to express appreciation for submissions of money-saving ideas; publishing house-organ recognition for winners and feature articles on "challenges from our competition"—both foreign and domestic; obtaining a congratulatory message from the president expressing, richly, his gratification in the way everyone has pitched in, and collecting other assorted congratulatory messages from customers, suppliers, stockholders, and so on.

But there is another way of viewing the cost-reduction campaign. To someone at a different vantage point—say, closer to the factory floor than to the communicator's typewriter—it looks like this: A flurry of activity by supervisors; a gradual decline in the flurry of activity; (sometimes) a new communications shot-in-the-arm; (sometimes) a brief new flurry of activity; a quicker decline; and extinction.

The cost-reduction or quality-improvement campaign's life cycle may be as short as a few months, or as long as a year or even a year and a half. It is seldom longer. In some companies the message is not much more than an exhortation to "do better."

Nobody can prove whether or not cost-reduction and quality-improvement programs really reduce or improve anything. There are almost invariably upswings recorded on the big tote boards, but for the old line foremen who turn in the numbers that go to make up the scores, these are not too difficult to generate. The production supervisor has learned how to be responsive to the idiosyncrasies of the front office. And if the personnel department wants higher unit numbers and lower scrap numbers on the production reports, he can usually oblige without disturbing the equilibrium of his operation too much. Certain work can be delayed, maintenance jobs can be postponed, scrap rates can be fudged, at least for a while, and routine methods improvements which would have been made anyway can be credited to the cause.

The reactions of production workers themselves to the exhortation programs are often apathy, amusement, or even downright hostility—though these are seldom reported to the personnel men. In a major study of more than a thousand employees, General Electric's Behavioral Research Service found that employees exposed to *"an intensive, quality-oriented communications campaign,* which would accent such themes as pride in top-quality workmanship; the growing customer demand for superior product quality, the relation between high quality performance and job security, etc." showed *no change* in their attitudes toward quality. In fact, quality of production by groups of these employees actually *declined* after the communications program, as measured by scrap costs.[9]

For the most urbane and grandest-thinking specialists, there is another facet of communications that is most intriguing. It is called "economic education." Economic education is an off-

[9] The researchers found that a combination of communications and job instruction did have favorable effects on productivity. GE activity in communications research is almost as impressive as its efforts in communications application, though it is not clear that the appliers pay much attention to the researchers. If they did, the lack of employee responsiveness to the intensive quality-improvement campaign, for instance, might set them to wondering about what Boulwarism communications were really achieving.

spring of the anti-inflation crusade, and it is being widely promoted among employees on all floors of the corporate house. The core of economic education is, of course, the teachings, large and small, about free enterprise. And despite the complications wrought by Messrs. Galbraith, Hayek, Schumpeter, Berle, and others, the task of the grand-thinking communicators is to make it a cinch course for all its pupils.

The communicators do pretty well too. For instance, from *The Celotexer* (September–October, 1961), company magazine of the Celotex Corporation, comes a series of sprightly explanations of such economic terms as capitalism, productivity, buyer's market, profit, capital investment, and depreciation. For "capitalism," under the illustration of a little boy standing by his "LEMONADƎ—2¢" stand, the following: "If your youngster sold lemonade in front of the house this summer, he was taking part in capitalism. By investing his money (or your money), his effort and initiative in the enterprise, he hoped to make a profit. The economic system called capitalism assures us all of the right to own property and to risk our savings in hopes of making a profit. Capitalism also breeds free competition, which provides vast benefits to the consumer. It was once thought that capitalism meant Big Business. Not so: of America's nearly 4.7 million businesses, ninety-six percent have fewer than twenty employees."

There are also the less sprightly, more ominous tones of the Singer (sewing machine) Company's April, 1965, *Executive Office News:* "It is truly shocking that a broad cross-section of the American public can be so ill-informed about economic facts that they assume that manufacturing profits are four times greater than they actually are . . . But there is now no excuse for Singer employees to be ignorant about these matters. All they need to do is examine the facts set forth elsewhere in this issue of *Executive Office News*."

On the still slightly abstract, but more specifically tailored, level, economic education can also be shaped to fit individual needs. The threatened assault by Congress several years ago on the favorable depletion-allowance tax provisions enjoyed by the oil industry stimulated some very innovative communicating by Gulf Oil Corporation. Aiming at the hearts of its twenty-one thousand employees, and their potential impact on additional thousands of their relatives, friends, and acquaintances, the Gulf communicators made a movie, *It Never Rains Oil*. In light, nontechnical words and pictures, *It Never Rains Oil* told the story of the benefits of an ample oil supply and the problems of depletion. In addition, Gulf communicators spent six weeks at company headquarters training six apostles to travel with prints of the film, answer questions, and pass out supplementary pamphlets. By 1962, the last year for which figures were available, 270,000 pamphlets had been distributed. Gulf's presenters were on the road several months and covered every company location. In a thoughtful departure from the competitive spirit, Gulf also made its communication program available at cost to its fellow oil companies.

The Gulf company's use of a motion picture is not at all uncommon. Movies, including animated cartoons, film strips, slides and other visual aids, have become standard equipment for the communicators. Some less common devices include specially pressed phonograph records sent to employees' homes, closed circuit TV, and the "secret telephone number." This last is particularly clever, and like many great inventions it was made by accident.

The original intent of the telephone technique was to provide confidential information to supervisory personnel in easily accessible form. It was used especially during labor negotiations or other crisis periods. By dialing a secret number at any time of the day, any supervisor could be tuned in on a recorded bulletin on late developments. Unsurprisingly, it was not long before the secret number leaked to nonsupervisory employees, and a new number had to be set up. Or more often, recognizing that further leaks were inevitable, the whole idea would be abandoned. So the cycle went, until one day some nameless

hero of the communications past made the brilliant decision
to retain the system, but to *shape the messages* appropriately
in light of their changed audience.[1]

What has the payoff been? What are these billion-
dollar employee-communication programs really buying? It
must be something—and something big and important. How
could it be otherwise? Any reasonably normal mind *demands*
that the spending of a billion dollars (or even a hundred million) produce something big and important.

But it just doesn't seem to.

The evidence is limited, to be sure, but what there is, is not
encouraging. In 1961, General Electric's J. S. Parker said that
there was a need for "aggressive advertising and merchandising." In 1964, Continental Can Company's Ellison Hazard said:
"We in industry have been inarticulate [and] this must change!"
But back in 1952, William H. Whyte, Jr., wrote in *Is Anybody
Listening?:* "Never before have businessmen appeared to be
gripped with a single idea . . . to spread the gospel before it is
too late . . . we must tell the business story; above all, we must
sell Free Enterprise."

"And," concluded Mr. Whyte, "sell we have. But it is not
worth a damn."

In the years since 1952, the studies of the behavioral scientists have not seemed to contradict his conclusion. The cost-
reduction and quality-improvement campaigns do not seem to
improve output nor change employee attitudes. Even management people appear unmoved by the "economic messages"—
either ignoring them entirely or forgetting them soon after they
are read. D. M. Goodacre of General Electric's switchgear and
control division reported in the January-February, 1962, issue
of *Personnel* on a study of the impact of economic information

---

[1] In some companies where employees have grown wise to this ploy
it is nevertheless continued as a frankly employee-directed information
source. At General Telephone of Indiana, during one negotiations period,
an interesting variant occurred. The union—telephone conscious too—
installed its own dial-a-message system in competition with the company's.

distributed to foremen. Only about one third of the foremen said they had even read the information, and only *10 per cent* were able to recall the essence of it. Goodacre believes that 10 per cent may well be a generous score, since a number of those included in this figure required prompting, and there were indications that their information came from sources other than the company-distributed material.

In repeated studies within one of the largest corporations in the world, headquarters men went out into the field and tested and compared the credibility of the company's messages to hourly employees against the credibility of the union's messages to those same employees. And they found great numbers who believed *neither* source.

According to the communications litany, all would be well if only employees *understood*. With understanding would come contentment; and with contentment, co-operation, unity, and progress. A logical-sounding assumption. Except that there is no evidence that understanding begets contentment, and there is some evidence that it does not. A 1961 study covering more than a thousand management personnel[2] indicated that there was *no* significant relationship between individuals' expressed understanding of company salary-administration programs and their satisfaction with their pay. Chris Argyris, professor of industrial relations at Yale, reports similarly that "there is evidence that there is *no* relationship between how much a person knows and his morale or productivity."

Argyris also theorizes on the ineffectiveness of the corporate communications programs in changing employee attitudes, by drawing parallels to prior research on mass communications in the area of racial prejudice. He notes that even when information communicated on this subject was valid and well presented, those who found it contradictory to their own beliefs rejected it by ignoring it. In some cases they became even more tenacious in holding to their original views. Thus, Argyris hypothesizes, so long as employees feel a basic conflict of in-

[2] An unpublished research program in which I took part.

terest between themselves and management, the communications programs are more likely to increase hostility than to decrease it.

If Argyris is right, it would appear that efforts to change employee attitudes by communications cannot really do much good until *after* employee attitudes have been changed. And this would seem to leave the communicators in an ironical sort of bind.

12

⊨====⊧

Free Enterprise for Sale— Wholesale and Retail

WHEN MOST PEOPLE CONSIDER how corporate messages are transmitted to the outside world, they think about Madison Avenue public relations firms and the big-institutional sermons which emanate therefrom. This view is not inaccurate, but it is only partial. Madison Avenue has indeed been assigned responsibility for the big spray job, which is to cover all America with a friendly coat of enlightenment. But it is the chore of another species of personnel man to do the small-brush work —prime where the rust patches are particularly bad, and touch up the chipped spots. More specifically, this is called community relations, and it is the province of personnel men who are called community-relations specialists. They get a great deal of help from the communications specialists we discussed a while ago.[1]

There is no very clear boundary distinguishing public relations from community relations, once you have turned east or west off Madison Avenue. But if public relations is the supermarket-chain outlet for the corporate world, then community relations is the corner grocery. Both carry a lot of the same merchandise, but the local merchant handles some specialty items, and the service he provides is more individualized.

[1] Most often they work very closely together. In smaller plants one man frequently handles both functions.

The best way to understand the ways in which companies nowadays try to shape their connections with local communities is to look backward briefly. There was a time when a good many companies owned towns, and ran them. For the most part, these companies, in turn, were owned by the families who had started the towns, or at least had lived in them for many generations. Thus, they felt certain parental responsibilities toward them. They built schools, libraries, and hospitals, and sometimes, as in the case of the Duke family of Norfolk, Virginia, even a railroad. This was pretty nice for the local townsmen, but it was even nicer for the town owners. Aside from the baronial urges it satisfied, it also meant sustained community power and dependable community support in case of trouble—like a strike, for example. If the local workers were ever so rash as to walk off their jobs and onto picket lines, there was little doubt about which side of the argument the respectable local folks would be on. For politicians, police, merchants, and tradesmen, respectability was, by definition, being with the baron and against the rebellious ingrates who were snapping at his generous hand.

But the American economy has changed, and baronies are no longer the prevailing mode. Local operations of the corporate megacomplexes are seldom run by the sons of native first families—seldom in fact, by natives at all. These are the days of movable managers, executives who can be and are shifted from place to place much more easily than the equipment over which they preside. Most often both the company branch and its manager are newcomers to the local province, and affluent though they may be, they are not always warmly accepted by the townsmen.

Today pre-eminence as a community power also means preeminence as a community target. In times of economic troubles, production cutbacks, and employee layoffs, it is the most prominent employer who is often most prominently identified in the local press. The largest companies in town are also the ones toward whom the solicitors for causes turn most often and most expectantly for contributions. Biggest companies are blamed for the economic cruelties of automation, and hit hardest for the legal, ethical, or moral transgressions of their executives.

The appraisal of communities for business purposes has recently become an important specialty performed both within corporations and by business-serving organizations such as the U.S. Chamber of Commerce and the Employers Labor Relations Information Committee. These experts in community assessment warn employers against high tax rates, high ultility rates, inadequacy of the locally available skilled labor pool, inappropriateness—from the company point of view—of area zoning laws, general unfriendliness among the local population, and specific unfriendliness among the local politicians. And the company will need to think about such things as the adequacy of housing, recreation, and schools too. If it foresees probable population growth from any cause, it ought to consider how much the accompanying increase in police and fire protection, sewage disposal, and so on are likely to cost in future taxes. And, for certain kinds of businesses one also ought to examine the local community with an eye to how well it measures up as a potential customer for the company's products.

But most of all, if you are in a business that uses production workers, you look at the labor scene. You look long at the past history of labor relations in the community, deep at the state labor laws, and hard at the political influence of the local unions. You check back on how much of a problem jurisdictional disputes have been, and whether the union you will likely be dealing with is a warlike one. You find out how rigidly seniority rules are held to, and whether the union shop is accepted practice in the area.

If you are wise, you also look at the community attitudes toward labor, and how the local newspapers and broadcasters stand on union-management issues. You estimate whether you are likely to get support, neutrality, or hostility from people, politicians, and police, if and when you do find yourself embroiled in a strike.

In the best of all possible worlds, a company ought to analyze the local soil beforehand and if that soil is too acid it should choose some more fertile place. But, as the community-relations specialists recognize, most plants are already planted where they are planted, and their uprooting and replanting is a very drastic (though not unthinkable) thing to do. The alternative is to improve the local soil.

The prime objective of a community-relations improvement campaign is to capture the affection of the politicians—the mayors and councilmen, and the governors and legislators.[2] At the local level, it is city hall that influences the mood and manner of the police in the event of labor troubles and decides to whom contracts will be awarded for automobiles and building supplies, and for sewers and street lights. It is here, too, where zoning decisions and taxing decisions are made. From the state house comes the legislation determining the fate of "Right To Work" crusades, unemployment compensation rates (and whether or not benefits will be made available to strikers), income tax laws, and sales tax laws.

However, though the politician may be the prime target, it is rarely possible to win him outright unless you can also befriend a goodly share of his constituents. Or, as one company's community improvement manual sees fit to remind its management readers: "So long as we have a government by consent of the governed—so long as government officials depend directly or, in the case of appointed officials, indirectly upon the results of the ballot box—public officials will be responsible to the wishes of the electorate."

The simplest and most typical approach corporation men

---

[2] The union people seem to be aware of this too. Solomon Barkin, formerly director of research for the Textile Workers Union, and Albert Blum report in the March, 1964, *Labor Law Journal* on a survey of 38 union presidents and 47 additional union staff personnel. On a list of 22, the two top items the union officials called for in order to improve the climate from their standpoint were "Improve legislation" and "Increase political action." Barkin and Blum catalogue some of the new legislation proposed by their survey respondents. For the most part the collection reads like a mirror image of typical management proposals—exactly their opposite.

have taken in attempting to convince the community electorate that it ought to feel warmly toward the corporation is to tell them so in speeches. The speeches are generally delivered by operating executives, but are almost invariably written by communications specialists. They call for a light, modest approach, but one that touches all of the important items. Such as: the number of local residents on the company payroll; the dollars spent in the area buying supplies and services from smaller firms; the taxes paid; the amount the company spends on wages, salaries, pensions, and insurance; the amount contributed by the company and its employees to local charities, including the number of pints of blood turned in to the local Red Cross Blood Bank; and the various special scholarships and other academic programs the company supports.

In general, the tone of these speeches has a kind of virtue-is-its-own-reward flavor, but not always. J. S. Parker of General Electric's relations services, a man we have heard from before, probably bears no particular grudge against virtue, but in this case he does not see it as particularly relevant. Said Parker to other personnel men: "Community relations is growing up . . . Once regarded as primarily a process of charitable contributions and participation in civic activities, community relations is increasingly being practiced as a *quid pro quo,* something-for-something, two-way proposition between a job-producing plant and the local community. This is a healthy development, as is the increasing competition between communities for new industry."

Whichever mode the speakers—or the communications specialists—choose, however, there are some serious limitations to speech-making as a method. The main trouble is that the business-boosting speeches are made mainly to audiences that are already business boosters. They are made at chamber of commerce meetings, and Rotary meetings, and manufacturers' association meetings. And that usually means big business managers talking to little business managers and owners. While this process is by no means useless, it pretty substantially misses the great unwashed, except to the extent that the local corporate voice is reported and read about in the community newspapers.

The job of expanding that extent, incidentally, is one of the responsibilities of the local team of community-relations and communications specialists. It is their charge not only to write the senior executive's speech, but also to write the press release, get it to the local editor in timely fashion, and induce him to print it in a prominent spot. In localities where major corporate branches are abundant, major corporate spokesmen tend to make speeches in abundance on abundantly repetitive themes. Under the circumstances, even editors who are generally sympathetic to the corporate cause may get a bit skeptical about the news value of the stuff and feel self-conscious about putting it into print. The executive orator, on the other hand, seldom has any doubts about the cogency of his remarks, and he usually hunts for them avidly in his evening paper. If he does not find them, it may mean unhappiness for his community-relations communications team on the following morning.

Fortunately, oratory is not the only vehicle for carrying the company tidings. The mass media—local radio and TV spots, newspaper ads, and the like—are other ways of speaking to the natives. And there is also the United States postal service, for direct delivery of the company point right into the households of its community neighbors.

Most channels for company-to-community messages lie dust-dry except at crisis times. Then, there may come a torrent which overflows all. Recently, leading community-relations communications theoreticians have been advising their fellow specialists that there are advantages in maintaining a modest but constant flow. The weakness in the currently typical pattern, they say, is that like most flash floods it is indiscriminate, extravagant, and impermanent. It may saturate the local ground enough to germinate a lot of company seeds among the population, but without follow-up irrigation not many survive.

So far, we have been talking a lot about community relations of the moment. The focus has been upon quick responses, short-range objectives, and general audiences. There are also long-range community-relations strategies. For community-relations men, the long view focuses on special audiences, and it calls for more subtle and patient approaches.

Some of the most splendid artistry of those who promote the enterprise view is bestowed upon the young and their teachers. To win educators there are business-sponsored scholarships, community science fairs, and outright gifts of dollars and equipment to the local schools. There are also more novel approaches. For example, there are "Business-Education days," when the business community hosts the educational community, and under the careful stage direction of the community-relations men in charge also instructs it and flatters it through a carefully planned day of plant tours, fine lunches, and executive speeches. While the speeches do not neglect the virtues of the business world, they concentrate mainly on the "vital role of the educator."[3]

Ford Motor Company has taken the concept of the Business-Education day and literally carried it a good deal farther. Ford has established what it calls a "flying faculty" which goes from college to college to hold after-dinner seminars with professors, on subjects from science and engineering to labor relations and economics. The group of Ford executives who make up the flying faculty have, according to the company, met with 6,400 professors from more than five hundred colleges and universities over the past nine years.

There are more intensive programs to educate the educators, too. Early in 1964 General Electric announced that it was granting summer fellowships to three hundred professors, teachers, and guidance counselors. A hundred grants were for the guidance counselors; two hundred went to secondary-school teachers and college professors in the field of economics. J. M. Bertotti, secretary of the General Electric Foundation, which runs the program, pointed out that although economics was seldom taught under that name in secondary schools, it was

[3] There are also, incidentally, Business-Clergy days.

becoming more important as one of the group of subjects which comprise the social studies. It is not instruction in the historical perspective of economic thought that GE's Foundation is encouraging. Rather, according to Bertotti, the plans are "to stress current developments in economic analysis, comparative economic systems, and economic trends in our present society." And, as part of the program, there will be scheduled trips to GE facilities and talks by GE personnel to supplement the special university courses.

The General Electric effort follows a direction set in 1949 by an organization called the Joint Council on Economic Education. The council was an outgrowth of a still earlier group, the Committee for Economic Development, an assembly of two hundred businessmen concerned with what it perceived as a terribly low level of economic awareness throughout the country. In 1962 the Joint Council issued a policy statement titled "Economic Literacy for Americans." Its recommendations included: "Begin early; Exposure to economic ideas can start in the first grade; Plant more economic concepts in other courses —history, geography, arithmetic, civics; Give 12th graders a semester of economics; Help social science teachers get training in economics."

One way of encouraging the young to acquire enterprise wisdom is through learn-by-doing projects. One of these is the Junior Stockholder Plan developed by the Washington Gas Light Company. Washington Gas Light donates one share of stock every year to each of the forty outstanding high-school students in its community. The aim is to enable the young recipients to experience first-hand the joy of receiving dividend checks and the fascination of Dow-Jones averages. Arrangements are even made for special Junior Stockholder annual meetings, which are presided over by real company officers.

Pioneer among the catch-them-while-they're-young projects is the Junior Achievement movement, which was begun in New England in the early 1920's by Horace A. Moses, chairman of the Strathmore Paper Company. Junior Achievers are teenagers who form miniature companies that produce and sell such items as ash trays, letter openers, and dolls. They are recruited, organized, guided, and financed by committees of local business men; and these senior achievers are, in turn, usually organized, outfitted, and coached by their companies' community-relations specialists. But though Junior Achievement certainly captured the affections of the business community (there are now several thousand chapters throughout the country), the business way of life has unfortunately not sufficiently captured the affections of the young. In a 1964 survey of 1,723 high-school seniors made by the Opinion Research Corporation, only 26 per cent named corporations as their first choice of a place to work.

The reasons for the decline in corporation popularity, according to the business-sponsored survey specialists, are that the young people see business as too restrictive, lacking in challenge, overemphasizing money, inhibiting creativity, and unable to provide a feeling of accomplishment. But, proclaims Opinion Research Corporation editorially, of course, they're all wrong. "As every corporate executive knows, American business abounds in both excitement and opportunity to be of service to others." The trouble is that "companies have not been able to picture the world of business in a way that keys in with the idealism and motives of service that are so important to many young people."

There are other special audiences to be wooed besides the young and their teachers. Among the more discerning of the personnel men who are responsible for the community-relations effort a consensus has grown that with few exceptions communications programs ought to be aimed at and tailored to the *individual* interests of *particular* groups if they are to be most effective. Thus, clergymen and lawyers, doctors and farmers, businessmen and stockholders, all have become particularized targets.

About the largest of the particularized targets is women. Women own outright a major portion of the wealth of the United States, and through their buying habits they control an even bigger share. Women comprise about a quarter of the nation's work force and an approximately equivalent proportion of union membership. They hold what has probably become *the* influential role in family affairs. They have come to be a significant power in community affairs and a prime power in educational affairs at the elementary and secondary-school levels.

Women, to put it redundantly, are a force to be reckoned with. From the viewpoint of business that force has not been an especially friendly one. According to combined studies carried out during the 1950's by Opinion Research Corporation and Group Attitudes Corporation, another survey specialist, these are the particulars: Only 57 per cent of the women surveyed were convinced that big companies are producing high-quality goods. Sixty-eight per cent believed that big business squeezes out little business, and 61 per cent thought that big companies bought up smaller ones to get rid of competition. More than half the women surveyed also held such negative notions as these: that big companies conspire to fix prices, that they are controlled by a few wealthy people, that they are too tight in their contributions to charity.[4]

One thing that ought to occur to you almost immediately if you are a reasonably perceptive community-relations specialist is that a considerable number of the women in your community are also the wives and mothers of the men who work in your factory. This makes them even more important than other women, and that means they ought to be given special treatment. For instance, then can be invited in for a visit.

The plant open house for wives is a featured item in a number of company community-relations programs. Sometimes it is ornamented with interesting details. International Harvester provides a factory tour which allows a wife to spend half an hour or so at her husband's work station. Borg-Warner does this

---

[4] The surveyors asked their questions of men too. In general, the men were about 5 to 10 per cent more favorably disposed in their opinions of the big-business mode.

too, and also arranges for the wife to be introduced to her husband's boss. The Quaker Oats Company combines its hospitality with a folksy lesson in business economics. The cereal-producing firm invites the wives and mothers to a lecture during which a blanket is torn apart to illustrate what happens to the company sales dollar—18½ inches for taxes, 52½ inches for wages, and so on, until only the barest shred remains for profit.

Besides these projects on the entertainment level, though, there is a more basic effort being made to establish and maintain contact with the ladies behind the men behind the company machines and desks. A major frustration for the communications specialist has long been the difficulties in getting management's messages to the women. Though he tailored special articles in the plant newspaper to appeal to the feminine reader (including "Hints to the Homemaker" columns), repeated studies showed that the newspaper seldom got any closer to her than a wastebasket on the way to the company parking lot.

But what won't be carried by a husband will be carried by a postman. So the important messages are now often mailed to the employee *at his home.* And when they are contained in the format of a "personal" letter from the plant manager they become almost a sure thing for capturing the attention of his wife too. Sometimes mail delivery time and domestic patterns are such that they get to her *before* they get to him.

Just about the abrasive apex of this technique is the occasions, generally during a labor crisis, when the letter from the plant manager is addressed *directly* to the wife, poignantly describing the suffering which a strike invariably brings to everyone. One can only speculate on how the plant manager might react to a production employee who tried to go over *his* head.

Businessmen also talk to each other a great deal. Not only in the thousands of speeches they make at chamber of commerce, Rotary, and manufacturers' association meetings, but in scores of books, newspapers, and magazines as well. The currently prevalent style of corporate conversation is moderate. But it would be a mistake to conclude that all sectors of the business world have marched along the road of progress at an equal rate. Some have moved exceeding slow, and others have not budged.

One of the long-established interpreters of American business's stand-fast segment is The Foundation For Economic Education, Inc.[5] Located in Irvington-on-Hudson, New York, the FEE, speaks to businessmen with a simple consistency which rings pure and clear in these times of complication and ambiguity, and it deserves particular consideration.

The principal products of the FEE are its "Ideas on Liberty," and they are packaged monthly in a neat, pocket-sized magazine called *The Freeman*. According to its own description of itself, The Foundation For Economic Education, Inc., is a "nonpolitical, nonprofit educational champion of private property, the free market, the profit and loss system, and limited government." That is a pretty hefty load for such a little magazine, but it is shouldered regularly each month. The many-faceted shape of *The Freeman*'s burden comes clear with a glance at the table of contents in a few copies. For example, from the December, 1964, January, 1965, and February, 1965, issues come the following titles, with accompanying editorial plugs:

The Labor Monopoly—Professor Benjamin Rogge finds in compulsory unionism perhaps the most flagrant current example of abuse of government-granted monopoly power.

Is the U.N. Really Necessary?—When William Henry Chamberlin asks about the necessity for the U.N., many readers will have an answer; but here is some additional ammunition.

Why Social Security Must Fail—Social Security promises something for nothing but affords no way to get your own money back.

And, finally, the truly big question:

[5] Not to be confused with the American Economic Foundation, which could easily be seen as a slightly left-of-center outfit by comparison.

Is God a Keynesian?—Though not ordained, William Henry Chamberlin takes it upon himself to question the trend among religious leaders to look to government as their brother's keeper.

The Freeman is really great stuff, but it is not unique. There are also *Spotlight* and *Human Events* and others. You find them sometimes in company offices, being passed along from name to name on mimeographed distribution lists.[6] The Foundation For Economic Education has been with us since 1946, supported by contributions. It speaks to businessmen, and some of them are no doubt captivated by the uncompromising iron of its spirit and its unashamed rejection of half a century of history.

I would enjoy talking more about *The Freeman,* but we had better return to the matter of those who approve of the businessman and business.[7] Doctors, for instance. The American Medical Association believes in the free-enterprise system. So much so that at the sixth Medical Public Relations Conference, a portion of the program was devoted to "Selling Our Economic System: How Others Do It." The AMA invited a number of admired industry experts to come in and instruct the assembled body healers on how best to heal the body politic of such ills as creeping socialism, government interference, and similar inflammations.

From industry's point of view, there are a number of good reasons for having the community doctors on your side, besides the comfort of their moral support. Doctors are the ones who make out the charges on company-insurance-covered medical claims, and doctors certify or decline to certify employee disability claims.

Another appealing thing about doctors, and about lawyers,

---

[6] I found the three issues mentioned on a dusty shelf in the office of a communications specialist friend of mine. When I asked him what he thought of *The Freeman,* he said he preferred comic books about Cardinal Richelieu.

[7] You can get *The Freeman free* by writing to its offices at Irvington-on-Hudson. That makes it a sort of free-enterprise give-away program.

clergymen, and teachers as well, is that they are considered to be "community thought leaders." The thought-leader theory holds that these professions are the elite ones. Therefore they contain the community's superior people, and such people are the most influential. One principle of the community-relations specialty we noted earlier called for concentration on special interest audiences. Another principle calls for capturing the community thought leaders.

There are some complications, though. For one thing, the traditional idea of what makes a thought leader does not seem to be holding up. The traditional idea is that a man or woman who has attained success in one of the high-status occupations will at the same time have won the respect and admiration of the whole community. And under a kind of big halo effect, his attainment in his occupation would automatically be accepted as evidence of his competence and wisdom on most subjects. Thus, when he spoke other people would pay special attention. That is the premise, and it is still pretty broadly applied.

But the social scientists have been active again, and the evidence they have turned up has not been very supportive of the big halo theory. A research project by Clark T. Cameron and Joseph R. Goeke of Opinion Research Corporation points to a fairly pronounced erosion in the last several decades of the influence of typical authority figures in the community. Cameron and Goeke believe that not only specialization but also the *idea* of specialization is now an integral part of contemporary life. As a result, even the least sophisticated segments of the local community tend to look to subject matter experts, rather than to heroic figures, as best qualified to speak on particular subjects. What is more, many of the people who currently occupy the status occupations have themselves become so busy maintaining their roles in their own specialized groups that they now tend to speak more and more exclusively to each other and less and less to the public in general.

In many ways things can be difficult for the personnel men who drum the company beat. The odds in his favor are not especially good. Too many high-schoolers think the Government ought to take over business, and too many women think that big businesses squeeze out little ones. But that is not the worst of it. For those who have been assigned the responsibility of inspiring community enthusiasm for management's cause, the worst of it is that it is so very hard to inspire enthusiasm among those they strive to serve—the local plant managers themselves.

There are a number of reasons for this. A basic one is the manager's personal value system. In the minds and eyes of many business managers there is very often only a single point of clear focus, and that is *the business*. To those at the peak of the corporate structure this means the *whole* business. To those lower down it means only that part of the business for which they are responsible. For the local plant manager this is directly translated into *production and sales*. For these managers, joy in its highest state is a kind of nirvana in which they are left alone to do *the job*. And the job is to make and sell things.

By the very fact of their presence, community-relations specialists are disturbers of management tranquillity. They do not leave plant managers alone. Instead, they are continually urging them to speak up and be active. Of course, if union problems are interfering too severely with the making and selling of things—if production workers are walking picket lines outside the plant gate—then this does not matter. The managers may as well be talking. But if the landscape is relatively peaceful, the idea of speaking up, with its accompanying risk that someone may speak back and that all at once there might be an unpleasant fuss, is an unappealing one. Not that the plant manager is unduly demure. It is just that getting involved in such frivolity is liable to divert his attention from the serious purpose of making and selling.

Still another obstacle which stands against the operating manager's entry into the full wash of his community's affairs is the underlying reality that the corporation itself remains the primary community for many managers, regardless of how long or short their stay in one locale happens to be. Their careers, their occupational connections, and even their social connections are made, not within the town or city in which they temporarily reside, but in *the company,* which is considerably more permanent and more relevant. It is hard to get wrapped up in town politics when company politics are so much more cogent. There is not much appeal in devoting substantial personal time to civic affairs, not because of laziness, but because so much personal time is already being devoted to company affairs. It is less interesting to follow the patterns of state legislatures and legislation than to attend the rise and fall of company executives and the changes in company policies. And, ultimately, it is more important to be well beheld in the light of corporate opinion than in the light of community opinion.

These are some of the unseen barriers impeding the community-relations mission. If left to be confronted by the community-relations man's power alone they would almost certainly remain unmoved. But the community-relations specialist has allies, potent ones, who sit at the top of the corporate structure, who do focus on the *whole* business, and who do have longer time perspectives that encompass production and sales not only *now* but in the future as well. While factory managers may move often from place to place, factories do not.

So participation in community affairs has in many companies become a formal requirement, written into the job descriptions of plant managers at the direction of presidents and vice presidents.[8] The plant manager is implored and encouraged to meet his responsibilities as a business citizen. If necessary he may even be shamed or coerced into doing so.

Fortunately, when the plant manager is eventually inspired he discovers the chores are really not so bad. Being a community leader is less trouble than it used to be. In the days of the company town baronies, the barons spoke authoritatively and individually. Often they acted as though they owned the place

___
[8] The participation push has gone so far as to include urgings from executive vice presidents that plant managers move out of the suburbs and into the cities in which their factories are located. But this, so far as I know, has not been pressed very hard.

—and frequently they did. The mode of present-day local corporate chieftains is different. It no longer involves either the high-handedness or the *noblesse oblige* of the past. These days, it is usually a choir of voices which hums the business themes to the townsmen. And if on some rare occasions there must be a confrontation of the local community, it is made by the business *community*. That is the preferred style.

The business community is an organized one. There are about five thousand chambers of commerce, and there are merchants' associations, manufacturers' associations, and merchants' and manufacturers' associations. There are Rotary clubs and Lions clubs. The forms and functions of these associations tend to be similar. But one was different.

In the late 1950's there came into being a movement called "Practical Politics," a particularly determined kind of associating. One of the first practical politics adventures began in 1957 in Syracuse, New York. Local management men from about twenty companies participated in the pioneering, including representatives from branch operations of such major leaguers as General Motors, General Electric, Crucible Steel, Chrysler, and Allied Chemical and Dye. The effort was boosted by a kick-off speech from still another major leaguer, Vice President Richard M. Nixon. In the words of the Syracuse Manufacturers' Association committee that acted as midwife at its birth, the objective of the program was "special training of a hard-hitting character and of a truly practical nature for management in connection with the hurly-burly of practical politics—particularly participation and action."

The objective was to be met through five steps, which included preparing a manual of action, the "Political Primer for Management," a promotional dinner called "Tell & Sell," and a two-day seminar to tutor a special cadre of course instructors. The instructors were then to instruct other groups in an eleven-week series of in-plant training courses. The idea for the Syracuse program grew out of a report on the state of the Syracuse business climate. The outcome of a study by 125 top executives in the area, the report did considerable viewing-with-alarm on such items as high corporation income taxes, high individual income taxes, and high average costs to employers for unemployment and workmen's compensation insurance. It also cited the general lack of affection for business and industry that permeated Syracuse and its environs.

What the subcommitte recommended, as we noted earlier, was hard-hitting training for the hurly-burly. Specifically the hurly-burly turned out to include writing a personal letter to a congressman, attending a local council meeting, personal contact with state legislators and district committeemen, a close look at the local tax rate, and most important, the pushing of twenty neighborhood doorbells per man for the 1958 fall election.

How did the practical politics programs make out? Not well, not well at all, and the reasons are interesting. For one thing, management men did not take very naturally to doorbell-ringing, nor to envelope-stuffing. What they wanted to do was to manage and to organize. But the local and state party groups already had organizers, and these entrenched veterans were somehow unconvinced that they ought to step aside in favor of the eleven-week wonders. They were, in fact—and this came as a terribly unpleasant surprise to the practical politics grads— consistently inhospitable.

For the tastes of the veterans of ward and district politics, the management men were too "idealistic" and sometimes downright nutty. They would, for example, if they got the chance, march blithely into solidly workingman precincts and blithely campaign for right-to-work laws. They wanted to change everything all at once, and they wanted to win on every issue. In general, they got in the way and made pests of themselves. Some, in zeal or in angry response to the rebuff of the established party machine, determined to run for office independently. A few succeeded. But more often, in their first encounter with the rough-and-tumble (the step beyond hurly-burly) of political in-fighting, they felt the burn of personal insult and hurried quickly away.

They made mistakes, and sometimes made enemies out of former friends. When they blatantly trumpeted the damning results of their business climate studies in speeches and in the frightening portents of their widely circulated brochures, they pleased each other with the display of their outspoken collective courage, but they displeased the hell out of legislators of *all* political persuasions. There was, after all, the chance that others outside the city or state might actually take the stuff seriously, and a decent chance for a new plant would be killed.[9] There are two statements that I feel nicely sum up the practical politics movement. One is by Joseph J. Eley, president of Public Affairs Counsellors, Inc. In a *White Paper on Corporate Public Affairs,* Eley makes his assessment against a starkly salient criterion: "For all the much publicized efforts, the movement of business into the public affairs area has not been attacked by the anti-business elements of the country! . . . The fact is that political efforts of business do not as yet constitute a threat to the power of anti-business elements."

They may, rather, constitute a threat to the probusiness elements. Or as one informative community-relations veteran put it: "About the only good practical politics did that I can think of is that some people listed it on their résumés as a course they had taken. Maybe it impressed somebody and helped them get a job. One thing I know is that the only practical *politics* there is, is the kind that amateurs stay out of."

9 For instance, in 1957 a group of Rhode Island business climate improvers called the Weekapaug Group got hold of an advertising letter from the Director of Industrial Development in Dallas, Texas. The letter, for circulation among businessmen, was headed "Want To Cut Labor Costs?" and showed that Texas unemployment insurance tax rates were the lowest in the country. In contrast, it showed that Rhode Island's rates were highest. The letter also spoke of a number of other advantages Texas offered. The Weekapaug enthusiasts featured a full reproduction of the letter in a newspaper ad. This may or may not have had some healthy effects on Rhode Island unemployment tax rates in the long run, but if I had been a company president looking around for a spot to build a new plant, in the short run, I'd pick Texas. And if I had been the governor of Rhode Island, Weekapaug wouldn't be one of my favorite words.

All that is left is to bring us up to date. Much we have seen so far has been gloomy. Junior Achievement has been tutoring America's youth on the excitements of business adventure for two-score years, but the high-school boys and girls are less enchanted now than before with a corporate world they perceive as too restrictive and too mercenary. Practical politics flared brightly, with accompanying bugles and drums, but now, less than a decade later, lies dark, and—for some of its one-time sponsors—gratefully quiet.

Is there a lesson here? Is there a sudden realized truth? For instance, that the public is not inclined to put its trust unreservedly into *anybody's* story, nor willingly allow an unrestrained hand to *any* of its biggest institutions—whether it be government, labor, or business. And is there an accompanying realization that such a condition is really quite a healthy one? Has there possibly been something profound learned about the statics and dynamics of the apposition of enterprise and community? Not on your life.

Joseph J. Eley, the public affairs consultant we quoted a moment ago in a cool view of the realities of business and politics, seems to forget them all only a few pages later. In his *White Paper* Eley joins the choir and calls for business to speak out about its good works in the community and where it stands on political issues. He warns the faithful of the perils of government control, and entreats them to remind employees "that politics is their business." He calls for businessmen to unite in common fronts and reminds them of the beneficial effects of economic education and the advantages of training the wives of management men for political activism.

The same 1965 Opinion Research Corporation report which grieves that "companies have not been able to picture the world of business in a way that keys with the idealism and motives of service that are so important to many young people" concludes with corrective recommendations which include such frantic "innovations" as clubs for twelfth-graders with guest speakers from industry, and career guidance for *ninth-graders,* including invitations to visit industrial plants and offices.[1]

It is hard to believe. There is an unreal sound here which should not be heard from the most heroic figures of pragmatism that ever were. Business has gathered a pile of fallen leaves which it cannot sell. And it tells itself to paint them green, and when that doesn't work, to paint them blue. But they won't sell even whether they are painted green or blue or orange or purple. Not if their bulk is doubled, nor if they are called by some other name. It is a new year, and old leaves are not in demand.

---

[1] Other ORC suggestions included: Business-Education days, Junior Achievement, and direct advertising through radio, TV, and teen-age magazines.

Part Three

THE
CHOICES

13

⟨══⟩

Human Relations—
Stews and Ragouts

SOCIAL SCIENTISTS have been passing through the doorways of American companies with increasing frequency during the last couple of decades. Even sociologists and anthropologists now saunter familiarly down the corridors, not only at company headquarters but in many cases at the satellite plants in Lynn, Des Moines, and Louisville as well. A number of companies, including Standard Oil, General Electric, AT&T, and IBM, have their own behavioral research staffs, and there is hardly a psychology department at any major college in the country which does not have at least a few consulting contracts with major companies.

There are a number of ways to account for the social science surge. If you like simplicity and cynicism there is one that explains the whole thing as simply the latest style in management devices for getting people to work harder. In the 1930's management finally learned, to its profound sorrow, that there were serious defects in the old-fashioned push-and-pull methods of handling employees. For one thing, it took too many supervisors to stand guard over the system, and if they didn't watch closely —or sometimes even when they did—employees found a lot of ways to beat it. Sometimes quite unpleasant ways, such as committing industrial sabotage, forming labor unions, and from time to time even getting the Government to step in on their behalf. So, retaining the simple and cynical view, management in its infinite resourcefulness turned to some new advisers called social scientists and a new strategy called human relations. But the basic objective is still the same—more output at less cost.

There is undoubtedly something valid in this point of view. The fact is that the smoothest sector of the present-day human relations movement (or probably more appropriately, human relations *movements*) is what can be called modern manipulation. Its objective is indeed to get people to do what you want them to do—but with a minimum of fuss. If you are really good at it you may even be able to get them to think it was their idea. Some of the slickest social scientism goes to support the techniques of modern manipulation and, reciprocally, some of the heaviest corporate financing goes to support those psychological research and development programs which expand the manual of manipulative knowledge.[1]

But I think it would be entirely inadequate to dismiss the human relations surge as nothing more than a retooling of the voracious urges of the economic-management man, even if you are cynical. You would miss some very important subleties. Like the discomforts of power.

In 1902 a red-blooded executive named George F. Baer said: "The rights and interests of the laboring man will be protected and cared for, not by Labor agitators, but by the Christian men to whom God in His infinite wisdom has given the control of the property interests in this country."

But half a century later another management man, Moorhead Wright of General Electric, said: "The social revolution

---

[1] A concise illustration of the point: In a sort of self-appraisal report on its first five years of operations in 1964, the chief of one of the largest social science research departments in industry recommended to his boss that the research organization be continued and "that increased efforts be directed to achieving an even more improved focus of research effort on projects directly relevant to cost, productivity and profitability needs of the Company." And he concluded: "In our view the evidence is clear that this activity provides a major opportunity for needed investment that will produce a return many times its cost . . . " The recommendation was accepted; the research department survived and does to this day. Once more the cause of science triumphed.

. . . has greatly narrowed the gap between the top of the heap and the bottom. It has brought about a virtual disappearance of the lower class, and an expansion of middle-class society. The new middle classes are the ones we must manage. They are not serfs or slaves; they are people in their own right. They have a new freedom, and arbitrarily ordering them around won't work."

Americans seem to swim within some oddly eddying currents when it comes to the subject of power. For a while now, even the word has been sort of embarrassing. Poor Mr. Baer, who spoke his mind before the days of corporate images and without the aid of public relations counselors (to whom Mr. Wright has ample access), probably has been and will continue to be the cause of intermittent blushing among his descendants.[2]

It is not that Americans are unaccustomed to power. In international affairs we have used it from time to time, albeit often with reluctance, discomfort, or both. But here at home, visible power has been a commodity to be handled gingerly by those who own any substantial piece of it. It is something your opponents ascribe to you and you disclaim. This holds true even for our Presidents. To claim or even acknowledge the possession of power in the United States is to be arrogant, and to be seen wielding it is to be seen as tyrannical.

So, the managerial dilemma. The times make for high visibility, not only for politicians, but for corporations as well. These are the days of company images and public relations sensitivity, and few managers like the idea of being seen by the public as either arrogant or tyrannical. One of the appealing things about human relations is that it shows promise of being a way around the problem. The human relations approach, at least at first glance, has a nice, noncoercive motif.

There is another, more optimistic way to account for the rise of human relations in industry, of course. It is simply to say that managers are, after all, people just like you and me, and

---

[2] Baer's moment of indiscretion may eventually achieve the stature of an earlier royalist's "Let them eat cake." I found one version or another of it quoted in three books which I happened to have in my bookcase.

therefore they too have been touched by the liberal sweep of progress. Thus, not only are they concerned to avoid the public images of themselves as arrogant and tyrannical, but, more importantly, they do not want *to be* that way either. They would rather be good men than bad ones, contributors rather than exploiters. Their interests in their employees have become sincere and sustained rather than feigned and incidental. And their adoption of the human relations way is the most cogent evidence that it is all true.

Once again though if we stop here we have not gone far enough. There are further questions to be asked. What is the ultimate aim of enlightened management? Is it solely a firm resolve not to exploit subordinates, or something more? For a few managers, but mainly for a certain group of social scientist theoreticians, it is a great deal more. It touches on some strange and wondrous concept, such things as "healthy organizations" and "self-actualized" employees. And if you follow along closely enough, after a while some unusual things seem to happen to the practice of management itself. It begins to look less and less like being boss and more and more like mental hygiene. In the next chapter we will be coming back to this more radically different management, but there are some prerequisites.

In talking about human relations it is first necessary to recognize which human relations it is that you want to talk about. The term has been used by so many people in such different contexts that it now connotes too many different impressions. Some of these are very nearly the direct antitheses of others. The images "human relations" conjures up in assortedly conditioned minds span a spectrum, running all the way from a sort of pragmatic "be-kind-to-dumb-animals-and-they-will-be-grateful-to-you," through the methodological sophistication of modern social psychology, and ultimately to a kind of total life philosophy strongly linked to Existentialism.

Human relations history as it relates to the subject of this book began officially with the Western Electric experiments of Elton Mayo. But there is a kind of prehistoric period which started long before Hawthorne. We can call it the "say please" school—or sometimes, "say please, but carry a big stick." There is not much science in this primitive version, though there is often a considerable amount of religion. The fashion of the "say please" school was, and is, benevolence. The dynamic is autocracy. And the tools are words—good, old-fashioned, tried-and-true, common-sensical words. From the manager's standpoint the idea is that you do just about the same thing you always did, but in a more polite way.

At its Bayonne refinery in 1915 and 1916, Standard Oil of New Jersey found itself in the midst of the worst labor strife in its history. The company's relations with its employees had deteriorated to the point of repeated and violent conflict. William B. Maloney, at that time assistant manager of the employee relations department, recalled in a 1957 speech on "Jersey's Employee Relations Philosophy" that it was this harsh time which inspired the beginnings of Jersey's version of human relations. Because, as a result of its unhappy experience, the company decided to hire a man named C. J. Hicks. Hicks, recalls Maloney, was "a man who had dedicated his life to the teaching and application of Christian principles in industry . . . and he was charged with the job of building a philosophy of human relations for the Jersey Company . . ."

The keystone of that philosophy, one that Jersey has been building upon ever since, according to Maloney, was the golden rule. Except that in Maloney's version it comes out a little differently than it once did: "That rule is—do the thing that has to be done in the way you'd like to have it done to you, if the positions were reversed." Mr. Maloney does not say who decides what "has to be done."

There are many examples in the personnel literature of the late thirties and early forties of the "say please" advice, particularly on the subject of supervisory training. The fascinating thing, though, is that there are also examples in the late fifties and even in the sixties. For example, there is the wisdom of a classicist whom we have already met, James Stiles of Abbot

Laboratories. Said Stiles in 1957 to an American Management Association audience: ". . . Employees want to talk—and be talked to—about their 'private' lives, to some degree. The fact is that every person likes to talk about his own family, the community in which he lives, the church he attends, even the schools he once attended—because a part of his life has gone into each of these things. When anyone, and especially his employer, takes an interest in the things that interest *him* . . . he feels just a little bit closer to that person. If it is his employer, he begins to feel that that otherwise abstract and sometimes menacing creature, The Company, is actually interested in his activities to which he has devoted a substantial part of his life. And pretty soon he talks about The Company as the best place for a man to work in the community."

It is not really clear where the primitive "say please" school of human relations ends and the next higher step in human relations development begins. But there is a next step. All in all, it can probably best be thought of as a kind of Mulligan stew of loosely interpreted Elton Mayo.

Mayo's early work gave birth to a theme that seemed to speak of the importance of both the informal work group and the beneficial effects of management's paying attention to employees. For the average personnel man-in-the-plant the first concept was new and unfamiliar, but the second fit easily and appealingly into his tool kit. A deluge of personnel gimmickry soon began to flow from the Mayo postulates, and continued to do so for thirty years. Most of it had little legitimate connection with Mayo's work, but the temptation to pin some of their own pet notions to the theory of a high-style social scientist was irresistible to a good many personnel men.[3]

[3] There is some sort of sad irony in the fact that while Mayo's work provided a jumping-off place for all sorts of harebrained formulations, one would be hard put to find any going program of the present or past, excepting Western Electric's itself, which could be thought of as "pure Mayo." With hardly even a polite hesitation, almost everybody reshaped the Hawthorne work to suit his own fancies. Such rudeness eventually generated considerable irritation among the early Mayo team members.

The one jewel of truth that gleamed more brilliantly than all the others that came out of Hawthorne was that everybody in the working world wants to feel important. From this gem of a discovery came a myriad of methodologies. A full-page advertisement in the July-August 1963 issue of *Personnel Journal* headlined: "The psychological aspects of recognition and incentive programs—challenging goals can be achieved when the reward has both tangible and emotional value!"

"Man's desire for acclaim is the key," says the Omega Watch Company. "A job can be a lonely thing or it can be a wonderful experience with stimulation all day long. The difference is not in the job but in the attitude of the job holder and the knowledge that he or she is recognized and understood by management." And Omega agrees there needs to be a symbol of that recognition and understanding. Understandably, Omega prefers the symbol to be a watch.

Many participated in cooking up the post-Mayo Mulligan stew, from personnel men through production superintendents to company presidents, but mainly it was fed to first-line supervisors. Nutritionally, it was guaranteed to build managerial muscle and a smooth complexion which would produce admiration and affection in both superiors and subordinates. Most often the ingredients consisted of about a pound of recommendations and a matching pound of warnings. For example, the good supervisor should: request rather than order, be objective and calm, get all the facts before he acts, be honest and loyal, talk things over with his men, give praise for good performance, accept responsibility, give others a chance to express their opinions, use "we" instead of "I," and, of course, keep production up and costs down. The good supervisor should not: shout or lose his temper, brag, blame his boss, bawl a man out in front of others, bribe or threaten, tell people they are wrong undiplomatically, favor one employee over another, get too close to his men (though he ought to know what is troubling them in their personal lives), pass the buck, lose control of his group, or forget he is a *management man.*

There were supervisory training manuals, foreman hand-books, and management lectures to convey the "new" human relations principles to the supervisors. The favorite vehicle for enlightenment, though, was itself a product of human relations discovery. It was, and still is, called "the conference." The conference is composed of a conference leader, a conference leader's handbook, and a lot of other people called participants or trainees. Its major premise is that people do not get as bored listening to someone else talk if they have a chance to talk too —even a little. Another of its premises is that the conference leader can best get his points across by getting other people to make them, so the trick is to ask questions in such a way that "right" answers become almost unavoidable. For example:

CONFERENCE LEADER. When you want to get a man to do something, do you yell at him?

TRAINEE. No.

C. L. Why not?

TRAINEE. It just makes him mad.

C. L. Right. What about handling a guy who has been goofing off. Do you just let it go?

TRAINEE. No.

C. L. Then, do you call him in front of all the fellows and chew him out?

TRAINEE. No.

C. L. Why not?

TRAINEE. He's liable to get the shop steward in on it, then you might have to back down and you come out looking like a damn fool.

C. L. (*Frowning*). Anybody else have any other ideas?
     (*Silence*)

C. L. Well, how would you feel if you got bawled out in front of this group?

TRAINEE. It would be embarrassing.

C. L. Right. And would you like the guy who bawled you out?

TRAINEE. No, I wouldn't.

C. L. Good! The idea, then, is that you don't reprimand people in public because this is embarrassing to them, and in the long run it's likely to get you a lot of ill will, not only from the guy you reprimand, but from the other people in your group as well. Do you all agree with that?

TRAINEE. Sure.

There were other ways for serving up the Mulligan stew. One was the "open-door" policy, which in many cases became a literal as well as figurative description of supervisory practice. Employees were to be encouraged to bring their problems— both work-oriented and personal—not only to their immediate bosses, but, if they liked, to higher-level management as well. In some companies this invitation extended all the way up to the general manager or even the president. Thomas J. Watson, Jr., describes how his father, "T. J. Senior," founder of IBM, instituted the policy: "If a man was not getting along, or if he thought he was being treated unfairly by his manager, he was told to go to the plant or branch manager. If that did not work, he was then invited to come and lay his case before my father."[4]

Still other variations of the same diet are the semiannual pep talks by general managers to assembly-line and clerical workers, personal write-ups of production stars in the company newspaper, individual gold-lettered honor rolls of monthly cost-saving champions, and, of course—with a bow to Mayo's groupism—pennants for championship teams.

As one theory had it, the key to everything was in convincing each and every employee that his was an absolutely vital job, essential to the business's success. For a long time there had been a profound personnel slogan which held that all work was important and essentially of a kind, whether it was the work of

[4] From *A Business and Its Beliefs,* by Thomas J. Watson, Jr. In many firms today anachronistic vestiges of the policy are still to be found. In a literal sense, the prevailing mode, even in the executive suite, is the open door. But the placement of the executive desk is such that he cannot be seen from the corridor, and besides, there is usually a very smooth but tough secretary placed just outside. It takes a very daring (or desperate) man indeed to hurdle these ramparts.

the sweeper or the vice president, the drill-press operator or the manufacturing superintendent. It was a comforting thought—as is "We are all brothers under the skin." One could grunt about it in satisfaction and then proceed to other matters. But among many personnel men the grunts began to be eloquent and sustained. For if employees could only be convinced, there would come true revelation of the managerial enlightenment, and with that, surely, a more sober sense of responsibility.

Thus emerged the communications campaigns, pointing out clearly and profusely that as in days of old, when for want of a blacksmith's nail a war had been lost, so too for want of a quota fulfilled a company could be lost. And from the even higher-soaring imaginations of some personnel men came an even more enchanting idea: What better road to the managerial enlightenment than to have every man think of himself as a manager—a manager of his own job. As the plant manager managed the work force of the plant, the accountant would manage his ledgers, the lathe operator his lathe, and the sweeper his broom. It was an enthralling concept, and it too was liberally sprinkled onto the supervisor's plate. If he gagged a little at first, eventually he got used to it.

Other contributions to the simmering pot were called "applied psychology"—mostly by people who knew little if anything about theoretical psychology. Strangely enough, however, a substantial number of "management-oriented" psychologists greeted these chunks of pragmatic cleverness, not with the frosty disdain one might expect from the professional purist, but with hearty congratulations. For example, there was the tissue-paper éclat.

In the early days of World War II a "human relations" problem of serious proportions arose in a newly built Midwestern aircraft plant. The factory, in conformance with blackout requirements, had been designed without windows or skylights. It was, however, fully air-conditioned. But despite the air-conditioning, employees of the plant, who were primarily rural people accustomed to outdoor work, complained about excessive heat and humidity. Engineers were called in to check the system and found it working perfectly. This was made known to the employees, but the complaints persisted. Then one supervisor had an idea. He fastened bright tissue-paper streamers to the air-conditioning ducts and as they fluttered gaily they also incontestibly demonstrated the fresh-air movement. Soon employee complaints tapered off. The problem was solved. As professor Keith Davis of Arizona State College pronounced admiringly in the introduction to his book *Human Relations at Work:* "That which was technically right had been made *humanly* right."

Not all the ingredients in the big stew were fresh. Many were warmed over. Someone rediscovered old-fashioned suggestion systems and happily noticed that they had been human-related all the time. Said one vice president of U.S. Steel to an assembly of the National Association of Suggestion Systems in 1960: ". . . But people crave more than money and group benefits. They want warm human appreciation of their essentially human personalities . . . That the suggestion system provides this recognition and respect is perhaps no better illustrated than by the man in one of our plants . . . who has submitted more than 250 suggestions, has had 44 of them accepted, has 10 more under investigation right now—and always has to be reminded at least once to cash every award check. 'I don't need 10 or 15 dollars that bad,' he grins. 'The big thing I get out of the Suggestion Plan is that people know who I am now . . .' "

For the most part, American cuisine has not been especially admired by Continental chefs. The same cannot be said, though, for American human relations recipes and their appeal to Europe's management cooks. That the American "production machine" did very well during the Second World War is no news to anybody. What may be news, though, is *why* it did so well. *Human relations.* At least, that was the conclusion of many European businessmen and they wanted some too.

Chris Argyris of Yale, a long-time examiner of human relations fads and fancies, tells of thousands of European top managers who visited the United States in the postwar years to learn our production technologies, and of the hundreds of reports they produced. In more than 95 per cent of the reports is the inevitable conclusion: "The true secret of American success is human relations!" "Where do they get this information?" Argyris asks. "One look at their crammed schedule and it becomes obvious that there was little time for interviewing employees. Usually they obtained this message from management."

But no matter. The marvelous conclusion had been drawn, and it was carried home, as befits any hero, on the shoulders of the highest and most modern European executives. When it arrived it was cheered loudly and examined hardly at all. One does not examine heroes very closely, particularly when they belong to top management. The situation was not without some awkwardness, however, for while almost everybody loved human relations, almost nobody knew what it was.

Argyris recounts his experiences as a member of an American assistance team in Europe. In discussions with more than two thousand top representatives of management, unions, and governments, the most frequent questions asked of the American experts included: "What *is* human relations?" and "What isn't human relations?"

But from time to time there were exceptional mixtures, combinations of more subtle sauces and sophisticated seasonings, prepared in smaller quantities for more highly developed tastes. Ragouts, perhaps, rather than stews. Probably the most notable of the human relations ragouts was the one slowly and patiently prepared by R. W. Johnson, chairman of the board of Johnson and Johnson.

Sometime after World War II, Johnson became deeply interested in the application of human relations to industry. But instead of snatching up any of the precooked versions already available, he decided on another approach. Johnson met with a group of businessmen and clergymen with similar interest in the subject. Their objective, as he described it, was "to put their ideas into a form that made practical business sense." The product of the group's deliberations, later referred to as "A Magna Carta for management and the worker," is probably the most thoughtful and explicit statement of human relations values made by anyone up to that time. Clearly, Johnson's Magna Carta was not typical of business thinking and in many ways it went radically beyond conventional espousals.

First, despite the fact that its charter called for it to concentrate on "practical business sense," the group reached the inescapable conclusion "that the problem was one of ethics." Further, it acknowledged in a more than superficial way that business did exist within a larger society, and even that it had a responsibility to this larger society. The report admitted the possibility that employees' desires for a guaranteed annual wage might not be merely a manifestation of socialistic heresy, but rather a legitimate expression of their security needs. It also suggested that it might be possible to soften, at least a little, the antagonism between management and unions.

When the Johnson report descended from abstraction and spoke of the translation of philosophy into principles for action, its radicalism diminished, however. Here once more were the familiar rules and devices: the need to recognize that "men crave recognition," that they have "social instincts" and tend to associate in informal groups, that they need to be *made to feel* that their work is important. Here too were the management guides for *adjusting the worker to the job,* and the advice that employees must be sold on changes in production policies so that often ". . . they feel that the policy is their policy, even though they did not originally agree with it."

Assessment of the Johnson committee's report is not a simple matter. It certainly represents a more than usually significant statement of a "progressive" management position. *But it is not a Magna Carta.*[5] And, curiously, the differences between it and that A.D. 1215 document are cogent. The differences are these: First, the original Magna Carta was not a unilaterally determined statement. It was a feudal contract, a product of the confrontation between a king and his antagonistic barons, and for the moment, at least, the barons had the upper hand. Second, the document signed by King John contained a *clear surrender of power* by him in favor of the barons and it provided the barons with a specific base for the exercise of their newly won power. The Johnson committee report surrendered nothing, either in fact or in theory. On the contrary, it rather advised that if the corporation king be judicious and benevolent, he need never face the crisis of a Magna Carta.

But though the Johnson report is intriguing it did not represent the prevailing approach to human relations of its time. It was the Mulligan-stew mixture that was characteristic of the myriad of foreman training programs initiated during that period. And what did these programs actually produce? In the mid-fifties two fairly solid research projects were conducted on the effects of the supervisory training programs. Both tested by questionnaire employees' perceptions of their relationships with their supervisors *before* and *after* training. For human relations enthusiasts the results were unhappy. At International Harvester Company, the first of the testing grounds, researchers Fleishmann, Harris, and Burtt of Ohio State University found no gain in supervisory-subordinate relationships occurred after the extensive company human relations training program. There was, perhaps, even a slight deterioration. In the second investigation, which covered two divisions of the Detroit Edison Company, University of Michigan researchers found some improvement in one division, but some loss in the other.

---

[5] The difference is not a matter of nobility of motives, though. The original was not nearly as grandly democratic as we have subsequently come to think. It was more like a union contract negotiated between two tough bargainers, one of whom happened to have more trumps in his hand at the moment.

Overall, there are a number of people who feel that the human relations diet of the first-line supervisor probably contributed more in the way of nervous indigestion than nourishment for him. It complicated and confused his life. On the one hand he was confronted with the plain message from above that a good foreman was one who could handle his men, not in the old bull-of-the-woods way, but in a manner that inspired their confidence and affection. By the new human relations standards a disliked supervisor was by definition an unsuccessful one. What is more, there were easy ways for workers to indicate their lack of affection for a supervisor so that his superiors would know about it—a sudden rash of minor grievances, a few group visits to the personnel office, a concentrated refusal to work overtime on rush projects. It did not take long for the workers to recognize that management had presented them with this subtle but powerful gift.

On the other hand, however, the basic management expectation of the first-line supervisor had not changed. He was supposed to be a *management man* with a management outlook. His job was still to get the production out and spread the management word. It was an unpleasant dilemma.

To survive it, many of the supervisors turned to the political arts. The popular foreman was the one who became one-of-the-boys. The way he did it was by not pressing his men too hard, talking the time-study man into setting lower output standards, sympathizing with or even joining in the men's gripes against "the company," and covering for them when they violated minor codes of management. In return, the crew under the good-joe foreman protected him by meeting the minimum production requirements set for the unit, by keeping their written grievances to a minimum, and by keeping the foreman informed (through their almost invariably superior intelligence systems) of what higher management currently had on its mind.

Frequently, the result of all this was a pleasant and easygoing *détente*. Sometimes there was even an active alliance between supervisor and workers *against higher* management. In either case, what management unknowingly had wrought often resembled a barrier against its objectives more than a support for them.

To a few people, the taste of the human relations Mulligan stew had been sour right from the start, and even as heaping ladlesful had been generously distributed at home and abroad they had disapproved. To the discriminating palates of the old Hawthorne classicists, the stuff was especially offensive. It was loose, impure, and sloppy, and it threatened the irremedial corruption of work to which they had dedicated substantial parts of their lives.

Finally, in 1951 Fritz Roethlisberger, a principal member of Elton Mayo's Hawthorne team, spoke his irritation openly. In the September issue of the *Harvard Business Review,* Roethlisberger said: "For some time now I have been impressed by how ineffective and unrealistic many of these programs are . . . That we teach supervisors such 'untruths' does not bother me so much. I realize there are some important and useful 'half-truths.' What does bother me is that this kind of nonsense goes on in the name of common sense, realism, and practicality—and that the grim, earnest, and serious discussion of these silly little points is not even helpful."

But even as Roethlisberger spoke the mixtures continued to bubble as gaily as ever—and the same *Harvard Business Review* continued to print new variations of the basic recipe. For a number of personnel departments, especially the smaller, slower ones, it is still an admittedly favorite dish. The style-setting personnel leaders, however, were eventually to lose some of their taste for its jumble, and turn instead to tidier and more sophisticated fare.

There are a number of explanations for the gradual decline of this style of human relations. Most of the movement's structure was based on bad theory—a collection of loose, intuitive notions, insufficiently tested and inappropriately generalized by too many overeager personnel men. And, gradually, the consequences began to show. Uncharitably, some rude researchers had begun to explore the cherished "golden rules" and the answers did not come out right.

Investigators discovered that many of the highest-producing employees in the plant were *not* well-integrated group members but isolates. Other researchers found that effective leaders did *not* try to understand and be friendly toward their subordinates. On the contrary, they tended to be quite critical. Perhaps worst of all, a whole series of re-examinations of both office and factory workers by some of the best young turk researchers around clearly indicated that there was *no* systematic relationship between productivity and satisfaction or morale. As Robert L. Kahn of the University of Michigan Survey Research Center put it, after an extensive survey of the research reports on the subject: "I would like to begin by asserting, without qualification, that productivity and job satisfaction do not necessarily go together. The persistence with which managers and managerial consultants place them in juxtaposition is much more revealing of their own value structure, I believe, than it is indicative of anything in the empirical research data on organizations."

And that applied to the particulars too, including job satisfaction, financial and job status satisfaction, satisfaction with supervision, and satisfaction with the company. Even pride in one's own work group did not seem to tie in in any special way to high productivity.

It was a blow. But actually, a great many personnel men hardly noticed it. It is somewhat more likely that the loss of Mulligan-stew popularity was at least equally attributable to two other causes. First, the simple fact that people do tend over a period of time to tire of even the most appealing sort of thing (even televised wrestling); and second, the fact that in a wild moment of indiscretion somebody threw a very peculiar new ingredient at the kettle.

The new ingredient was called "permissive management," and it is not at all clear whether it ever actually got into the pot or not. Nevertheless, the mere idea that it might have was enough to spoil forever a good many management appetites.

The theory of permissive management was that you left people alone to do whatever they felt inclined to do, and somehow through a kind of benign higher law things turned out better and more smoothly than they would have if you had ordered the people around. The rationale for permissive management is probably to be found somewhere in the early works of such managerial logicians as Mary Parker Follett.

Follett had magnificent faith in orderliness. For her and her fellow logicians the root of the most serious troubles of industry was in the giving and receiving of orders. Being bossed naturally aroused antagonism in the recipient, and with the accumulation of incident upon incident eventually came covert opposition to management, or even overt strife.

Mary Follett's solution was to "depersonalize the giving of orders, to unite all concerned in a study of the situation, to discover the law of the situation and obey that." Thus the greatest cause of industrial unrest could be eliminated, for, as Mrs. Follet said: "If orders are simply part of the situation, the question of someone giving and someone receiving does not come up. . . . This gives, does it not, a slightly different aspect to the whole of business administration through the plant?"

It did indeed! But not, so far as I know, to any plant that ever existed in the United States. There was a good deal of talk about permissive management in the world of the theoreticians, and Mary Follett's books were studied in any number of management courses. But if anyone actually tried the theories of permissive management in any real way his valor went unnoticed and his name is lost forever to the roll of heroes.

If permissive management had any impact at all on American business aside from the fright it produced in some managements, it was that it may have served as a kind of rickety bridge to the two other styles of human relations: participative management and a bogus variant of it which is now a major element of modern manipulation.

The chances of discovering a full-fledged version of participative management in the United States are only slightly higher than the chances of running into a real case of permissive management. Furthermore, there have been a number of oversweet, "academic" descriptions of participative management which tend to make it hard at times to see much difference between it and the permissive approach. Another complication is that some of the most genuine experiments in what could be called participative management according to the definitions set forth in this book are not actually called that by those involved in them. In fact, the best examples tend not to be identified under any name at all, while some of the programs labeled participative management are in reality merely examples of a sort of participation-plated paternalism.

The root sources of participative management theory are deep, august, and varied. For some people they are in political philosophy, an extension of the ideas and ideals of democracy into industrial life. In essence, as the political philosophers see it, there is a dreadful incongruity in a society that cherishes universal suffrage and self-determination among its fundamental concepts, yet sanctions and even blithely encourages autocracy as the accepted mode of one of its major institutions, the industrial organization.

For others the roots of participative management are in humanistic psychology. It is not so much the global and abstract essences that matter, but rather the more personal and immediate needs of individual human beings to grow and fulfill themselves as human beings. And only as each person is enabled to take a genuine part in making the decisions which will effect his own destiny can such fulfillment be realized.

For still others the point of participative management emerges neither from political philosophy nor from individual psychology, though either or both may be invoked for public relations purposes. Rather, it is a matter of "effectiveness." Participation—real participation, not merely its outward slogans and symbols—is a way to a greater optimization of human productivity.[6]

The idea of participative management is simple. Subordinates are encouraged and enabled to contribute substantively to the decision-making processes that take place within their organization. The techniques and devices provided for them come in a variety of shapes and are called by such names as "multiple management," "consultative management," and "democratic supervision." There are task forces, problem definition groups, permanent advisory committees, and *ad hoc* working committees. There are "vertical groups," combinations of people from two or more organizational levels; and "horizontal groups," combinations of people at the same organizational level, but from different functions.

As we remarked earlier, it is difficult to identify examples of companies in the United States in which genuine participative management is the prevailing mode. Rather, there would seem to be growing efforts within some organizations, by some managers, to experiment with the approach.

If for its sincere advocates the fundamental of participative management involves a true marriage of human and organizational interests, the more common pattern of current industrial human relations practice is seduction. And, as often happens in the ordinary variety of the two processes, a lot of the words used in the latter approach are the same as those used in the former.

We are talking about modern manipulation. The idea of modern manipulation is to help you to get other people to do what you want them to do because they like to do it, or because they like you, or because they think you are wise, or because they want to be part of the team, or because any other non-

---

[6] In actuality, of course, making a trichotomy out of these views is a considerable oversimplification. Some theoreticians see all of the elements as individual but intertwined. Others have not troubled themselves at all in deciding which represent the prime motives and which the secondary.

coercive reason.[7] A good deal of what is currently described under the heading of participative management is in reality something else—a combination of its premises and principles reduced to slogans and glued firmly to selected pieces of organizational trivia. For every real adventure into the frontiers of the still-unfamiliar territory of participative management there have probably been at least a score of ersatz armchair excursions which unashamedly flew the participative flag.

For the practitioners of modern manipulation, "participation" has been translated into an elaborately advertised advocacy of allowing subordinates the privilege of choosing between equally inconsequential alternatives within the framework of unimportant situations. Or the similarly well-advertised encouragement of employees to provide their individual suggestions on *how to implement* the minor details of decisions management has already made.

The personnel literature of the 1950's brims with tasty samples of this kind of participation. How our employees decided whether to hold a dance or a bowling meet, or how they resolved the issue of whether to take their morning coffee break at nine o'clock or ten. The way in which our mail clerks decided to deliver to the third-floor offices before the second-floor offices (and saved eight minutes). And so on.

In January, 1951, an article appeared in the *Harvard Business Review* authored, participatively, no doubt, by Elizabeth and Francis Jennings, a well-known husband and wife team of human relations consultants. It has subsequently become something of a classic, I suppose, and has been reprinted in a number of human relations anthologies. The Jenningses' article was titled "Making Human Relations Work," and it deserves more than average attention. There is a special fuzziness about the Jenningses' style, and an illogical construction even in their

---

[7] President Eisenhower, a great admirer of business and its men, described leadership as "the art of getting somebody else to do something you want done because he wants to do it."

wishful thinking which in a somewhat extreme way characterizes the period.

Groups, begin the Jenningses warningly, are an essential fact of organization life, but that is not necessarily a good thing for management because groups can become antagonistic. For instance, the Jenningses note, they can become "overorganized," as in the case "when workers lunch together so frequently that they become bored with each other and can think of nothing except their problems."

What can be done about this dangerous situation? Provide a list of interesting topics for discussion? Shorten lunch hours? The Jenningses do not tell us. Their collective gaze is fixed on less pedestrian courses. What is needed, they advise, is "to develop group cooperation through which workers may pool their knowledge, develop strength as they hear their opinions voiced and begin to express themselves, give each other courage, satisfy their need for the esteem of others, promote enthusiasm and sound morale—and eventually group efficiency."

If it is a bit difficult to find the precise logic upon which this optimistic sequence—from co-operation through courage to efficiency—is based, it gets harder as we go along. For the Jenningses assure us that not only will the worker grow more efficient through participation, he will also come to realize the validity of management's authority structure and the need for him to conform to its standards.

But it is not so much its disjointedness that makes the Jenningses' statement of human relations at work significant. It is that in their curious selection of illustrative case studies they help to make clear what "participation" in its emaciated version really looks like. There is, for instance, the Jenningses' description of the case of a young woman supervisor with "a deep sense of values" who had been angered by the fact that her coworkers had pretended to their division head that they had read and admired some material he had prepared, when in fact they had not. Her fellow supervisors explain their deception to her as "just good politics," but the young woman remains angry and disapproving.

And what is the moral drawn by the Jenningses? It is that the young woman is reacting bitterly as a result of "her rigid determination to mold individuals to her own liking and to judge their behavior." The whole matter obviously is the young woman's problem and nobody else's. Which might have been a bit difficult to see without the Jenningses' reassuring interpretation.

The Jenningses are dependably reassuring. For example, there is their response to "the president of an organization" who asked: "Do you mean to tell me a stock boy can help me manage my business?" No, replied the human relations counselors, this is not at all what is intended, "and anyway the stock boy would be extremely uncomfortable [doing so] . . . But a visit with the stock boy and some of his fellow workers for an exchange of opinions and experiences would give the president some idea of how to manage the stock boys."

One final object lesson from the Jenningses on participation and its happy consequences. It seems that in one client's company there had been a long-standing practice among employees of taking up collections for engagement parties, wedding gifts, anniversaries, and even to comfort girls who lost their pocketbooks. The solicitation parade had reached chaotic proportions. Anybody could start up a drive, anytime, for any reason. And, according to the Jenningses, "It took a courageous soul to ignore the collection basket . . . [so] lacking the courage to refuse, but wanting to, [a number of employees] went to the management for aid." Management's response, naturally, was to invoke its version of the participative mode. It decided to call a meeting of the workers.

At first, the workers were reluctant to express themselves, but after a word or two of facilitative encouragement from the chairman—"Large families require a lot of money these days"—all agreed that large families did indeed, and after that all also decided on a brand-new policy which substantially curtailed the collection drives.

The Jenningses' human relations lesson here: "The announced policy contained a paragraph that it had been written by workers' representatives in collaboration with the management. Had an arbitrary policy been issued, all that would have been needed to set hostile reaction in motion would be for one disappointed collector to say, 'Who do they think they are, telling us what to do with our money?' Here, in this case, is the essential difference between a dictatorial method of control and a participating method which utilizes the worker's individuality through the group's collective responsibility."

There is, I believe, high significance in the Jenningses' trivial tales and morals. It is the very fact of their triviality. What a paltry concept of "worker individuality" they have. A young woman is angered by deception and the lesson is that she needs to become better adjusted to her fellow workers' foibles. An executive is comfortingly promised that if he opens his ear to the voices of the lowly inhabitants of his kingdom he need not fear to hear a challenge to his omniscience or omnipotence. The victims of "collectionism," lacking courage, are helpless, and only through the intervention of management's superior parental comprehension of psychological affairs can they be rescued from their self-imposed trap.

The Jenningses' message to management is clear, and it is an attractive sales talk: Try "participation." It is so easy to please the worker-children, and quite safe, and it costs so little.

14

⟫━━━⟫

Therapeutic Management

FOR A LONG, long time there have been arguments about what sort of a man Man is. Is he a noble savage corroded and corrupted by the acids of civilization, or a wicked cannibal covered over and inhibited from his natural destructive urges only by his thin plating of civilization? Some speculators on the human condition have felt that most men are by nature selfish, shortsighted, and mean, or even that all men naturally hate their fellow men, and, as Thomas Hobbes put it, "only by a common power to keep them in awe" could they be kept from exercising their innate urges to eliminate each other.

On the other hand, there have been a few viewers of Man's course who have found it not quite so bleak. While they were not unaware of the troubles and vicissitudes, they nevertheless felt that natural man was, in Rousseau's words, "naturally good," or at any rate, he did at least have a choice between goodness and badness.

In some ways these philosophical disputes are going on at a very practical level in organizations, and their outcome may produce some significant difference in the ways companies approach the matter of dealing with their employees.

In the good old days managers tended to think and act according to certain assumptions about themselves and about the natures of those who worked under them. These assumptions were hardly ever made explicit or catalogued, but by and large they were there. They went about like this:

1. The job of running the business belongs to management and *only* to management. Management holds sole responsibility for profit or loss and therefore it must have sole authority for determining the allocation of funds, resources, equipment, and people. To manage is to control.

2. People would prefer not to work. People work only because of the raw demands of economic necessity. They work then only at a minimal level of exertion unless management can devise means to coax or coerce them into a higher level of effort. Management has the responsibility to do so.

3. People prefer to be told what to do and how to do it. They dislike responsibility and the risk which accompanies responsibility. They prefer that management assume both the responsibility and the risk. Management must do so.

4. Though it is the source of their livelihood, nevertheless most people (not all) are indifferent to the fate of the organization, and some are even hostile to the organization. Management must be on guard to protect the organization at all times.

5. Most people are shortsighted, unintelligent, and easily misled by the radical elements in society. They are not readily influenced by the logic of the business point of view, which is usually beyond their ability or desire to comprehend. There is probably little that management can do to change people's attitudes, but management must maintain a strong position to protect the organization against subversion.

For many managers, especially older ones and those at lower organization levels, these five premises remain as adequate today as they were yesterday, in theory as well as practice. In 1961 Opinion Research Corporation surveyed more than two hundred managers on their attitudes and assumptions about subordinates. Between 60 and 79 per cent of those at the middle and lower level indicated agreement with statements such as the following:

—The boss who expects his people to set their own standards for superior performance will probably find they don't set them very high.

—Because most people don't like to make decisions on their own, it's hard to get them to assume responsibility.

—Usually when people talk about wanting more responsible jobs, they really mean they want more money and status.

But other managers, especially the products of the new business schools and a portion of those at the higher levels of the organization, apparently are not so sure. In response to the same survey, only 56 per cent of top managers agreed with the first two statements, and 39 per cent with the third.

There are probably a number of factors contributing to the apparent change in outlook, and it is difficult to determine the degree of conviction behind the changes. There are the discomforts of the modern managers with overt power, the fond management hope that people can be inspired to like to work, and to work hard if a way can be found to touch their spirits, and so on. There is also the influence of one of the newest behavioral science ventures into the organization world. We shall call it industrial humanism.

If for economic man business is merely business, for the industrial humanist business is a significant human institution. If, as the economic man sees it, people work in order to live, as the industrial humanist sees it, work is an essential part of life. The points are made more specifically by people like Dr. Harry Levinson, head of the Menninger Foundation's industrial mental health division. Work, insists Dr. Levinson, is a great deal more than a way to earn money. "The fact that someone will pay for [a man's] work is an indication that what he does is needed by others, and therefore that he himself is a necessary part of the social fabric. He matters—as a man."

But at the same time that the fact of work's importance is proclaimed by all industrial humanists, the style of work required by the present-day industrial organization is deplored. As they see it, and as their more eloquent radicals describe it, work has become an alienated experience. Too many managements have a shining vision of optimum productivity, and it incorporates the worker as an optimized production tool. The glare of this shining vision has blindingly obscured all else that matters.

As the individual, minute motions of each component part of a machine have been predetermined, measured, and adjusted, so now are the individual, minute motions of the component parts of a man. Refined versions of Frederick Taylor's and Frank Gilbreth's original systems have been applied extensively in the prescriptions of methods to be used in production as well as in determining standard rates of output expected from the individual worker. Bright, young, management-inspired technicians concentrate heroically to translate the factory methodologies into comparable systems for the office, and highest management sighs longingly for that hallelujah day of universal application—even to the ranks of *lower* management. Thus, the efficiency-oriented industrial chief, probably not such a bad fellow when he is at home, has become a sort of super Dr. Frankenstein at the plant. He strides heavily up and down the aisles, draining out the workers' individuality and injecting *therbligs* in their place, producing apathetic automatons by the thousands.

The worker has been dehumanized and toolized, continues the humanist complaint. The processes of production have been designed, divided, and distributed solely to facilitate their own accomplishment and without regard to the worker who performs them. The worker plays no significant part in determining what, where, or how the work will be done. These determinations are made by specialists. The resulting products of this approach are jobs which involve only fragmented, meaningless pieces of the whole, operations which are minutely specialized, severely repetitious, deadeningly dull. The worker thus becomes bored, lethargic, and uninvolved in what he is doing. He may take flight from his unhappy situation by daydreaming or by developing avoidance techniques (goofing-off), or he may, in rebellion, develop antisocial—or anticorporation—behavior.

The toolized approaches are wrong, insist the industrial humanists. They are complicated, cumbersome, and inaccurate in their premises. The attempt to derive a single most effective way of performing an operation by pasting together slices of motion to make a whole pattern ignores individual differences. But worse still, the effort to rigidify human actions into preset patterns is itself something less than human.

Some interesting inferential models of the toolized view of the worker have been put together by the industrial humanists. One of the early formulations was by Chris Argyris. In a 1957 book, *Personality and Organization,* Argyris drew a number of connections between the normal biological patterns of growth and maturation in an individual and the effects of typical organization life on these processes. As Argyris saw it, the normal development of a person takes him from an infancy in which he is totally passive and dependent on others through a gradual maturing process during which he acquires increasingly more active purposefulness and independence. At any rate, that is the way individuals are *supposed* to develop. In most corporations, however, maturity is not a prized quality. On the contrary, the infantile qualities—passivity, dependence, submissiveness— seem to be hallmarks of "good employees."

The organization tends to discourage individual maturity in endless ways. To begin with, there is the very foundation of the organization itself, the formal hierarchy and manner of leadership. Once again, as in his childhood, the individual worker finds parental-style authority and a barrier to his independence. His goals and course are planned at the management level. In the formal organization are prescribed pathways to management authority which he must take for the resolution of any question or problem he may have. From the management-parent come regular inspections and checkups to make sure that things are done "right," as the management-parent sees right. And here too are the processes of judgment, reward, and punishment. Again analogous with those of childhood days, they are simple, swift, and materialistic.

In *Personality and Organization,* Argyris's concentration is primarily focused on production and clerical employees, but others have seen some relevance of his concepts in the functioning of higher-level personnel as well. A number of organizational strictures often bind professional and even supervisory people in equal, if less obvious, ways. At times there are even some special manifestations. For instance, there are the father-son relationships between individual junior-senior executive pairs, and the waiting-for-the-master's-pronouncement syndrome, in which no member of the management "team" has any opinion until the captain announces his. And perhaps most striking of all, there is the worship of the company kings. The degree of apparent devotion to and dependence on the heroic father figures of top management by middle managers frequently reaches proportions which transcend anything to be seen among the common troops of the factory or office.

Management's classic assumptions about workers set forth earlier in this chapter were derived in part from the writings of the late Douglas McGregor of the Massachusetts Institute of Technology. McGregor called the mode of industrial leadership which resulted from such sets of assumptions Theory X management, thereby attempting to avoid placing evaluative judgments on this management style (which would be inherent in the use of labels like "autocratic" or "authoritarian"). Among McGregor's fellow theoreticians, and subsequently among a number of personnel men and practicing managers as well, Theory X has become a commonplace abbreviation for "traditional management."

Conversely, McGregor's Theory Y has become an equally well-known designation for an alternative management style. The assumptions which comprise Theory Y were first set down systematically in Douglas McGregor's book *The Human Side of Enterprise*. Probably more than any other brief writing, they reflect the basic credo from which much of industrial humanism has grown. The Theory Y assumptions are as follows:

I. *The expenditure of physical and mental effort in work is as natural as play or rest.* The average human being does not inherently dislike work. Depending upon controllable conditions, work may be a source of satisfaction (and will be voluntarily performed) or a source of punishment (and will be avoided if possible).

2. *External control and the threat of punishment are not the only means for bringing about effort toward organizational objectives. Man will exercise self-direction and self-control in the service of objectives to which he is committed.*

3. *Commitment to objectives is a function of the rewards associated with their achievement.* The most significant of such rewards, e.g., the satisfaction of ego and self-actualization needs, can be direct products of effort directed toward organizational objectives.

4. *The average human being learns, under proper conditions, not only to accept but to seek responsibility.* Avoidance of responsibility, lack of ambition, and emphasis on security are generally consequences of experience, not inherent human characteristics.

5. *The capacity to exercise a relatively high degree of imagination, ingenuity, and creativity in the solution of organizational problems is widely, not narrowly, distributed in the population.*

6. *Under the conditions of modern industrial life, the intellectual potentialities of the average human being are only partially utilized.*

McGregor's formulation is not particularly unique. There are a number of familiar themes, a few of them even faintly echo from the Mulligan-stew past. There is also the underlying premise, clearest in point 3, that the goals and purposes of organization and individual are indeed susceptible to a common integration. This we have certainly heard before. The difference is that McGregor's concentration is on *convincing management men* that they ought to go along with *what is good for their employees,* because in the long run it would be good for them too. The obverse is the more typical message.

Nor are McGregor's suggestions for the practical application of Theory Y very revolutionary. In many ways they are recognizable as a version of participative management, in which man and manager sit and reason together on the requirements of the subordinate's job, the determination of goals to be met, and the subsequent review of performance. The mode in which these processes occur, however, is different. Under Theory Y, when the supervisor slides away from his traditional role as boss, he does not merely slide into the role of "senior partner." He becomes a "colleague-consultant." His primary mission is to bring out his subordinate's own ideas, and to contribute to their formulation into proposals. The supervisor must avoid dominating the interchange.[1]

For the most part McGregor's Theory Y assumptions are readily understandable. The concept of "self-actualization," however, may be less clear. Self-actualization is the term of Abram Maslow of Brandeis University, still another active industrial humanist, whose specialty is human motivation.[2] Maslow sees industrial man, and in fact all men, as insatiably striving animals. In contrast to a number of economic men who also hold that view, however, he does not believe that men merely strive for more and more of the same. Rather, according to Maslow, the nature of men's needs tends to change even as they are met. They grow increasingly less simple and substantive, and more complicated and abstract. But for the needer they continue to be vitally important.

Maslow believes that the lowest order of men's needs is at the physiological level—food, shelter, clothing, and so on. In the

---

[1] The differences are subtle but significant. It may help to think about them in this somewhat oversimplified way: The Theory X boss would say: "This is what you will do"; while the garden-variety participative manager might say: "This is what we ought to do. What are your suggestions on how we ought to do it?" But the Theory Y manager would probably ask: "What should we do, and how should we plan to do it?"

[2] The industrial humanists do indeed tend to be more than usually activist in behalf of their cause. Professor Maslow is, among other things, a consultant to Non Linear System, Inc., of Del Mar, California, one of the few companies highly involved in Theory Y experimentation.

context of the twentieth-century American environment these basic needs are translated into such items as pay, working conditions, fringe benefits, and other things economic.

But for most Americans these lowest-level needs have already been met. Thus, for the majority, while striving continues, it changes its focus to one of the four higher levels in the Maslow "needs hierarchy." These are: At the second level, *safety* needs. In the industrial setting such needs would be met through assurances of job security, stability of earnings, and adequate retirement income. At the third level are *membership* needs— the desire to belong and to be accepted by one's fellow workers and by management. Fourth are the needs for *esteem*—for the demonstration of one's adequacy, and competence, and the need to be recognized and to have status. And finally, at the fifth and highest level are the *self-actualization* needs—the needs for the realization of one's potential, the chance to grow and to fulfill one's self.

To a few very sophisticated personnel men the Maslow needs hierarchy has significant implications, for they raise the question: In trying to motivate our employees are we appealing to the most appropriate needs level? If the Maslow theory is valid it may well be that we are not, that we are still working too far down the scale, on needs which have already been satiated.

Among those intrigued by the Maslow formulations was Opinion Research Corporation. In a study reported in 1961, focusing on the perennial question of how to make better managers, ORC made an attempt to find out where management men were to be found in the needs hierarchy. The results of the ORC study were mixed. On the one hand ORC reported: ". . . esteem and self-fulfillment needs are high on the list of unsatisfied needs for the managers in this study, offering much greater leverage for motivation." But on the other hand, the researchers also found that the single most frequently expressed need on the part of their management population sample was at the lowest "physiological" level—68 per cent of them wanted "a chance to earn more money."[3]

One of the central ideas of Theory Y is that the manager gradually stops being boss. Instead, he becomes a kind of counselor, whose primary responsibility is to bring forth the latent forces of his subordinates—their ideas, energies, creativity, and so forth. In *Personality and Organization,* Argyris describes one such manager, a man named James Richard (his organization is not identified). Earlier in his career Richard, now an executive vice president, had been production superintendent of the company. And as the man in charge of production, Richard had apparently worked at nothing so hard as he had worked at not being in charge. As he explained to Argyris, he had tried *not* to maintain order and control over his subordinates, *not* to keep things moving on the right track, and *not* to make decisions. Instead of issuing orders, giving assignments, and following up results, he put the problems raised by individuals and departments into the group's hands and left it to the group to handle them from there. Underlying his actions, said Richard, was the fundamental belief that there was more wisdom, good judgment, and creativity stored up in the group as a whole than there could be in any one individual—himself included.

Thus, at the primary level the Theory Y manager is most of all a facilitator. He aspires to relationships with his men in which he can be a colleague rather than a superior, a relationship in which he is seen not as a menace, either active or potential, nor, according to some theoreticians, even as a benevolent judge of their work. All in all, it would seem to be a relatively simple role. But it can become complex.

There are stages of managerial wisdom and proficiency beyond this primary one. If for managers who have attained the

---

[3] Actually, this may not be so clear an indicator of managerial primitiveness as it first appears. It may be that "more money" has become a fairly universal symbol for a great many things, including evidence of esteem, and perhaps in a funny way even self-actualization. Like: If I had enough I could tell them all to go to hell and go off to Pago Pago and paint seascapes.

first order of Theory Y wisdom the task is to search out and remove the external organizational and environmental barriers which restrict their subordinates' functioning, for managers who have attained the second order of such wisdom the task is deeper. At this higher level some, under the tutelage of the industrial humanists, have come to perceive their responsibilities as including the searching-out of the barriers *within* their subordinates' emotions, and their own emotions as well. And thus have we come to the newest and perhaps the ultimate in industrial humanism, the "therapeutic" approach to management.

If the manager is to be effective in this new and very different role, he must learn to be exceptionally sensitive to each of his subordinates, not merely as a worker but as a total and individual person. He must become aware of those conditions within his subordinate and within himself which are preventing the subordinate from fully utilizing his talents, and which may in some cases be restricting other work-group members from using theirs. He must learn to recognize, understand, and respond to fairly deep dynamics of human psychology—the conditions of men's minds and emotions, *including his own,* which lie below the level of their immediate words and actions.

A simple illustration of this new human relations perspective can be drawn in the commonplace context of the performance appraisal process. Performance appraisal has been in trouble recently, but it remains a continuing tradition, as applied to professional personnel. A key assumption of the process is that every subordinate wants and needs to know how he stands in the eyes of his superior—his strengths, his weaknesses, and his potential, as evaluated by the boss.

Under the penetrating lights of the new, deeper analysis that is not so clear. The manager who listens with a more sensitive ear to what each employee is saying when he "asks" for judgments on his work may hear different messages from different ones. From a few may come the cool request for an "objective" analysis of the quantity and quality of their output. But from others he hears a plea for positive reassurance. They may feel that the job they are doing is being done adequately, but they

need confirmation and encouragement. Some subordinates who
ostensibly seek the manager's assessment of their work are in
reality seeking yet another kind of comfort, and that is a quiet
pause in the hectic routine of their days in which they can re-
establish personal contact with their leader. In the usual pattern
of the organization function many busy supervisors may go for
exceedingly long periods without even seeing some of their
subordinates. At other times, even when contacts between man
and manager are daily their content is often limited to
quick, automatic exchanges of fragments of data. Given this
condition, especially when it is coupled with the dependency
needs of many employees, it is not difficult to understand the
sense of separation, even isolation, which they may come to feel
over a period of time.

The therapeutic manager may detect even subtler needs below the surface of this "simple," standard personnel practice.
Some employees only desire a means for determining whether or
not they are getting the credit and recognition they believe they
deserve, while others approach the performance appraisal with
mixed fascination and terror. They are about to test the
frightening possibility that their manager may indeed know that
they are performing as poorly as they themselves think they are.

Thus, in the traditional performance appraisal process, the
manager who responds with the classically correct, objective
"balance sheet" of positives and negatives, supported by specific
incidents and quantified justifications of his judgments, does
not at all meet the real needs of any of these more deeply need-
ful employees.

In a quite real way therapeutic management calls for
particular psychological skills. The insights and analytical abilities required of the manager bear a significant resemblance to
those of the therapist. Though the manager is seldom called
upon to deal with people whose problems have made them
"sick," he is often called upon to deal with people whose problems have made them difficult. But few managers come to their
jobs from a specialization in therapy, nor have many been psy-

choanalyzed themselves. How, then, do they acquire the skills?

There is a way. It is called "human relations laboratory training"—or sometimes, "sensitivity training"—and each year an increasing number of people are going through it.

To some, laboratory training is a cult, made up of a collection of semi-mesmerized subjects, led by a loose-knit coterie of overly intrusive academics. The cultists preach odd and dangerous gospels of amateur psychiatry in quiet soft-sell voices. To others, laboratory training is, at last, a real hope for a meaningful behavioral science contribution to the world—probably the most important development in the social sciences so far.

According to National Training Laboratories, or NTL, the small administrative nucleus based in Washington, D.C., around which clusters an exceedingly free-floating network of the fellows and associates who comprise its activists, laboratory training is a methodology. Its goals, as enumerated, for example, in a 1966 NTL brochure, are to foster learnings in:

Personal Growth—Self-awareness and Introspectiveness, Openness and Sensitivity to others, Freer expression, Better listening, More effective interpersonal relations.

Group Development—Understanding dynamics of groups, Development of group leadership, Building better teamwork, Increasing productivity.

Organizational Improvement—Effective change processes, Intergroup competition and collaboration, Effective communication, Problem analysis and change strategies.

Which might to the casual ear sound like the blurb for anything from a Dale Carnegie course in friend-winning to a Joe Oneshot seminar on dynamic foremanship. But it isn't. Laboratory training and NTL are neither platitudinous nor kooky fringe movements. On the contrary, there is within the network a highly impressive collection of distinguished people and institutional connections, though, with characteristic unconcern, NTL personnel seldom bother to mention this.

The NTL national board of directors has a broad spectrum of representation from the Camp Fire Girls to the IBM Corporation, and from the Methodist Church to the Hotel Corporation of America. NTL's fellows and associates, while mostly academic Ph.D.'s, also include a significant and increasing sprinkling of psychiatrists, psychotherapists, and industrial managers. Its affiliations touch universities and colleges across the country, including MIT, UCLA, Arizona State University, Boston University, Case Institute, the universities of Colorado, Wyoming, and Nevada, and dozens of others. The list of its clients is an awesome one. On it are such industrial mammoths as IBM, Standard Oil of New York, American Telephone and Telegraph, Humble Oil, Aluminum Company of America, Boeing Aircraft, Dupont, Eastman Kodak, General Electric, Goodrich, United Airlines, United Parcel, Monsanto Chemical, and Westinghouse.

And there are others that one might think of as strange bedfellows for the aforementioned corporate giants. For instance: The National Council of the Episcopal Church, the National Council of Juvenile Court Judges, the Peace Corps, the International Office of Public Health Service, the Commonwealth of Puerto Rico, the Air Force's Maxwell University, and the United States Department of State.

Nor is this nearly the full story of NTL's scope. Laboratory training by NTL affiliates extends not only across the country but to every continent in the world. Under the auspices of the Ford Foundation, for instance, NTL associates like Dr. Thomas A. Wickes have carried the laboratory training methodology into several newly formed African nations in efforts to help key government personnel prepare for their new roles.

In Scandinavia, England, India, and elsewhere training of industrial, governmental, and other institutional personnel has been expanding steadily. Both in the United States and abroad, training programs at the college level are also multiplying.

The concept of laboratory training originated in 1946. It was an accidental birth, though a legitimate one by most standards. The founders of the method were recognized social scientists, and its theoretical construction can be related to the group dynamics work of Kurt Lewin, a formidable figure in the field of psychology.

In the summer of 1946 a large group of educators and social scientists were brought together for a three-week conference on social science applications. By the standards of that day, the conference design itself was planned to take advantage of many of the latest developments and techniques of human relations. At the beginning the conference proceeded in more or less the usual way. There were lectures, demonstrations, group discussions. The conferees took notes, asked questions, agreed with each other sometimes and disagreed with each other sometimes. It was all quite pleasant and even informative, but similar meetings in the past had been also.

One thing, though, was not typical. A small group of social scientists had been asked by the conference planners *not* to participate in the sessions, but rather to sit in on them as observers. The task of this group was to watch the lecturers and discussants and to make notes on what effects they were having on each other. Without anything quite specific in mind, the conference planners felt that the gathering of such information might help in improving teaching methodologies.

It was the custom of the observer group to meet informally after dinner to compare notes and discuss their observations. Gradually, a few of the regular conference participants became curious about what went on in these small evening meetings and asked if they might sit in and observe the observers. The observers consented. And that was how it all started.

There was a striking difference between the subject matter of the observers' meetings and that of the formal conference. The observers had not been particularly concerned with *what* the lecturers and participants had been saying, but rather *why* they were saying it, and *how*. Why had one member of a discussion group, for instance, almost invariably disagreed with another member? Why had still a third participant lapsed into sullen silence after the group had seemingly rejected his proposal for a slight change in subject matter; and why, in fact, had the group rejected his proposal? How had these individual participants attempted to make their points—by persuasion, by aggression, by ignoring opposing points of view? And what effect had these varied styles had on others in the group?

When the observers had met alone, their discussions on these questions had been calm, clinical, and impersonal. But with the arrival of their guests, often actually the very people who were being discussed, the meetings were entirely different. The guests' interest was personal, and grew increasingly intense. Soon they were unable to remain quiet listeners. Instead, they questioned and even challenged the social scientists' observations and interpretations, and soon after that they were excitedly questioning and challenging each other.

Subsequent evening sessions became the high points of the conference, so a modified version of the same process was incorporated as a regular part of the conference. Discussion groups chose their own observers, and after five to fifteen minutes of discussion the observers would be called upon to summarize what they had observed—who was doing what, which group members seemed to be working for consensus, which were opposing or obstructing, which were dominating and which were retreating.

Under the stimulation of the new technique the entire character of the conference changed. While it had at the beginning been academically interesting and informative, it now became exciting and immediately personal. Where earlier discussions had dealt with the comfortably distant questions of back-home problem situations, they now dealt with much less comfortable discussion of "here-and-now" behavior among the participants. Where initially each participant might have expected to gather from his fellow practitioners theoretical diagnoses and advice in response to *his own description* of his professional problems, he now got direct and sometimes surprising reactions to himself as a person. It was indeed a different experience.

Laboratory training at present still rests essentially on the conceptual base of its earliest days, though it has changed and continues to change in techniques and design. Experimentation is still under way in many directions, including, for example, a programmed instruction approach, and "marathon" groups which go on for two or three days without pause. People sleep when they have to by curling up in the corner of the room, or for that matter, right in the middle of the group, if they like.

Most often, however, training laboratories, particularly those held for businessmen, are conducted under more comfortable conditions. In fact, *very* comfortable conditions. They are held at some of the nicer country clubs, resorts, and converted mansions in the United States—Arden House in upstate New York, a ninety-six-room mansion built by the Harriman family in the early 1900's; the Seaview Country Club near Atlantic City; the Kings Bay Yacht and Country Club in Miami; the La Coquille Club in Palm Beach. The Florida work conferences are thoughtfully scheduled during the winter months. Training laboratories for public administrators, educators, students, and community leaders are held at somewhat less plush but still quite pleasant spots like Bethel, Maine, and Lake Arrowhead, California.

The typical laboratory training program lasts either one or two weeks. For the busy executive population the one-week version is now most common. Its basic parts consist of "T Groups" ("T" for Training—not Therapy), theory lectures, and a wide variety of simulation exercises. Each program element is different from what might be considered its counterpart in a traditional management conference or seminar, but most different of all is the T Group, and the T Group is the heart of laboratory training. T Groups are a controversial subject, but one thing about them is clear—they are almost invariably a very strong experience.

What is a conference like? Something like this. The delegates, as the trainees are called, begin to arrive at Arden House or Seaview or some similar quietly luxurious spot at about noon on a Sunday. This is just about the time the regular, less serious-minded week-end guests are beginning to depart.[4]

The laboratory workday starts at about nine o'clock, with lunch at noon, and following that, usually a period of free time until three or three-thirty in the afternoon. There are evening sessions scheduled until about ten, which often go until midnight or into the early morning hours. Laboratory life is not easy. Even the noon-to-three period often becomes "work" time. The lines of distinction between working and leisure time tend to blur. The essential mode of the training laboratory involves people in combinations—from very small to fairly large groups. Thus, in time almost all that occurs becomes relevant. The only difference is the degree of intensity or casualness with which the delegates deal with it.

Typically, the first official session of the laboratory begins after dinner on Sunday night. The delegates, usually about fifty to seventy-five of them, are primarily from large and medium-sized companies. A few may be from the military services and other major Government branches. They are assembled in the main auditorium and welcomed. They are told that the hotel or club is happy to have them, that dress will be informal, except perhaps at dinner, when they will dine in the main dining room, and they are given a description of the laboratory method and purpose.

The description is brief. It includes the point that the laboratory emphasis is upon "learning from our own behavior" so that we may better understand ourselves and our effects upon other people. As the training week progresses, it becomes more

---

[4] One thing, incidentally, that has always been striking to me is the contrast between the patterns of dinner-table conversation among the participants on that first Sunday night—it much resembles that of the more leisurely week-end guests who have not yet left—and the pattern of conversation on the last evening of the laboratory. There is a quality and content to that final night's conversation that is very different. My guess is that were the early arriving country clubbers to overhear what was being said by these staunchest members of upper and upper-middle management they might become quite nervous about their common shares.

and more apparent that little of the introduction was really heard by the delegates. Their *expectations* of what a training program *ought* to be were much louder in their mind's ear than the words of the speaker. And that is a fairly important lesson in itself. Many may eventually come to realize that the same phenomenon occurs in their experiences outside the laboratory as well.

After the introductory general session the delegates divide into their separate T Groups. Generally, an effort is made by the training staff to avoid placing two or more men from the same company in the same T Group. Each T Group has one or two laboratory staff members, called trainers, and about twelve to fifteen delegates. And so the strange and serious work begins.

There is no single pattern. Trainers have different styles, and diversity is not only tolerated but encouraged by the mores of NTL. Most often, however, the T Group session begins with a very brief statement by the trainer. Essentially, it is a reiteration of what the delegates were told in the general session: We are here to learn about how individuals behave in groups, and we may best do this by learning how we ourselves behave in this group. Often the trainer adds a disclaimer about his own role in the group, a statement that he does not expect to behave in the usual manner of teacher or group leader. *He then stops talking.*

What follows almost inevitably is a long, uncomfortable silence. It is finally broken—nervously, or irritably, or cautiously—by one of the group. He suggests that it might be a good idea if we all introduced ourselves. Perhaps something like this:

> DELEGATE A. Well, if nobody else has any better ideas, maybe we ought to start by introducing ourselves. At least we can find out who's who.
> (*Silence*)
> DELEGATE A (*To the man on his left*). Why don't you start?

DELEGATE B (*Reluctantly*). I'm Bill Smith. I'm with XYZ Company.

DELEGATE C (*Also reluctantly*). My name is Joe Brown and I'm with PQR Company.

DELEGATE D (*Not at all reluctant*). I'm Sam Jones and I'm vice president for marketing of MNO.[5] I'd like to say a few words about why I'm here too. (*Glances at the trainer*) I've heard a lot of good things about these conferences and I expect that by the time we finish with the course we are going to know a lot more about handling people effectively.

The introductions continue and now each of the delegates includes not only his company affiliation but his position as well. Few can match the marketing vice president. Many also volunteer reasons for their presence at the lab. These range from generalizations similar to those of the marketing man to more personalized expressions like: "I'm here because my boss thinks I'm rough as a cob, so he figured this charm school business would smooth me out. I doubt it, myself." Or: "I really don't know why I'm here. My boss called me in one day and asked me if I wanted to go. I know some other guys who have been up here and they're real comers, so I feel pretty honored, and I can see by the kind of group this is that my impressions were right."

Finally the round is completed and abruptly the group falls silent again.

DELEGATE C. Boy, when it gets quiet in here it really gets quiet.

DELEGATE E. It's nerve-wracking. (*He smiles*)

(*Silence again*)

DELEGATE D. It seems to me that what we need to do is to organize this outfit a bit. Maybe get a chairman and set up an agenda. (*Turns to the trainer*) What would you think of that approach?

---

[5] This, of course, has been the first status bid. Good, but not as good as the response by one puckish trainer I know: "My name is Fred Green and I own the western half of the United States. What do you do best?"

TRAINER. Does the group feel that it wants to organize and develop an agenda?

DELEGATE F (*To the other delegates*). You can forget about asking him questions. From what I heard from some other fellows who have been through this snake pit before, these guys never answer questions, they just ask them back at you.

DELEGATE C. Sounds like a good job to have. I wish mine back at the plant was like that. When I get asked something I'd pretty damn well better have the answer right now or somebody will start looking for a replacement.

DELEGATE A (*To the other delegates*). You know, I sure hope for his sake that he's going to do more than that. I'm the first one my company has sent to one of these things, and when I get back they're going to ask me for a recommendation on whether or not we send anybody else.

DELEGATE B (*Laughs nervously*). That's okay. Your company may be asking him for a recommendation about you too.

DELEGATE A (*Chin out*). That doesn't bother me a bit.

DELEGATE B. Look, I think these leaders know what they're doing, so I don't think we need to worry about it.

DELEGATE A. Maybe they do and maybe they don't. I've heard some stories about some guys who have cracked up going through these things.

DELEGATE D. Gentlemen, I'm not sure that this is really getting us any place. I think there is a motion before the floor that we elect a chairman and develop an agenda for this meeting. I think if we did that we would be able to get to the problem here a little more systematically. Don't you think? Does anybody want to make any nominations for chairman? (*Silence*) Well, then, does anybody feel that he would like to take on the role of chairman—say, on a temporary basis?

(*Silence*)

TRAINER. There are some things that seem to be happening here in the group. Maybe someone would like to comment on the process as he has seen it.

(*Short silence*)

DELEGATE E. It seems to me that *nothing* seems to be happening. That's the trouble. We're just going around in circles.

TRAINER. Why do you think that is?

DELEGATE E. I don't know. Maybe it's because we're all pretty nervous about this whole thing.

DELEGATE A. Speak for yourself. We're not *all* nervous.

TRAINER (*To* DELEGATE A). You're not nervous or uncomfortable?

DELEGATE A. Hell, no. Why should I be? I don't think anybody here is *really* nervous.

But, of course, they *really are,* and eventually—perhaps not in the Sunday night session or even in the Monday series, but soon—they will look back upon their first night and vie with each other in their descriptions of just how nervous they really were. They will also recognize, since this pattern will be repeated in subsequent sessions, many of the other things that actually were going on below the surface of their words. For instance, their discomfort with the ambiguity of this unstructured and undefined milieu, and their quest for identification and status recognition, through the introductions. Their expressed need for an authority figure (the trainer) who would tell them—as they were used to being told—what to do. The dependency of some of them upon the trainer, and the counter-dependency of others.

They will recall the bid for leadership made by the marketing vice president, and his rejection by the group. And as the week or two of their group experience goes by, they will learn other things. Most valuably, they will learn that they can trust each other and help each other. To many of these hard-bitten men of enterprise, this will come as the most startling point of all.

While the T Group is the key element of laboratory training, it is supplemented by other processes too. There are brief, simple "theory sessions" which by and large are directly tied to the experiences the trainees are undergoing in their individual T Groups. And there are also a wide variety of simulation exercises, focusing in microcosm upon the phenomena of group competition and co-operation. One of the principal lessons to emerge from these exercises is that sometimes competition can be an inappropriate mode of operation, while co-operation can be a very effective one. For some that may be an entirely new idea.

One simple exercise that is used to exemplify the point is the nickel-bidding game. In it the trainer offers to a group of several delegates the opportunity to bid for nickels during a limited period of time, perhaps five minutes. He has a pocketful of them, so for this short period the supply is essentially unlimited. Bidding begins, and before long, in the heat of the contest, nickels are selling for seven, ten, even twenty-five cents each. When the five minutes is over, the trainer almost invariably is richer and the delegates, poorer. They are also sheepish, for the point is, of course, that if they had co-operated and each in turn had bid only a penny for each nickel, they all could have profited.

Another exercise that remains vivid in my own memory was a much more elaborately designed one in which combinations of T Groups were formed into teams in order to compete against each other in designing and constructing an edifice which would "best symbolize the laboratory." The materials supplied for the project were the same one might provide to any group of kindergarteners under similar circumstances: colored paper, Scotch tape, scissors, paper clips, and so forth. But the other aspects of the task were not childish. Each competing group was to simulate a business organization. They were to select a general manager, an assistant general manager, foremen, and workers. Each phase of the exercise—organization planning, design development, and actual construction of the "symbol" —was to be accomplished within a specified time period, and the final products would be judged against each other by a small group of "impartial" referees elected from the delegate body itself.

The laboratory staff that had designed the exercise felt it might produce some interesting phenomena for later review by the groups, but at the same time the staff was also a little uncomfortable about whether such an elaborate make-believe could capture and maintain the interest and real involvement of these upper-echelon management realists.

It did. In fact, it did beyond the most optimistic expectations of the staff, and very nearly beyond the control of anybody, including the management of the plush resort hotel at which the laboratory was held.

Several unprogrammed events burst in rather wild disorder from the formation of a "labor union" by a disgruntled group of management men—"workers" who did not like their "managers" and decided to strike against them. There were suddenly picket lines and picket signs in the hotel corridor just off the main lobby, and then just as suddenly there were "goons" and strike-breakers, and pushing and shoving. Perhaps it had started as a gag (and later it was to be recalled as one by the embarrassed participants), but at its peak it was not funny at all.

The "competitive spirit" continued even after "negotiations" finally brought the striking workers back to their jobs. There was, for instance, industrial sabotage, as men pilfered each other's paper clips and scissors. There were charges of unfair competition as one team apparently prolonged its planning period beyond the prescribed time limits of the exercise. And there was genuine industrial heroism as the "chief judge" (in real life a major company executive who looked every inch the part) rose to announce the judging group's decision, faced the boos, catcalls, and taunts of the losing teams, responded to them masterfully, and eventually stared his hecklers into silence.

What are the lessons learned from the laboratory exercises? It is difficult to say. In the case of the nickel-bidding game the moral is obvious, but the situation is so simple and tricklike that it is hard to translate its implications into other, "more real" situations. In the construction exercise there was a complexity which did in some measure approximate the real world. For the perceptive man here indeed were some clues to the roots and courses of industrial relations conflicts. But there were no clear lessons on how to avoid them.

All this would seem to indicate that the laboratory experience is a totally rugged one, and it is not. For as the laboratory moves onward from session to session and from day to day, some unfamiliar but pleasant things are happening to its delegates too. They are coming to be *interested in,* to *know,* and to *understand* each other. And it is a different kind of interest, knowledge, and understanding, at a deeper and more meaningful level, than many have ever experienced before. The theme of the T Group is concentration on the here-and-now rather than the there-and-then. The subject matter of the group is itself and each of its members, and while there may be momentary flights of attention back home to the office situation, or to abstract philosophy, or to the general affairs of the industrial or national society, or whatever, inevitably the group returns to that most intense, most immediate, and most relevant entity—itself.

It knows what is really important. The exploration of its members' relationships to each other; their individual introspections, sometimes painful but almost always rewarding; their tentative testings of the freer expression of their own real feelings and the often joyous discovery that in such expression each man is not rejected but rather even more wholeheartedly accepted by the others.

The products of these patterns of interaction within the T Group are most often the growth of mutual affection and regard, warmth more easily expressed, empathy, and understanding. And in this climate long-dormant seeds of thought and feeling grow, at first hesitantly, and then strongly, to be rediscovered. Men speak of things they have literally never spoken of before, their personal and private hopes, anxieties, and confusions. And they find among their fellows comprehension and often common cause.

A top-level executive fears that he is not really adequate in his job; he has always felt that way, even as he climbed rapidly up the hierarchal ladder. Another believes his subordinates are contemptuous of him. The thought pervades his every contact with them, almost to the point of immobilizing him. Still another has attained a company-wide reputation for his devotion to his work. His perpetual travels on company business, his late hours at the office, are the admiration of his superiors and held up as examples for his peers. But he does not really love his work. Rather, he cannot abide his home. He is alienated from his wife and son, and he knows of no way of bridging the chasm in his family relationships.

And as each expresses his trouble he receives neither ridicule nor disdain from his fellows. Instead there are concern and compassion, a willingness to share experience and a genuine desire to help. The strong and solitary chieftains of organizations, for this brief time, at least, have put aside their awesome painted shields and stand revealed. And nobody laughs.

For many I know personally, it is an experience they will never completely forget.

15

With Feeling

IN TALKING about industrial humanism we have not merely been cataloguing one more new wrinkle on the old face of human relations methodology. We have really been talking about some drastically different views of the ways people in organizations ought to relate to one another. That means that we have been talking about breaking away from a management trajectory that has been climbing along nicely for a couple of hundred or so years. The main departures are these: First, as the industrial humanists see it, work itself is not just a way for people to earn money. Rather, it is one of the most significant of all human activities. What happens to men at work and what men cause to happen at work is of the utmost importance to them, not just economically, but humanly. Second, in the humanist view, men in general are a lot better in a lot of ways than a lot of people think they are. They have large untapped resources of imagination and intelligence. They can be reasonable and responsible, and they have the capacity for self-control.

There are some striking differences too in the ways the industrial humanists have been pursuing their assumptions. In contrast to the main line of human relations tradition so far, they have not been concentrating very much on what needs to be changed in *workers' attitudes*. Instead, they have been concentrating on what needs to be changed in *managers' attitudes*.

The humanists see the organization as a place where all people can and should grow, develop, and fulfill their individual potential. Management's responsibility, they think, is to facilitate these processes.

Interestingly, for the archtypes of both classic entrepreneurship and classic liberalism the verdict on industrial humanism is clear—and negative. To the business traditionalists the whole matter is nonsense—or worse, subversive—and among the fighting liberals there is a curious similarity of view. There are, in fact, a number of anti-establishment men who sneer or even get downright mad about the idea of trying to get people to like their work and work place. Sociologist David Reisman, for instance, feels that business ought to concentrate on productivity in the interests of getting as much of it as possible, and let people get their "meaning" and fulfillment in increased leisure time *away from the job*. Other nonadmirers of the business way are irritated by the presumptuousness of the corporation in even pretending to assume responsibility for "developing" people. That, say they, is the province of the home, church, and school, but clearly not the business of business.

Robert N. McMurray, a well-known and long-time management consultant, is not enthusiastic about industrial humanism, either, mainly because he is a pragmatic man and he does not think it will work. He makes a counter case for what he calls "benevolent autocracy," which he does think will work. First of all, says McMurray, most top managers today are hard-driving, egocentric men who don't really believe in democratic leadership, and without their real—not just verbal—support, no substantive change in the corporation's operating mode can be sustained by those below. Secondly, the individual parts of major company organizations are too interdependent and delicately balanced together to allow for much meaningful small-group independence in the decision-making processes. Third, and most significant, as McMurray sees it, large business organizations are, by and large, established bureaucracies, and for this reason, they draw to them people who tend to need security and who *want to be loyal, obedient and subordinate*. Expecting these people to be otherwise will bring you nothing but frustration, and them nothing but high anxieties.

But McMurray's views are seldom heard from the newer breed of consultants, or from the really forward-looking inside management men either. On the contrary, in these modern times it probably takes the protection of a deep conservative trench, a close-to-retirement age, or a great deal of courage for anybody to publicly denounce the cheery optimism in postulates like those of Douglas McGregor's Theory Y. Among many of the younger managers of the big, image-conscious corporations, some of industrial humanism's espousals have become not only acceptable, but quite fashionable. It is probably even true that in that compartment of the averagely enlightened managerial mind which is reserved strictly for philosophical theories about "humanity," a little place has been found for this one too.

So much for industrial humanism in general. What about laboratory training in particular? The answers again run the full gamut from overflowing homage to overwhelming scorn. In between there are those who see the NTL methodology as not awfully consequential one way or the other—a sort of ineffectual puttering-about which does not produce much in the long run, though in the short run it may provide a bit of a catharsis for the temporary relief of the emotionally constricted executive.

There are those who cherish and those who damn the therapeutic style; those who see it as an unwarranted and outrageous invasion of men's private lives, and those who see it as, at last, the beginning of the corporation's acknowledgment of its human responsibilities.

George Odiorne of the University of Michigan's Graduate School of Business is probably, among academicians, the archantagonist of laboratory training. Odiorne believes that personnel men, managers, and all other organizational minions ought to keep their noses out of other people's psyches, and he tells them so. In an article in the January, 1965, *Training Direc-*

tors Journal titled "An Uneasy Look at Motivation Theory," Odiorne says: "Most training aimed at teaching motivation ends up prompting managers to probe into the personal privacy of others and practicing amateur psychology without having a useful effect on job performance or supervisory results. That this pointless and widespread invasion of privacy is resented is increasingly apparent." Besides which, he adds: "The body of literature which deals with *needs* of men[1] is not strictly speaking behavioral 'science' at all, but a rather heart-warming and pleasing kind of philosophical speculation which draws on bits of evidence, combined with personal and private systems of explanation and modes of expression."

By the early 1960's National Training Laboratory activities had become noticeable enough on the American business scene to deserve the attention of *Fortune* magazine. *Fortune* decided to send a man around to sit in (as an observer) on an NTL laboratory held at Arden House. In August, 1961, the writer, Spencer Klaw, described his "Two Weeks in T Group." While the reactions of *Fortune*'s man were not entirely unfriendly, he concluded: "In the end, what one makes of T Groups and laboratories depends on a number of things; on how one feels about the propriety of intimate conversations staged, as it were, under institutional auspices and with a tape recorder running;[2] on one's tolerance for talk about helping and caring and adventures in growth; and on the degree to which one shares the assumption, seemingly held by many people who serve as trainers at human-relations laboratories, that there is not much wrong with the human condition that a little social engineering cannot cure."

On the other hand, the editors of *Factory* magazine, a stand-

---

[1] Maslow's needs hierarchy, for instance.

[2] Tape recorders are almost standard equipment for T Groups. The point is emphatically made by the trainers at the very beginning of the sessions, however, that the tapes can be listened to *only* by the members of the group, and that all tapes are erased immediately after the laboratory. In all my experiences with laboratory training I know of no unauthorized use of the recordings.

ard journal among manufacturing men, were a great deal more positive in their reactions to T Groups, as well as folksier. Said the July, 1959, issue in reply to the negativists: "Most of the critics, unfortunately, are throwing rocks over a wall at something they have never seen . . . And the something on the other side is not one thing—or even one concept. It's a patchwork quilt of management concepts and theories that are being applied with success today in isolated cases in industry. The lab's quilt of theory doesn't have any edges or any definite form, because the many quilters are feverishly sewing new patches on all the time. But the center of the quilt is warm and durable, as a good quilt (or management theory) should be."

At the moment it certainly seems that an increasing number of people and companies are getting ready to snuggle under the quilt. Year after year the number of NTL laboratories for management men grows larger and more diverse. Only a few years ago a special "interne" program for the training of industrial trainers was begun, and immediately afterward, in response to enrollment requests, the program was doubled. In a similar pattern, a special laboratory for company presidents was started in 1964, and here again the subsequent demand was such that NTL's plans for August 1967 through July 1968 include three presidents' labs plus two "alumni" labs for chief executives who previously attended.

The reactions of Robert C. Hood, president of Ansul Chemical Company, one of the first chief executives to try out a laboratory, illustrate the way most of the growth has come about. Says Hood: "In 1952 I attended the National Training Laboratory at Bethel, Maine, and came away so impressed with their advanced approach to leadership training that I have seen to it that eight of my principal top executives have participated in subsequent laboratories.[3] I feel that what they have gained from this experience has measurably improved the caliber of my management team."

---

[3] The laboratory "ethic" would not altogether approve of Mr. Hood's having "seen to it" that eight of his subchiefs attended labs. NTL believes that laboratory attendance should be voluntary, not forced.

But pro and con, the reactions of the *Fortune* and *Factory* writers and of Mr. Hood have so far been individual, anecdotal, and subjective. Perhaps, on the favorable side, they really reflect no more than fond recollections of the comfortable warmth beneath the laboratory quilt, and on the negative side, only the sulky contrariness of old-guard cynicism. In the words of the T Group itself, "gut-feelings." And the business world does not, at least according to its own description of itself, operate according to gut-feelings. It operates by facts and figures.

What are the facts and figures on the subject of laboratory training? There are not many. Until a few years ago there was almost none, and what is more, hardly anybody in the field seemed very concerned about gathering any. Not many are even now. Most activists in laboratory training strike some people as irritatingly complacent. They have no doubts at all about the validity or worthiness of what they are doing, and they seem little concerned about whether others agree or not. What is still more exasperating, they don't even point to the growing popularity of the laboratory method as proof of its worthiness.

When efforts have been made to find the figures and to deduce some at least approximate facts about the effects of the training, the results have been inconclusive—often uncomfortably so. In the first comprehensive volume on the subject, *T-Group Theory and Laboratory Method,* published in 1964, Dr. Dorothy Stock of the University of Chicago's Department of Psychiatry, one of the contributors to the volume, concluded that "The studies reported [so far] demonstrate how difficult it is to answer this apparently simple, but actually complicated, question [of] what people learn from their T-Group experiences, and how many actually do learn anything."

One of the more interesting assessments of the effects of laboratory training on participants is contained in an unpublished draft memo to the NTL Research Committee by Henry Reicken of the National Science Foundation. After reviewing about two dozen studies on the subject, Reicken concludes:

"The results have been extremely varied and there have been many failures in the sense that the research uncovered no change following training or no differences between trained and not trained persons. (Obviously these 'failures' could be training failures or research failures, and we'll never know.)" (Author's parentheses.)

"Where effects of laboratory training have been detected," Reicken continues, "it appears that about two-thirds of the participants display changed behavior following training, mostly changes of a positive or desirable sort." But he also points out that where control groups have been used to check the significance of laboratory training, about one third of the *untrained* people also show similar changes of behavior, and where comparisons have been made between laboratory and more traditional kinds of training, about one half of those trained under the latter approach also show such changes.

Reicken further notes that the standard kinds of psychological tests, especially personality tests, do *not* seem to be useful for measuring the effects of laboratory training. The dimensions of personality and competence which do seem to be changed in those individuals who are affected at all seem to be difficult to describe in any precise psychological terms. They tend, Reicken observes, "to be rather global factors" having to do with personal effectiveness, improved abilities to communicate and to listen to others, and other interpersonal functioning.

For those who may have begun to wonder whose side Dr. Reicken is on, let us clarify. Reicken is not only an NTL fellow, he is also a member of NTL's national board of directors. A fascinating thing about the NTL researchers who are significantly involved in laboratory training is that their innate confidence in and devotion to their cause does not seem much to impair their ability to see the counterevidence. But then, the counterevidence does not seem to shake their confidence or devotion much either.

Still another NTL fellow, Dr. Paul C. Buchanan, at the time a personnel researcher for Standard Oil of New Jersey, expressed concern about the tie-in of laboratory training to organizational situations. In a 1965 study report he describes an "organization development" program in a company (unidentified) that utilized a modified form of laboratory training as its major component. The project, begun in one large department of the company, progressed for about two and a half years with "increasing success." So much success, in fact, that it attracted the interest of other company departments, and eventually the attention of the company president. Here progress and success both abruptly stopped. In so hard and decisive a manner that the shock dislodged the department head who had initiated the program, and his entire organization development staff as well. The problem, according to Buchanan, was that the company president neither liked nor agreed with the laboratory-inspired mode of operation. Buchanan believes that his lack of sympathy for the program was attributable to poor planning and execution by the personnel men who introduced it to him.

In contrast to this unhappy debacle, however, Buchanan is able to point to more favorable experiences in another firm in which the introduction of the laboratory approach and four years of operations under it produced highly favorable results: "The organization shifted from a condition of tight centralization of power to one of wide participation in decision making, from high distrust and lack of confidence of one level of management for another and of older 'practical' people for young, technically trained people, from separatism and lack of cooperation across unit lines to cooperation among work units; and there was a substantial increase in profits during the four years, a large proportion of which was attributed to the development efforts."

"Thus," Buchanan concludes, "in assessing information regarding the contribution of laboratory training to the development of an organization we can see both successes and failures. But we can see enough to say that such training does have an impact upon the individual and what is needed is more attention to strategies of organization development and to adapting laboratory training theory and methodology to fulfill the strategy, and to devising ways of assessing the impact of such programs."

After his own survey of research studies, Henry Reicken's view of laboratory training's impact on organizations was on the whole less cheerful than Buchanan's. Reicken examined an even broader array of research results on the attempted installations of this new-style management and came away with an even broader range of troubled conclusions. Said Reicken: "In contrast [to indications of improved competence in some functions], there is little or no evidence for improved competence in diagnosing and solving problems, effectiveness in group decision making, management of inter-group relations or tensions and the like. Correspondingly, there is little positive evidence (in spite of many attempts to measure it) of change in *intra*personal dynamics, character structure, tension level, anxiety management, aggressivity, rigidity, and the whole host of personality qualities, traits and attributes that laboratory training is supposed to affect."

The principal labor of this book has been to identify and criticize what I think is wrong with a particular agglomeration of prevailing theories, activities, fancies, and rituals which, in a broad view, fall within the scope of what is presently called personnel work. The other side of this same project involves trying to find some alternative modes which show greater promise. I believe that industrial humanism is one of these. It makes sense—not the whole sense, but a part of it.

I need to make it clear, though, that being for industrial humanism does not mean that I have discovered in it any universal solvent. I have not, for instance, found any easy means to wash away the objections raised by those who are affronted by it, who believe that the corporation's influence is already too intrusive a factor in American life. That is a point. I think that there is little chance of things being otherwise. Big organizations —corporate, government, and labor—are just there. Like mountains, they are part of the landscape and we are not likely to get rid of them nor, realistically, should we want to. It might, however, be worth remembering that there is no immutable law which insists that influence must flow in only one direction. It is just possible that if we think big we may be able to come up with some ways for American life to intrude somewhat on the corporation, as it now intrudes on American life. There are things about industrial humanism which might very well help in that process.

My case becomes no easier when I come to the specifics of laboratory training and its applicability to management. I have not forgotten Michigan University's George Odiorne or *Fortune*'s Spencer Klaw. Odiorne is right in several ways. Psyche-probing is a delicate business, and it can be a damned annoying one, especially when it is done by amateurs. What is more, it is far from clear that such diddling can be justified according to the standard criterion of entrepreneurial pay-off—more pieces of stuff getting out to the plant shipping dock faster. *Fortune*'s man is right too. T Group language can sound odd, or perhaps more to the point, it can sound uncomfortably un-he-manly. My only response is that I do not find any of these objections damaging enough to offset the useful things that so many people feel they get out of their laboratory experience.

Most of all though, I am mindful of Buchanan's, Reicken's, and especially my own personal observations of the fumbles and failures when some people have attempted to carry the laboratory training mode into an industrial context. What is to follow in the next several pages is an examination of some ways laboratory training has been applied in organizations. A good deal of what will be said will be critical. But let me be clear at the outset; it is my conviction that industrial humanism offers great promise. It is truly, in its potential, a means to the extension of a more meaningful life for the individual at work. Further, I believe that laboratory training is, *in itself,* a unique and valuable opportunity for personal growth. The fact that an ever increasing number of people from the industrial community and from other segments of our society are participating in laboratory training is an important and positive phenomenon. At the same time, however, I believe that a number of those who have attempted to transport both the spirit and the substance of the training laboratory into the individual environment have moved with more zeal than effectiveness. I admire their pioneering courage, but too frequently they have neglected the preliminary requirements for confronting and understanding the current realities of organizations.

Therapeutic management is group centered. The group motif per se is not universally admired. Over a period of time it has provoked some brisk antagonism both within and outside corporations. Outside, the anti-togetherness people condemn groupism as one of the more reprehensible forms of conformity producer and individuality killer. Inside, a number of prominent philosopher-executives have for some while been scowling at "committees," and talking about the committee style as one that inevitably produces compromises which tend to reduce the quality of the work to the lowest common group denominator. What most often come out of the committee room, according to the critics, are decisions which are traditional, safe, devoid of spirit or imagination, and consequently mediocre, at best.[4]

True enough, say the therapeutic management advocates, for *ordinary* committees. But in laboratory-oriented groups there is a difference. These are not the usual aggregates of suspicious men warily jockeying for position, stifling each other's expression for fear that someone will show up as more quick, brilliant, or influential than someone else. Rather, they are assemblies of individuals who have come together to work on a common problem, a group in which people trust each other—really trust each other—because they really know each other. And also a group where there is recognition that different kinds of problems, or even different phases of the same problem, may call

---

[4] For instance, in the December, 1965, issue of *Nation's Business* there is an article by Joseph G. Mason aptly titled "No, Not Another Committee." Among other things, Mason recommends that any time a situation calls for action the best thing a manager can do is to think twice before calling a meeting.

for different expertise, so that the "dominant" role is not a perpetual trophy to be fought for, won and clutched, but a functional tool that may shift easily from one member to another, without threat, jealousy, or hesitation.

Ideally, the roles of all members of the therapeutic manager's team are flexible, including his own. They are not locked in either by the predeterminants of the organizational hierarchy or by the members' needs to protect their status. And if the members do not have to exhaust the major part of their collective energies in defense of their egos, they may instead use it to attack their company's problems. In the climate of mutual trust experimental approaches are not stifled, they are freed.[5] The orientation of the group's members is not to judge but to help each other.

Sometimes, groups like this can be formed, although it is not an easy process and it takes a good deal of time. They do, incidentally, give a good deal of pleasure to their members. There is a remarkable kind of environmental warmth generated, and people can get surprising satisfaction out of assisting rather than blocking or finessing each other. The therapeutic-style group, in contrast to more traditional ones, frequently encourages individual expression, particularly among the usually reticent or weaker contributors. It is impressive, too, to see the change in behavior among the strong, articulate members who once tended to dominate and monopolize the meetings. They gradually begin to devote themselves, not to their own ideas, but to helping the previously inarticulate to develop theirs. Eventually this can become not a sacrifice but a genuine pleasure for the former dynamos.

But is the new style a pure blessing? Probably not, for some

---

[5] An underlying theory of a more common group process called "brainstorming" rests on a variant of the same principle: that by officially sanctioning the acceptability of silly ideas, under the ground rules of "free association," management men can temporarily stop worrying about their images and let their unconscious flow more freely. In practice, though, a lot of brainstorming sessions are shams. People spend hours in advance preparing to be "spontaneous."

other things can be happening too. One is that such a group can have a tendency to tyrannize in unobtrusive ways, not the weak and reticent, but the dominant and articulate. Thus, with minor irony, we have gone full circle to return again to the classic complaints against committees. Environmental warmth, as well as distrust and fear, can subdue the spirit of the bullish but superior operator. What we are saying is that it is likely that the gentle milieu does encourage many kinds of adventures, including attempts at creativity by people who have seldom if ever before felt unthreatened enough to risk trying such things. But at the same time it can also bring about a kind of self-imposed dampening effect on those who by nature or nurture were once the freest-wheeling idea-generators. Not because they *have to* repress themselves, but because the spirit of mutuality which pervades the group makes them *want to.*[6]

The therapeutically oriented manager may tolerate extended conversation and speculation long past the point where the more directive leader would have terminated it and made his decision, in order to avoid cutting off his subordinates' opportunities to express themselves. And in individual manager-subordinate relationships he may, in his emphasis on encouraging initiative and exploration by his subordinates, stifle his own impulses to overrule them, even if his ideas are in fact substantially superior to theirs.

According to the ideal of the therapeutic manager, decisions are not determined by his or anybody else's command. Nor are they based upon the democratic vote of the majority. The best decisions are, in fact, hardly *decided* at all. They are derived from *consensus.* The ethical rationale for this point of view is that no one is coerced. Instead, everyone acts according to his own free choice. There is an accompanying efficiency justifica-

---

[6] Really high-impact effectiveness and creativity are probably not distributed broadly and equally among the general population. Furthermore, Dr. Donald W. MacKinnon, director of the Institute of Personality Assessment and Research of the University of California, found in his research on "effective" and "creative" people that creative people tend to be "self-assertive and dominant."

tion: that free choice means individual, personal commitment, and with it comes the strongest of all motivations to make the decision succeed.

Again, in considerable measure the idea makes sense. The hazard is in trying to make a running rule of it. In the world of organizational reality the idolization of consensus can lead to paralysis. Groups can become too preoccupied with assuring not only each member's opportunity for expression but his satisfaction with the outcome as well. Discussions may become interminable. In a desultory search for understanding of each other's point of view conversations may expand in ripples of increasing irrelevance, the requirement for decision or action forgotten.

Commitment should not always be contingent upon one's full agreement with the action to be taken. There needs to be a balance, a recognition that sometimes commitment ought to derive from one's sense of responsibilty to the organization and its other members even if that means doing something one is not personally enthusiastic about.

One of the valuable learnings that grow from the training laboratory experience is that disagreements and conflicts are often rooted in misunderstanding or personal value differences. When these underlying factors are brought to light and faced, new perspectives are discovered, and so fresh opportunities for understanding and agreement. But some of the consensus seekers have become so devoted to this idea that they have forgotten that there are times when disagreement is real and substantive, when the choice of the *right* decision is not the inevitable and obvious product of a free, unblocked exchange of ideas. There are right decisions that are unsure, risky, and even unsupportable according to the prevailing logic of a group. They are derived intuitively, perhaps by a single bright person's insight. The organization that cuts off all opportunities for such individual, "nonpopular" decisions will suffer for it.

Feelings, says a fundamental tenet of laboratory training wisdom, are facts. They are indeed, and this holds true inside organizations as well as almost everywhere that people deal with other people. People have brought their "hidden agendas," as well as their official ones, to almost every gathering that has ever been held. And there are times when the items on those secret, personal lists of the mind are so compelling that they can distort or even block completely any progress on what is supposed to be the business at hand. Most people who have lived inside the organization houses for a time can easily recall local examples—the long-standing states of low-key warfare in which personal antagonisms between individuals or between organizational factions were so pervasive that one could almost be certain that any proposal at all made by one side would be opposed by the other, no matter what its content.

But such situations are not beyond help. The problems of the hidden agendas can be treated, not by outlawing them, but by acknowledging their existence and dealing with their contents openly and directly. This can be accomplished by establishing an organizational environment in which genuinely *full* communication is sanctioned, an environment which liberates each individual to deal with the underlying emotional as well as the intellectual content of what is going on.

Once more, however, there is a requirement for responsibility. Let to run with no rein at all I have known some "liberated" groups to gallop a goodly distance into the emotional backwoods. Long-standing feelings, pent-up frustrations, fixations, and desires that have belonged to their expressers for years become completely enthralling to the group; and while they may be real, significant, and important for the individual who owns them they can be carried to a point where they cease having an even peripheral bearing on the original purpose of the group.

Feelings can become a fetish. A visitor coming into the middle of some of the supposed work sessions of one group I recall might readily have concluded that the long, rambling anecdotes, philosophical discourses, and exchanges of recollections of mutually inspired annoyances were its primary agenda. The group's members were often so utterly captured by the psychological undercurrents of their own dialogues that they increasingly neglected any direct approaches to dealing with the more mundane subjects of their work together.

The difficulties described here are not inevitable. Avoidance of these self-entrapping situations does not require the group to ignore or suppress its members' hidden agendas. Rather, it calls for an initial definition of purpose, and sufficient self-discipline for the group to maintain a clear connection with its mission even while it explores other matters. At best all group members ought to share responsibility for maintaining the group's purpose, and they may remind and reinforce each other in doing so. When this does not occur, however, the responsible manager must feel free and able to exercise directive leadership, un-ashamedly—within a context that does not automatically stigmatize all such exercise as a failure of managership.

It is true that the therapeutic orientation tends to liberate a tolerance for individual differences and less guarded self-expression. It can also, however, release a tolerance for ineffectiveness and laxity. The task-neglecting pattern which becomes the hallmark of such meetings as those just described is one example. There are others. Let us look at three more. We can call them the "antistructure," the "simplicity," and the "self-confrontation" syndromes.

First, antistructure. According to the laboratory view, too many people depend too much and too often on traditional, pre-set configurations of thought and action. The use of old, established ways of looking at problems and developing solutions is familiar and comfortable for most people, but it is extremely limiting. If people could learn to live with a little more ambiguity they could be more open to new stimuli and they would probably be significantly more innovative. The point is a good one. Research outside the laboratory movement on similar hypotheses has produced encouraging results.

Again, though, the trouble is that some of the converts to this new view swing too far. In their zeal *all* structure is automatically condemned as restrictive, and randomness becomes a sort of new religion. It is difficult to run a complicated organization randomly.

Simplicity, the second syndrome, is in some ways related to the first. Simplicity is a quality highly prized by many laboratory devotees. Simple things are more easily expressed, more clearly understood, more readily amenable to consensus, and, at least apparently, more quickly responsive to "the situation."

The more plain and direct the solution to a problem is, the less likely it is to be encumbered by the heavy burdens of precedent, systematization, and policy. Simple solutions are *functional*, open, and responsive to the immediate need. Sometimes the solutions produced by the champions of simplicity are elegant, economical, and entirely adequate. At other times, however, they are naïve, irrelevant and entirely inadequate. Simple solutions work for simple problems. They do not work for complicated ones.

Finally, self-confrontation. A small number of people who go through training laboratories experience a very powerful encounter. It is an encounter with themselves. Not only with respect to their behavior and its effect on others—this is a common outcome among laboratory attendees—but at a deeper level as well. These people suddenly see themselves in total. Clearly, deeply, and realistically. The beauty of the experience is that it enables the fifty-year-old, tense, ulcer-ridden executive for the first time to recognize that he is not going to make vice president—that he lacks the brilliance, personal force, energy, or whatever that is required. This can be a traumatic but exceedingly healthy event for him, especially when he learns from his fellow T Group members that they neither condemn him nor like him less for not being a potential vice president.

Experiences in T Groups are often impressive ones, and sometimes they are adopted as models for back-home behavior. The concept of self-confrontation can be distorted in unhealthy ways too. The realization it brings is not always one of life's realities. Sometimes the so-called self-confrontation turns out to be no more than a capitulation to an easier, less demanding mode. And where the organizational environment is such that there is a too-ready and sympathetic acceptance of these "revelations of inadequacy," then in a curious way they can become almost fun to make. For the longer run, by admitting your "inability" to do certain parts of your job you may be able to avoid the need to do them. And nobody will blame you.

The Horatio Alger model may be a terribly sterile one to contemplate as the shape of the good life, but to abandon it entirely in favor of a new, easy-surrender model does not seem an improvement.

But these last several pages have been about extremes. They are intended as precautions, not as predictions of the inevitable. Not all "liberated" groups are so smitten or become so fixated. In speaking of therapeutic management's applications we have after all been speaking about a relatively new phenomenon, and my own observations of its practice have been limited to a small sample of cases. One explanation for some of the afflictions of therapeutic management I have noted may in fact be as much attributable to the individual natures of the group members as to the management style. It is likely that a group comprised of those whose impulses are not especially goal-oriented to begin with will tend to slide most rapidly and happily into the delicious pit where psyche contemplation is the main preoccupation. But, even so, the captivity need not turn out to be permanent. When the novelty wears off most people may outgrow it, just as most outgrow adolescence.

The long-range viability of therapeutic management is a possibility. It is not a certainty. Therapeutic management in its current form has deficiencies. The most serious of these derive from the fact that in most instances it has been developed merely as an extension of laboratory training, and laboratory training was never intended to be a management methodology. The way things are at Arden House, Seaview, and the LaCoquille Club are really not the way things are at U.S. Steel, General Foods, and the Ace Galoshe Company. Whether one is saddened by the fact or not, or even whether one feels the urge to make life at Ace more like life in a T Group, is really not the point.

There are indications that therapeutic management as a mere extension of laboratory training is not viable. Repeatedly, managers have returned enthusiastically from their experiences in T Groups, fully resolved to change their personal styles and operating methods toward greater openness and co-operation. But within a few weeks afterward they tell of their discouragement and abandoned resolve. Change has been impossible for them in the face of the unchanged counterforces of the organization environment. Other discouraging signs are also in evidence. Recently, a few of the firms that have devoted the most serious attention to the application of this new style of management show signs that they may be giving up their efforts.

There are hopeful signs too, however. At least one advanced technology company I know of, deeply involved in this area for a number of years, has carried its management theory beyond laboratory training theory. From the early days of its experimentation with new organizational relationships the company has given attention to its own total organization culture, rather than limiting its focus to individual management development alone. It has also made progress in confronting a number of the problems cited earlier in this chapter, including the development of a clearer, more congruent understanding of the need to integrate facilitative group process, task responsibility, and legitimate directive leadership.

16

The Loyal Opposition

THIS MIXED EXAMINATION of the personnel man and, more broadly, what we have enfolded under a generous concept of personnel work is almost concluded. To be added are only a few points of emphasis and some alternative proposals.

Very early in our tale we heard the sounds of personnel men mourning—about their inferior status, their lack of acceptance, their lack of recognition. The personnel men felt the scorn of the operating management men, the accusations that they interfered with rather than facilitated enterprise processes, that they used too big words, that they were impractical, ivory-tower dwellers who did not comprehend *business*. From the management theoreticians too there were harsh words. The personnel man's profession, observed the mentors, was a shallow one. His field consisted of little more than a collection of trivia left over, accidentally or disdainfully, from the more significant tasks of management. In summary, the personnel man was peripheral. He neither designed, made, nor sold the product, nor did he maneuver the money as it came in and went out.

More scorn and scoldings came from outside the organization. But they were different, often ironically so. To the anti-establishment critics the personnel man was *not* impotent or peripheral. He was the monitor of conformity. He was the master architect of the organization's dehumanizing systems, and chief instructor in the sciences of worker seduction. Thus, from varied vantage points has the personnel man's work been seen and condemned as inconsequential and diabolical, shallow and insidious, irrelevantly ritualistic and coldly calculating, inane and sinister.

None of these criticisms is, in my opinion, entirely accurate or adequate. The personnel man's basic chores in themselves are useful and necessary. As recruiter the personnel man is responsible for seeking out people to do the organization's work. As employment interviewer he must screen the suitable from the unsuitable. As wage and salary administrator he is the classifier and arranger of the values and prices of jobs. In companies, records must be kept about people; arrangements of all types must be made. Job-skill training, the processing of insurance claims, the discussion of employee complaints about working conditions, and so on, are all useful functions.

Nor can the results of the personnel man's effort be seriously thought of as "sinister." In the preceding hundreds of pages we have looked at what personnel men do or try to do with people. The concentration has been mainly on people inside organizations; occasionally, as in community relations, it has included people outside organizations as well. In cool perspective, without dramatic lighting, little of what we have seen has been really ominous. For the most part, the personnel style has not been especially subtle or cunning. More often it has been blatant and even awkward. Where the personnel methodologies have tried to be subtler, as in the scientisms of the human relations approaches, the successes seem no more remarkable. The high chiefs of business still decry worker and public unfriendliness. The bright and once-promising lights of Mayo's Hawthorne have dimmed. Their successors, those variegated versions of applied human relations blink on and off erratically. Management-designed incentive programs, cost-reduction and quality-improvement programs do not sufficiently inspire. Intricate and elaborate designs, when they are developed, bog down. Personnel cleverness and smoothness are met by countercleverness, and sometimes by devastating employee rudeness.

The fact is that there really is no master conspiracy here, and it is exceedingly doubtful that one is in the making. The personnel man's plans and plots (there are some plots) are short-range, tactical rather than strategic. The personnel man's idea of long-range planning is merely the recycling of his present programs in as many iterations as required by the time span he is planning for. To plan strategically one must have a purpose, and that requires a sense of past history and a perspective of its continuity with the present and the future. It also requires a philosophy, a context within which judgments can be made.

By and large, personnel men have neither a sense of history nor a philosophy. They have only catechisms borrowed from traditional business doctrine. What personnel men have been doing and continue to do is to try to win people inside and outside corporations over to what classic free-enterprise ideology says are the right ways of life. But classic free-enterprise ideology is hoary and out of date. The good old days are gone, if indeed they ever existed. Some businessmen are beginning to recognize this fact, but personnel men are not.

The personnel man's utter devotion to the ideal of profitability is the outgrowth of his capture by free-enterprise classicism. It is the ever-ready basis for his self-effacing acceptance of others' accusations of his unworthiness, the basis for the continual plethora of self-flagellation to be found in the personnel literature.

The personnel man's responses to his tribulations have been heard here too. Sometimes they have been despairing and hopeless, but more frequently they are bold and show high resolve to prove himself—to change his negative image among his fellow management men. First, of course, he will cast out from his midst the weak and wavering. And then, the mission is clear, the dedication is clear: The personnel men, all together, requiring only time and opportunity, will prove that they can—they *really* can—contribute to the money-making.

Thus, the personnel man concentrates his energies on trying to fulfill his overwhelming desire for acceptance by his business contemporaries. Not many, but a few high personnel men have, by their personal qualities, made their way into the top management councils of their companies. If they remain, though, it is most often as tolerated guests rather than as recognized members of the family. Their presence and their influence are based solely on their persuasive skills. No operating charter, formal or informal, exists that entitles them to—or better still, imposes upon them—responsibility for participation in the organization's policy-making. It is difficult to imagine a top engineering, manufacturing, or sales manager who would accept a similar status.

And so, in their unsureness and discomfort the "accepted" as well as the unaccepted personnel men continue to seek the devices, the gimmicks, the magic key which will open the door into the organization's inner circle to them, and keep it open. But they have not found it so far, and so long as the search continues to be restricted to its present ground it is unlikely that they will. The odds are against them. Other specialists are better adapted and more adept at exploiting the matters of efficiency and productivity—among them, industrial engineers, human factors specialists, and methods men. Their approaches are more direct and substantive, their technologies better developed and more relevant.

The personnel man hunts for others' acceptance. He stalks it, entices it, charges after it, but it eludes him. It will, until he meets its prerequisite. The essential for acceptance by others is, first, *self-acceptance,* and the personnel man has not accepted himself. Nor can he, until he is able to find and recognize legitimacy for the personnel function. What has been said in this book is that the personnel man is seeking his legitimacy in the wrong places; and his present preoccupations are so obsessive that they block his consideration of alternatives.

I believe that legitimacy for the personnel function may be won if and when the personnel man reorients himself and his work to accept two new and radically different missions. First, to become the corporation's man in charge of sensing and representing the interests of the *people* of the organization. Second, to become the interpreter and advocate of society to the corporation.

In performing the first of these functions the personnel man would need to examine and understand in depth the meanings of men and women at work. He would need to resist and eventually clear away the wishful fancies and obscurantist slogans of prevailing management folklore in favor of discovering realities. His primary concerns—clearly and unequivocally—would be with people, not with production, nor with *people as the implements* (or "human resources") of production. That does not mean that the personnel man would need to be antiproductivity. He could, even should, be proproductivity, but for him productivity would be *secondary* to people.

What I am talking about, of course, is just exactly the reverse of what is ostensibly the personnel man's present orientation. The personnel man would not be removed or apart from organizational and profit concerns. He needs to be aware of them, but at the same time he needs to recognize clearly that, in contrast to other organization specialists, they are the background conditions, the environmental facts, *not* the prime focus of his job.

Once the personnel man recognizes this change in his function he must acknowledge it straightforwardly. He must resist the ever-present temptation to hinge his proposals to the old justifications. At present, too often the calls to pay greater heed to the human elements of the organization are coming out of the same old cavalry bugles. The case is being set up on the same old presumptive base: *It will increase operating efficiency.* That is no good. Not just because it runs away from the main point, but also because it ignores the inevitable—that sooner or later a time will come for testing the humanitarian case against efficiency's criteria, and it may not test out sufficiently well.

So, eventually, because it was built on an unsuitable foundation, advertised in inappropriate ways, and inspected against the wrong standards, an underdeveloped but promising architecture will probably be judged as faulty, and may be entirely discarded. That would be tragic.

The point can be made more specific. Some of its enthusiasts claim that Theory Y is the *only* way to fly; that in these technological times businesses which fail to open up the full potential of all their employees through developmental management approaches are not likely to survive the rigors of competition against other companies which have. Only humanistic organizations, warn its fans, can provide for themselves an adequate supply of managers and men able to make optimum decisions, able to cope with increasing price and quality competition, able to anticipate and adjust rapidly to science and technology changes, able to sense and grasp new opportunities for growth in products and markets.

I do not believe this is true. It is far too extravagant and there are too many counterevidences both in social science research and in day-to-day observation. The roads traveled to business success have been varied, and some are diametrically different from others. There are big, rich, thriving companies whose styles are tight, formal, and authoritarian, and whose executives hold low opinions of employees and feel neither the need nor the inclination to change.

I know of one organization which is as close to an ideal characterization of Theory X, and another as close to Theory Y, as one is likely to find outside a textbook. Both are eminently successful leaders in their respective industries. Both contain happy and unhappy people. The differences are that there are proportionately far fewer happy people in the Theory X organization, and those who are happy enjoy themselves in a considerably more frantic way. The happy people in the Theory X organization are the winners. They are those who won in competitions against other companies for business, or against other people or departments within their own company for position, status, praise, or influence. Many times they fought as hard on the internal battlefields as on the external.[1]

It is an organization that prizes combativeness, that uses, and uses up, men. But it finds other men eager to take their places, and with the introduction of new men it produces new ideas. It is a business run by brilliant autocrats at the top, who have picked out and bought very bright autocrats to manage the levels just below them. Decision-making is the task of the few, not the many. But it is not a caste or class autocracy, and any superb fighter may climb its hierarchy at any time.

While this company went through the usual ritualistic professions of its belief in the importance of its "human resources" as other companies did, almost no one believed it. Its labor troubles were constant and continual. Its blue-collar workers, protected by their unions, contested management on nearly every ground they could. And many good *and successful* management men grew tired of and disgusted by its style, and eventually left. It produced ulcers, "nervous conditions," and actual breakdowns among its personnel, including some at the highest levels. It was generally acknowledged by almost everyone, including those who were still rising rapidly within it, as a damnable place to work.

For me, this fact, not efficiency, is the real point.

In contrast, there is the second organization, in which there is almost no anguish and few organizationally inspired anxieties. Where a great many people are made to feel free to speak their minds and espouse their views. Where co-operation between departments and functions is more often voluntary than coerced

[1] Many people feel that this form of internecine conflict is wasteful, that it obstructs the common purpose of the organization and uses up energies needed for external competition. That is not the whole truth. Internal warfare can be obstructive, but it can also clear away obstructions. By the process of Spencerian "survival of the fittest" can come the quicker victory of superior ideas or superior men (though sometimes too comes the victory of meretricious ideas or cunning men). And the stimulation and practice provided by the internal conflicts may well increase—as does prebattle training for troops—rather than decrease the capability of the participants for external encounters.

from above, and where many times disagreements are dealt with in other than battle modes. Here again there are some brilliant and many bright people. But these people are encouraged to exchange ideas with one another, and so to expand their own knowledge and bring to bear upon their problems as wide a scope of choices as possible.

The prevalent style of organizational relationships between managers and their men has become peer to peer rather than superior to subordinate. The ideal form of decision-making is by agreement rather than by imposition. Here are people who may enjoy a mutual satisfaction derived from *jointly* developed solutions to problems, not solely individual éclats. There is more willingness to acknowledge the contributions of others to one's own victories, and a management sufficiently sympathetic with the concept of co-operation to recognize and credit these indirect contributions. And here as well are more people willing to risk the exploration of new and possibly inappropriate solutions without the fear of immediate organizational decapitation if they are wrong.

But here too, it must be admitted, is often a lesser sense of urgency. The emphasis on agreement sometimes results in allowing each man to have not only his say but his way. And when different men have different ways, an impasse can result. The idealized peer-relationship between managers and their men at times produces a strong reluctance by managers to overrule or override. So here again, deliberations continue without conclusion and action is delayed.

My sketch is drawn. In simple lines, without shading, it is intended to show that industrial humanism's applications do not necessarily produce more efficiency. In fact, they may at times produce less. The point of all this is that if one is going to buy or sell industrial humanism or any of its parts, one ought to buy or sell them for what they are, not for what they are not.

But that is the maxim rather than the whole story. It needs to be said too that many of the troubles of the second organization I described a moment ago are not in my view inescapable penalties one *must* pay for humanism. Some are transitional difficulties that come with any new approach. Others are the results of flaws in theory or application. They can be and need to be corrected.

What should be done? There is no clear and single answer. Management remains an art and not a science, under Theory Y no less than under preceding theories. Judgments must be made, weightings of consequences must be derived, and conclusions must be reached. Almost all of the concepts of industrial humanism are new in their application to inside-organization dynamics and they require effort to make them right and to make them work. They will not get better merely by getting older.

The personnel man's responsibility and opportunity are here. He is in the right position to help managers and nonmanagers alike, to work through the problems at all levels of the organization. From a vantage point just outside the daily flow of organization business he can encourage and support, perhaps when necessary even arrange for the protection of budding attempts at new behavior patterns. He can recognize and help others to recognize those temporary difficulties and problems that result from the transition from one management mode to another. And he can also assess and point out the maladaptations—excesses of leniency, irresponsibilities, differences between appropriate power-sharing and utter power abdication, the need for basic organizational guidelines that do not stifle but do impose requirements of time and result, and ways to provide such guidelines. The personnel man can also make others aware of the preparatory work that ought to be done before a change in management theory can be applied.

These are not easy tasks. The personnel man who attempts them will often find no precedent. He will need to experiment, and his experimentation will have to be careful, and rigidly checked against reality. He will need to separate the genuine from the spurious. He will need to monitor the organization processes continually to make sure that new techniques of manipulation are not being exploited. His task is still to help others. The personnel man will have his chance to be tough-minded—not in money-making, but in his insistence on organizational integrity. This does not mean that he will always triumph in making considerations for people victorious over considerations for profit, but rather that when profit wins he will not try to convince others that it turned out the other way.

In approaching the second of his responsibilities, to become the interpreter and advocate of society to the corporation, the personnel man needs to change the way he views societies—the societies within the corporation, and the big society outside the corporation. Perhaps it is too much to ask that he become a partisan of the big society, but if not, then he must at least subdue his ardor for classic business ideology sufficiently so that he can remain cognizant of the trends of the twentieth century without anguish or anger. He must be able to recognize what is happening outside the corporate walls, to consider it coolly, to interpret it, and to transmit an undistorted picture to those in charge of his company. His mission must also be to try to make them understand the picture—not necessarily to approve of it, but to understand it realistically. And he must do all of these things—functions very different from the responsibilities of his fellow managers who are profit-oriented—without shame or apology.

One way of thinking about the change of roles for the personnel man advocated here is as a change from organizational "me too-ism" to champion of the loyal opposition. A recurring observation for some time among contemporary observers of our society has been that corporations are private governments. Adolph Berle, C. Wright Mills, Scott Buchanan, W. H. Ferry, and others have made the point. Earl Latham, a political scientist, has detailed it by pointing out that corporations, like public governments, have constitutions or charters, "legislating" systems, hierarchies and bureaucracies, systems to reward and punish those governed, and the means to enforce the common rules.

Further, there are patterns of identification, involvement, and loyalty for many people within companies which often appear as strong or stronger than most other allegiances. Nor do many corporations discourage such patterns.

If corporations are private governments, "loyal opposition" may be an apt phrase to describe the new role advocated for the personnel man, but that does not of course guarantee its acceptance. There will be objections. Within the corporation the point will be made that in focusing on people and society such a personnel man would not be the *opposition* at all, because the corporation has always had the best interests of people and society in mind and at heart. This general point is then likely to be followed by supporting detail which makes clear that: (1) the virtue of self-reliance has always been essential for both people and societies, and the corporation has long supported that virtue against all manner of antagonists; (2) the free-enterprise system has produced greater abundance for greater numbers of people than any other system; (3) the competitive enterprise response to the dynamic forces of the free market provides the quickest, most sensitive, and most efficient way to meet the expressed needs and desires of society; and so on.

On the other hand, from outside the corporation there will be other objectors to the personnel man as loyal opposition. Their grievance: that the personnel man would indeed be a *loyal* opposition, so this is merely another ploy, more finely shaped, perhaps, therefore even more insidious. Its objective, to subvert the momentum of the *real* and *disloyal* oppositions which now inhibit the corporate appetites. For these antagonists it is better to see the enemy clearly and know he is the enemy unambiguously.

There is still another serious point to be made against this proposal for a loyal opposition. It is that all businessmen, certainly including the personnel man, ought to stick to their own business knitting, and let the natural countervailing forces— unions, government, public opinion—work things out. Otherwise, we might wind up with a business-oriented welfarism, and ultimately even the serious erosion of the pluralistic qualities we value in our society. I do not agree. To me this argument has a curiously similar ring to the one made for free-enterprise classicism: that the only moral principles are immaculate ones, and the only real alternatives are those that are diametrically opposed. To the extremist of the enterprise view all modifications become the slither of creeping socialism, for the extremist of the separatist view all modifications are the clumping strides of business totalitarianism.

Both philosophically and practically, I find the purely separatist view no more useful than free-enterprise classicism as a reasonable way of addressing the real world. For one thing, countervailence isn't nearly so potent a hero as all that. Its power inside companies is not uniformly distributed. It is underdeveloped or entirely nonexistent in more areas than it is strong. In the mundane, day-to-day processes of the organization that affect individuals, only one institution really countervails effectively: the union. The forces of government and public opinion exist, to be sure, but their impacts are general. Government must legislate to correct. Legislation is important, yes, but it is broad rather than particular, eventual rather than immediate. Public opinion is real, but its development from a vaguely sensed undercurrent to a recognizable force usually requires an even more extended course. And in the long interim it is subject to multiple and even contradictory interpretations.

In fact, only the labor union local—and at that, only a *strong* local—is readily available to its members. Only it can react quickly to the particular situation and the individual case. But many people who work are not represented by labor unions. The majority are not, in fact, and there are distinct signs that in the future proportionately even fewer will be.

Corporations may be private governments, but they are not democracies, or republics. It is unlikely that, in the foreseeable future, they will be either. Nor am I saying that they ought to be, in the same sense that our public government is a democracy. But there is the possibility for a further "democratization" of the corporation. Without either socializing the country or destroying management's "inalienable rights" to manage, there is room enough to allow the "political" representation of all people who work—not just the unionized ones—and to allow their voices to be heard on a wider range of organization matters.

This is not exactly a new thought. In 1914 a congressional Commission on Industrial Relations, after a two-year investigation of "underlying causes of dissatisfaction in the Industrial situation," concluded:

> The question of industrial relations assigned by Congress to the Commission for investigation is more fundamental and of greater importance to the welfare of the nation than any other question except the form of government. The only hope for the solution of the tremendous problems created by industrial relations lies in the effective use of our democratic institutions and in the rapid extension of the principles of democracy to industry.

There is a potential role for the personnel man here. At his best he could help the organization and its people to "constitutionalize" their rights and obligations with respect to each other and to the public. He could help to bring common agreement and articulation to the concepts of equity, welfare, and justice in the organization context. If he did, he would also need to play a leading part in developing *means for implementation* so that these concepts did not become merely another list of company platitudes for use in employee handbooks and in vice presidents' semiannual speeches. Nor would the list be adequate even if it were more seriously regarded, if it had been unilaterally determined by management, and was interpreted by management, in accordance with management's logic alone.

What I have in mind is something quite different. These formulations would need to be *mutually determined,* translated into tangible policies, and made as genuinely operational as any production schedule. And here again, in designing administrative systems for their application, the best of the personnel men could help. The *very* best might even help the unorganized to organize.

It is undoubtedly true that men need acceptance—at least in the long run—for themselves, their ideas, and their institutions. One reason corporations need acceptance is very practical: It enables them to do what they need to do, and it keeps their antagonists from doing things to them that would be harmful. For the executives of corporations there is probably an additional reason. Simply put, it is that most men want to be recalled by their children and by posterity as nice guys rather than villains.

An August, 1964, survey by Opinion Research Corporation on "The Ethics of American Business" showed that its sample of the general public ranked corporate executives tenth in a twelve-position list on the question "How would you rate the ethical and moral practices of each of these groups?" The groups included scientists, physicians, professors, lawyers, government officials, small businessmen, and so on. Only advertising executives and labor union leaders ranked lower.

So, corporation executives are not looking very much like heroes these days, especially in the ethics-morality dimension, and that is probably not pleasant for them. Even more important though, the corporation itself is not everybody's favorite twentieth-century institution. And it has occurred to some sensitive company men that if things don't get better, they could get worse. Conceivably, so much worse that the corporation might even begin to lose its *basic minimum of acceptance,* that subsistence level of affection without which institutions become malnourished and sickly.

Business has attributed its relationship problems to the fact that the business word is not getting through to society, but that is because it is not a very relevant word. And that, in turn, is because society's word is not getting through adequately to business. An argument of this book is that the personnel man ought to listen carefully and intelligently to what is happening outside companies, and then to relate these happenings clearly to those inside. That will require a change in approach. Among other things, it will take especially broad, sensible, and resolute people to handle it. The personnel men who choose to pioneer this orientation will not have an easy time. They will frequently need to stand apart from most of their fellow managers of the more traditional mode.

But the scene is not entirely forbidding. A few corporation presidents have recently been heard talking in unfamiliar ways. They are hesitating over the ancient rituals and quieting some of the tribal chants. Much of the time, of course, the changes seem to be more a matter of form than substance, but even that may represent progress.

For illustration there is the December 1964 meeting of the National Association of Manufacturers, which concerned itself with business's public image. Lynn A. Townsend, president of Chrysler Corporation, spoke to his fellow executives on the hitherto sacred litany of the dangers of the welfare state.

Said Townsend: "First, I suggest that in taking positions on matters of public policy that affect business we might do well to place a little more accent on the positive and a little less on the negative. Too often in the past, businessmen have expressed themselves as being squarely against many things that the great majority of the people are solidly for. As a result the business community has got itself a reputation for dragging its feet on social issues and being opposed to anything that looks like a new approach."[2]

And in what from another source would surely have been heresy against the governmental interference gospel, Mr. Townsend also suggested that "it might be well for businessmen to talk just a little less about the evils of government and a little more about the many ways in which government can help business do its work more effectively."

---

[2] Townsend later noted: "This is pretty ironic—because in reality the businessman at his desk is for innovation—for expansion—for improved quality—for better service to the public—for building a better civilization, if you will."

Others are talking too, and sometimes there is a distinctly serious sound to the business chiefs' ponderings. For example, from David Rockefeller: "In social terms, the old concept that the owner of a business had a right to use his property as he pleased to maximize profits has evolved into the belief that ownership carries certain binding social obligations. Today's manager serves as trustee not only for the owners but for the workers and indeed for our entire society . . . "

There are also the vigorous articulations of Norton Simon, head of Hunt Food and Industries. Says Simon: "Most companies will say 'We are in business to make a profit.' I think the better companies could just as well say: 'Our primary purpose in business is sociological . . . ' We are beyond the day and age of need of capitalism for survival. We need it for only one thing— the betterment of the human being . . ."

Among the most promising of all the encouragements for the broader personnel man there are the ideas expressed by IBM's Thomas Watson, Jr., probably one of the least constricted of America's major executives. Watson should be heard from at length.[3]

> Business has demonstrated how successfully it can innovate and produce. What we must now do—it would seem to me—is to assign a higher order of priority to the national interest in our business decisions . . . Anyone particularly interested in some segment of the economy must increasingly recognize the force of public or national interest. Ultimately we are held accountable to it. We exist at its tolerance . . .

> Much as we may dislike it, I think we've got to realize that in our kind of society there are times when government has to step in and help people with some of their more difficult problems. This does not mean that we have abandoned our traditional faith in American self-reliance. It means we have recognized that changing times have pre-

---

[3] The quotations are from his book *A Business and Its Beliefs,* based upon a series of lectures Watson delivered at Columbia's Graduate School of Business in 1962.

sented us with changing conditions which sometimes exceed the limits of self-reliance. And these changes are characteristic of a system as dynamic as ours.

Watson then cautions:

> . . . when people insist on social betterment and justice they are not going to be dissuaded by cries of alarm at what they may be doing to the free enterprise system. They look on the system as a changing institution—one which must change with the times. And as their needs become greater, or as their wants and ambitions grow, they demand new laws and programs—trusting in the ability of that free enterprise system to bear the costs.
>
> What we must always remember is that countries and systems exist for the benefit of their people. If a system does not measure up to the growing expectations of those people, they will move to modify or change it . . .

There are other favorable harbingers on the horizon. In early 1966 the President's National Automation Commission, which included Mr. Watson and Edwin Land of the Polaroid Corporation, produced recommendations of a startling quality. They asked for consideration of a minimum-income allowance by the Federal Government that would bring every American family above the poverty level. They suggested too that the Federal Government might undertake the role of "employer of last resort," by having the Government establish a specific policy of employing those who would normally be unemployed.

In California the state government, in co-operation with a number of leading aerospace firms, is pioneering the application of the industry's huge research and development talent pools to "civilian" problems like handling adult and juvenile delinquents, air and water pollution, and mass transportation. In other locales other corporate-governmental joint efforts are being directed toward the complex difficulties of hospital administration and toward establishing job corps centers. In mending the torn and frayed places in the social fabric there is even talk of using private enterprise resources in such unlikely fields as social welfare and work with the mentally retarded.

In some of the corporate efforts required to prepare for and begin these novel study programs, companies will spend more than they receive in reimbursement from the relatively tiny (in comparison to defense) contracts. That can, of course, be easily sloughed off with the explanation that it is not just the immediate but the future profit potential which counts. That is true enough, and there may well be later big-money possibilities in a number of the projects. But there are other attractions. In and around the aerospace industry an increasing number of bright people, especially the younger ones, are rather looking forward to doing things in the people-helping instead of the people-killing business.

We are beginning to broaden our focus to encompass ways of living, rather than merely ways of making and using. That is true within corporations as well as elsewhere in the society. The growth of laboratory training is one evidence. Laboratory training focuses on men and the way they live as men. Management keeps sending more and more of its kind to the laboratories, despite the fact that there is no proof at all that it helps their companies to increase profits, or indeed that it has any significant and sustained impact on the *organization*'s operations. Probably, that is because managers are human as well as economic. And because a laboratory experience is an intensely personal one, rather than a public utterance such as a press release on free enterprise, foreign competition, or compulsory unionism.

There are problems within organizations which need to be addressed, and problems between organizations and the society. There are also problems in the society that could be helped by the talents available in the corporations—the impact of automation, the obsolescence of individual skills, the employment and training of Negroes and others of those known as the "culturally deprived." There are also challenges of our time which grow more subtly from the industrial scene. For example, the matter of work and leisure time.

There is a pressing need for a better comprehension of the anatomies of both work and leisure. Some work is interesting and absorbing and some is not. The industrial humanist claim is that all men should have interesting and meaningful work. But realistically, in the context of our current efficiency ethic, that is probably not practicable. By modifying the efficiency ethic just a little, some jobs can be redesigned to make them more interesting. The cost would not be high, and this ought to be done. But there are other jobs not susceptible to such modest remedies. A few more motions added to the job of the assembly-line workers probably won't do. It is not sufficient for the long run, even though its apparent immediate impact on the craft-starved assembly-line worker may be favorable. The immediate impact of the Hawthorne results, when management and Mayo's men began to notice that the relay-assembly girls were alive, was favorable too, but its continued exploitation as a cheap solution to the "human relations problem" eventually paled.

However, there are other things that might be done instead. Rotating people into and out of such work on short time cycles, or developing other activities to which men may devote at least a part of their time even if such time does not contribute to production maximization. If some on-the-job work cannot be made satisfying, then we may need to reconsider the possibilities of off-the-job satisfaction, but in a different way. Not as *escape,* divorced from and antithetical to work. Instead, new designs can be developed integrating the needs of society and the opportunities for men in both the organization and the community. Perhaps we need to change our ways of thinking about work, so that it can be considered as no less meaningful when it occurs *away* from the factory or office than when it occurs at the factory or office.

Some sociologists consider the do-it-yourself and hobbyist trends in the United States sad evidence of men's alienation from their work. But perhaps the avocational urge does not need to be alienated. It could be turned to integral purposes. For example, the products of personal craftsmanship could be marketed. A "job corps" of part-time workers, paid at least in part by corporations, to do work that might otherwise be uneconomic and therefore undone might be established.

With scrupulous intent and careful design to avoid the doctrine and dogma biases of the old "practical politics" approaches, help could be given to people in improving the skills necessary for *their own* political, social, and charitable purposes. Again, there is nothing new here. There are loud and continuing calls from almost all segments of the nation's leadership for more caring about what goes on, and more active participation by more people in the society's business.

The classical business espousal that its best interests are also the best interests of the workers and of society in general is not very compelling. The efforts to portray it as all we know and all we need to know have wrought little but bemused frustration for the message-senders and have obstructed understanding for everybody. One of the reasons corporations keep at this odd exercise despite its ineffectiveness may be that they just do not know what else to do. The obstruction obstructs both ways. It blocks the understanding of those inside the executive offices as well as those outside. The point has been made in this book that there are a great many people in companies who have charge of taking care of the corporate interests, but that there is no one in charge of representing employees' or society's interests. No one responsible for making things better between companies and their people—*from the people's standpoint.* No one responsible for making things better between companies and the rest of society—*from society's standpoint.* There needs to be. The point has also been made that the personnel function ought to take on this job, that perceptive, intelligent personnel men could help a lot. They are in the right organization place to learn about the needs and aspirations of other organization people, and with some perfectly feasible, though not easy, changes in orientation they could gradually establish genuine contacts with people and institutions outside the organization.

This, then, has been a new prescription for personnel legitimacy—one man's compound. It has called for the personnel man, not merely to be more concerned about people and society, but to become *people's and society's man,* to espouse their causes, to argue for them when it is required. Most drastically still, it urges him to abandon profitability as his prime concern —to recant his devotion to the very oldest and most revered of all enterprise gods. If this prescription does not quickly become a popular household remedy that will not be difficult to understand. For many it will seem an odd, perhaps even a toxic mixture. But that is not necessarily bad.

In fact, what has been proposed is not meant to be a patent medicine. It would not suit every personnel man's constitution. At this stage it is an experimental compound suitable only for the young and agile—in spirit, not necessarily in years. It would be useless for those whose insight arteries have hardened, and certainly unsuitable for those who suffer from an anemia of internal confidence or courage. In truth it will be personally risky even for the best of personnel men to try it. Nevertheless, I hope some will.

INDEX

ABOUT THE AUTHOR

STANLEY M. HERMAN *was born in Brooklyn, New York, in 1928. In his early teens he moved with his family to Los Angeles, California. There, after sampling an educational mixed grill that included journalism, economics, and the behavioral sciences, he eventually graduated from UCLA with a degree in sociology. Mr. Herman has spent the major part of his working life in the personnel field. He has also been a free-lance writer and has worked in public relations. He has held consulting and managerial positions in both government and industry. Currently he is a personnel director in one of the nation's major corporations. His articles have appeared in professional journals over the last half dozen years.*

A NOTE ON THE TYPE

THE TEXT OF THIS BOOK *was set on
the Linotype in a face called* TIMES ROMAN,
designed by Stanley Morison for The Times
(London), *and first introduced by that newspaper in 1932.*

*Among typographers and designers of the
twentieth century, Stanley Morison has been
a strong forming influence, as typographical
adviser to the English Monotype Corporation,
as a director of two distinguished English publishing houses, and as a writer of sensibility,
erudition, and keen practical sense.*

*Composed, printed, and bound by
The Book Press Incorporated, Brattleboro, Vermont*

*Typography and binding design by
Kenneth Miyamoto*